THE CENSUS
AND
SOCIAL STRUCTURE

THE CENSUS
AND
SOCIAL STRUCTURE

An Interpretative Guide to Nineteenth Century Censuses for England and Wales

Edited by
RICHARD LAWTON
Professor of Geography, University of Liverpool

FRANK CASS

First published 1978 in Great Britain by
FRANK CASS AND COMPANY LIMITED
Gainsborough House, Gainsborough Road,
London, E11 1RS, England

and in the United States of America by
FRANK CASS AND COMPANY LIMITED
c/o Biblio Distribution Centre
81 Adams Drive, P.O. Box 327, Totowa, N.J. 07511

British Library Cataloguing in Publication Data

The census and social structure.
1. England — Census — History
I. Lawton, Richard, b.1925
301.32   HA37.G7

ISBN 0-7146-2965-0

Typeset by MHL Typesetting Ltd, Coventry
Printed in Great Britain by offset lithography by
Billing & Sons Ltd, Guildford, London and Worcester

Contents

Tables

Figures

Appendices

Note on Contributors

W.A. Armstrong, B.A., Ph.D., is a Senior Lecturer in Economic History at the University of Kent at Canterbury

D.E. Baines, B.Sc. (Econ.), is a Lecturer in Economic History at the London School of Economics and Political Science

Joyce M. Bellamy, B. Com., Ph.D., is a Senior Research Officer at the University of Hull

J.A. Banks, B.A., M.Sc., is Professor of Sociology at the University of Leicester

J.M. Goldstrom, B. Com., Ph.D., is a Senior Lecturer in Economic and Social History at the Queen's University, Belfast

David M. Thompson, M.A., Ph.D., is a Fellow of Fitzwilliam College and Lecturer in Modern Church History in the University of Cambridge

CHAPTER 1

Introduction

RICHARD LAWTON

I

The census of population is a key source for any study of
nineteenth-century England. In association with parish
registers and, from 1837, the civil registers recording births,
deaths and marriages, population numbers and trends, the
essential dynamic basis of population analysis, may be
studied. Though the earlier censuses of 1801—31 are largely
simple population enumerations, they also include information
on the number of houses and families, some rather rudimentary data on occupational structure and, for 1821 only,
an age structure. But from 1841, the first census to be carried
out under the office of the Registrar General, and in many
ways the first full-scale 'modern' British census, had a considerable range of information on the age and sex structure of
the population, on birthplaces (affording some insight into
the very important question of population mobility), on
occupations (and hence on the distribution and structure of
economic activity) and on housing, in addition to basic
information on the numbers and distribution of people.
The nineteenth century censuses are, therefore, not simply
enumerations, but are basic documents for the analysis of
a great variety of demographic, social and economic questions.
As such they were of interest not only to contemporary
demographers but to administrators and policy-makers. For
the present day student they are an incomparable storehouse
of data for the historian and social scientist; indeed in almost
any study of the nineteenth century we must sooner or later
turn to the census for information.

Not only do the censuses of population provide information

for many *types* of study, but they may be analysed at many different levels and at different scales. The objectives of study may be very specific, such as an individual street or community — or general, such as a countrywide study of the location of the textile industry or of urbanised areas; they may be conceptual involving such themes as family and social structure or the process of urbanisation; or they may be systematic in approach, involving a specific theme, or regional, concerned with a more broadly-based study of a particular area.

These varied approaches may be followed at a number of levels from the local or micro-scale, to the national level or macro-scale, and encompassing a whole hierarchy of regional levels between. The tabulations in the published census reports themselves provide information on various subjects of census enquiry at scales ranging from small administrative areas (township or ward) through intermediate administrative and local government areas (for example, registration districts and sub-districts, borough and sanitary districts) to county and regional groupings, though these are often difficult to compare from topic to topic and from census to census (see below, Chapter 3).

From 1841, census information was collected by means of a standard printed household schedule and, though these schedules were subsequently destroyed, they were consolidated into enumerators' books from which the tabulations of the published Reports were compiled (see below, Chapter 2). Though subject to a one-hundred-years' confidentiality constraint before release to the public records, these enumerators' books provide a significant body of material for the period 1841–1901 at individual and household level which is of considerable significance not only to genealogists and local historians but also to the growing number of historians and social scientists interested in a widening number of thematic and methodological studies of Victorian society.

As interest in the nineteenth century has grown, in general and as a field of academic study, so the use of both published and manuscript census material has increased: indeed studies involving census data have become one of the academic growth industries of the 1960s and 1970s, to the extent that users of census records in the Long Room of the Public Record Office in Chancery Lane far exceeded other classes of users and led to a shift of the enumerators' books to more spacious accommodation in the Land Registry, Portugal Street.

Unfortunately, neither the published reports nor the enumerators' books of the census are as easy and straightforward to use as may at first sight seem the case: indeed they are full of pitfalls for the unwary. The changing bases of enumeration, in terms of the organisation and range of information gathered in the pre- and post-1841 censuses make comparisons over time difficult. Changing procedures for both enumeration and tabulation all create ambiguities, complexities and unconformities between different categories of information within individual censuses and, more particularly, between censuses. Thus various types of census information which may at first appear straightforward and comparable on closer investigation prove not to be so. Many similar sets of data require adjustment before they may be compared. Hence there is an increasingly felt need by users of census data for a practical guide to the contents and use of nineteenth century censuses. Until recently there was no comprehensive study of British censuses apart from the admirable and concise pioneer work of the late L.M. Feery of the, then, General Register Office. Published in 1951 under the aegis of the Interdepartmental Committee on Social and Economic Research: No. 2 of the Guides to Official Sources, *Census Reports of Great Britain 1801– 1931,* this standard and authoritative brief account of the background to the development of the census, and of the subjects of census enquiry and details of the tabulations of the reports has long been out of print, though a revised *Guide to Census Reports Great Britain 1801–1966* has been published since this book was first planned. The editor is greatly indebted to H.M. Stationery Office for permission to reprint many of the invaluable tables among the appendices to this book (see Appendix XI): most of the contributors have frequently referred to the old *Guide* (as it is hereafter called) in the course of their work.

Since the publication of the *Guide*, research based on census data has become involved not only with the technical complexities of tabulations in the published census reports, but also with the unpublished enumerators' books. Moreover, many problems faced by the investigator are concerned with the systematic appraisal and comparison of census data in both statistical and descriptive analyses of a theoretical and empirical nature for which a different, more systematic, analysis of census content by topics would be useful. Some years ago Dr D.E.C. Eversley conceived the idea of a series of essays focusing on the problems of analysis of major topics on which information is contained in nineteenth century censuses. Unfortunately Dr Eversley's move to the Greater London Council as its Chief Planner (Strategy) forced him to give up his editorship of this project. Happily for the present editor, most of the original contributors invited by Dr Eversley were still able to contribute. I am grateful to Dr Eversley for the pattern of the book, which closely follows his original blueprint, and to my contributors for their patience over the prolonged gestation of their brain-children.

II

The book has very specific and limited objectives. It is neither a history of census-taking nor a history of the demographic background to the censuses of nineteenth century Britain. While a fully definitive account of those themes has yet to be written, the *Guide* gives a very good basis of the history and contents of the census. Moreover two recently published studies both give a valuable insight into the wider context of census study. Professor D.V. Glass has written a most informative but concise study of the development and demographic context of censuses and vital statistics in Britain.[1] Professor Michael Drake is much more directly concerned with the history of and contemporary reaction to 'The Census, 1801– 1891'.[2] These questions are not specifically discussed in the present book, apart from a brief discussion of certain aspects of the development of the census-taking and of the contents of the census in a later section of this introduction, though they are inevitably involved in the chapters concerned with such general themes as the enumerators' book (Chapter 2) and urban areas (Chapter 3), and as related to specific themes in other chapters.

The present book is essentially an interpretative guide: an aid to the systematic study of census data as a basis for the analysis of key themes in the study of nineteenth century society. It is deliberately selective in both the themes which it follows and in restricting the geographical coverage to the census of England and Wales. Following this brief introductory chapter Dr Alan Armstrong discusses the method of taking the census in the period 1841–71 and indicates the material contained in the enumerators' books for those censuses which are now available in the Public Record Office. Much of this discussion is fundamental not only to micro-level studies using the enumerators' books but also to the problems of evaluating the accuracy and interpreting the classifications used in the tabulations published in the census reports. Therefore it should be read in combination with subsequent chapters (3–6) dealing with specific topics.

Chapter 3 is concerned with the data available in censuses for the study of urbanisation, a basic theme in social and demographic change in the nineteenth century. In addition to information provided by the census on urban areas, it considers the changing units of enumeration and tabulation of urban areas used in the census, a complex business which is basic to any analysis of census material on nineteenth century towns and which also sheds light on some of the basic problems of any census study involving change over time or spatial contrast.

Chapters 4–6 consist of a systematic evaluation of three major sets of information contained in the censuses from 1841 (birthplaces, occupations and the use of occupation in the analysis of social structure), each of which should be read together with Dr Armstrong's study of the material available in the enumerators' books for more specific and detailed study at local and household level. Dudley Baines deals not only with the varying information collected on birthplaces (Chapter 4) but also with the basic problems of interpretation posed by these questions and their tabulation. He suggests ways in which they may be used together with information on net migration, derived from the Registrar General's Annual Reports, in the analysis of population mobility.

Dr Joyce Bellamy is concerned mainly with changing occupational classifications and their reliability in the study of occupational structure and economic analysis (their 'industrial' classification) (Chapter 5). Discussion of the grouping of occupations into Orders and Sub-Orders and their value in the study of population structure is carried further in Professor Banks' study of social structure as seen through the census (Chapter 6). In tracing the ways in which early- and mid-nineteenth century census-takers saw occupations as 'socially distinctive' he shows how these led to Charles Booth's systematic use of occupations as a basis for the analysis of the social structure of mid-Victorian England.[3] Professor Banks links this to more recent census classification of socio-economic characteristics, particularly that devised for the 1911 census.

The two final chapters contain the first general critiques of the unique Education and Religious Censuses of 1851. Separate from, though associated with, the general census enumeration of 1851, both were supervised by Dr Horace Mann, the Assistant Commissioner for the census. These difficult and unreliable surveys, hitherto underutilised and perhaps undervalued, are considered in the context of other nineteenth century data on these subjects but are also brought into focus against the 1851 Census of Population.

Dr Max Goldstrom, an authority on education in the nineteenth century,[4] shows how the Education Census focuses on schools and attendance, rather than on the educational experiences of the individual (Chapter 7). From 1851 to 1881 the English censuses also gathered information on those who attended school (part or wholetime) or who received regular instruction, but these data are unreliable, though information on residential schools contained in the enumerators' books is of considerable interest. In the absence of specific and accurate information on those attending school, available only from 1921, this special census is therefore of considerable value.

Similarly, the unique Religious Census of 1851 contains the only official information on religion in any English census, since the experiment was not repeated in view of the opposition to it and the inconclusive nature of the results. Problems of collection and analysis are due to its being a voluntary enquiry concerning church attendance. Dr Thompson's analysis (Chapter 8) shows how many of the problems of handling and interpreting the Religious Census sprang from the restricted and oblique nature of the enquiry. He adds some extremely valuable regional tabulations which will be of great interest and value to those engaged in regional and local studies.

III

Although these chapters involve most of the principal topics covered by nineteenth century censuses they are by no means comprehensive. Of the subjects of census enquiry listed in the *Guide,* the information on housing is fragmentary and unsatisfactory even in the late nineteenth and early twentieth centuries, when questions were asked on the number of rooms in tenements of under five rooms (1891 and 1901) and, in 1911, on the number of families per occupied house and the number of rooms in each house. Information on the family is also limited and difficult to handle from the published tabulations of the *Reports* alone, though the material contained in the enumerators' books gives considerable insight into this fascinating topic (see Armstrong, below, Chapter 3).[5]

British censuses in general have always been deficient in direct questions on social and cultural characteristics of the population (including ethnic background), as witness recent problems of obtaining accurate census information on overseas immigrants into Britain, particularly those from the new Commonwealth countries. Apart from very limited information on education and the 1851 Education and Religious Censuses, the only such information on cultural traits is that on nationality (primarily associated with the question on birthplace) and on Gaelic and Welsh speakers in Scotland and Wales only (from 1881 and 1891 respectively).

More fundamental aspects of population study which could have been included in this book are the demographic structure of the population, by age and sex, and the components of population change. Information on natural change of population is derived from the Registrar General's registers of births and deaths which (as with marriages) became a compulsory civil procedure in 1837 in England and Wales (under an Act of 1836) and in 1855 in Scotland (under an Act of 1854). Once the collection of ages by the census was begun in 1841 (apart from an experimental and probably inaccurate tally in the 1821 census), the problems of comparative analysis of population structure are not great, though reference should be made to Dr Armstrong's chapter for problems encountered in the enumerators' books.

The components of population change have been considered incidentally, particularly in Mr Baines's discussion of net migration (Chapter 4). Nevertheless there is considerable scope for further studies of population dynamics, especially the relationship between natural and migrational change, at local and regional level, among both the census summaries of those components for registration districts[6] and the more detailed figures of births, deaths (and cause of death) and net migration for registration sub-districts contained in the Registrar General's Annual Reports. Indeed there are considerable potentialities for the linkage of census and other personal and population information (from both national and local sources)[7] in demographic and social studies of the nineteenth century. Such cross-tabulation creates considerable analytical and statistical problems, but at the level of the individual and household much progress is being made in the handling and analysis of linked population data by computer, particularly through the work of the Cambridge Group for the History of Population and Social Structure.[8]

The scope of this present book has been deliberately restricted in a second major respect in that the greater part of it is concerned only with England and Wales. The very interesting and valuable censuses of Ireland have a separate and distinctive history beginning with the first census of 1821. They involve somewhat different questions and tabulations and have no enumerators' records because, unhappily, most of the enumerators' books were destroyed in the Dublin disturbances of 1922. A useful guide to their utility may be seen in the study of the Ireland of the 1840s by T.W.

Freeman,[9] a considerable part of which is based on the 1841 Census of Ireland, the first accurate and complete enumeration for the country.

The censuses for England, Wales and Scotland were conducted under a similar organisation from 1801 to 1831 and the procedures in issuing schedules, coordinating these into enumerators' books and using those as the basis of tabulations in the reports were essentially the same in all three countries in 1841 and 1851. Scotland, which was without compulsory civil registration until 1855, developed a separate office of the Registrar General from that year. Henceforward the Scottish census and registration system developed independently of that in England and Wales. However, the two Registrars General have always closely coordinated their schedules and procedures, and collaboration over questions asked in the census has been close. Despite some differences in tabulation and administrative areas used in the reports, the material collected by the Scottish censuses is very similar to that for England and Wales as the *Guide* indicates (see below, Appendix XI). Nevertheless direct comparisons of Scottish and English census material impose some difficulties and it was reluctantly decided to exclude Scotland from consideration in this book, with the exception of the studies of the Education and Religious Censuses of 1851 (Chapters 7 and 8).

IV

In this last section a brief background is given to the objectives, machinery and presentation of the nineteenth century censuses and census reports for England and Wales, together with some observations on the parallel question of the recording of vital events which have recently been the subject of a fascinating study by D.V. Glass.[10] The taking of the nineteenth century censuses themselves has been described concisely by A.J. Taylor[11] and, more recently, by Professor Michael Drake,[12] while the factual background to the taking of the census and the content of the various reports and tabulations is authoritatively and concisely outlined in the late L.M. Feery's *Guide*,[13] certain tables from which are reproduced in Appendix XI of the present volume. In addition, the report to each census details very fully the legislative procedures and organisation under which the enumeration was carried out, the questions included in the schedule and the manner in which these were consolidated into the tables published in the reports.

The history of vital registration in Britain is less easily accessible, though Professor Glass (*op. cit.*) deals with it in the general context of eighteenth and early nineteenth century population. The use of parish registers as a basis for the reconstruction of population history has been the subject of an increasing number of local studies[14] and is being systematically developed through the work of the Cambridge Group for the History of Population and Social Structure.[15] The records of civil registration of births, marriages and deaths from 1837 under the office of the Registrar General for England and Wales are familiar to most people through the Registrar General's quarterly and annual reports, though partly due to the confidentiality constraints, partly to the sheer volume and cost of using them, the original registers (of Superintendent Registrars) and certificates (indexed by Somerset House and now accessible in the records of the Registrar General) have been less used than they might be for studies of nineteenth-century population trends and structure.

The study of population in the late eighteenth and nineteenth centuries falls into four distinct phases which may be used as a framework for this brief discussion. Prior to the first census of 1801, population analysis depends on local population listings and parish registers to provide estimates of population totals, trends and structure. The first four censuses of 1801–31 were relatively limited in their range and were supported by parish register abstracts for estimates of vital rates. Following the creation of the office of the Registrar General in 1837 the first of the modern-style censuses, that of 1841, was taken and a much wider range of census information was supported by civil registration from 1837, though under-registration of births — considerable at first — probably continued until the 1880s.[16] With more precisely formulated questions — especially relating to birthplaces and occupations — from the 1851 census, and the adoption of the registration districts and sub-districts as a basic element in the areal framework of census tabulations, a format was achieved which changed little until 1911. In that year a wider range of information on housing and on industries in which people worked, and a wholly new investigation on the fertility of marriage, together with the full-scale adoption of the administrative framework developed under the Local Government Acts of 1888 and 1894 and a new format for assembly and tabulation of the census results, marked a transition to a new era in census history.

1. THE LATE EIGHTEENTH CENTURY AND THE 1801–1831 CENSUSES

From the 1750s a notable controversy raged in England concerning the numbers and growth of population which had not ended at the time of the first census of 1801.[17] The data for estimating population totals and trends were extremely defective and, despite modern demographic techniques of analysis, the figures of fertility and mortality are still uncertain. Taking into account the considerable regional differences in trends and their fluctuation over time, it is not surprising that contemporaries found the situation confusing: indeed contemporary estimates of late eighteenth century population ranged from 9 millions for Great Britain and Ireland to 11 millions for England and Wales alone, as compared with the 9.2 millions derived from an uncorrected 1801 census total of 8.9 millions for England and Wales.

Estimates of population totals depend on national statistics collected mainly for taxation purposes and on local listings which include a number of valuable counts for urban areas[18] but which are, collectively, far from comprehensive. Without firm landmarks from which to work, calculation of population trends has proved difficult. Despite the relative abundance of data on baptisms, burials and marriages contained in parish registers, the incompleteness of recording — both in terms of the proportion of parish populations covered and the time over which continuous records are available — make these difficult to use, especially in areas with considerable numbers of Dissenters. However, modern techniques of aggregation to estimate fertility and mortality on the basis of baptisms and burials, and of family reconstitution, which in parishes with detailed and consistently kept registers is yielding a very full picture of population trends and structure, are being followed by the Cambridge Group and have added much to our knowledge of pre-census populations.[19]

It is in this context that the work of John Rickman, the organiser of the first four censuses of 1801—1831, must be seen. The first proposals for a national population census were made in 1753 when a Bill was introduced into Parliament '. . . for Taking and Registering an Annual Account of the Total Number of People and the Total Number of Marriages, Births and Deaths'. The Bill passed the Commons, despite violent opposition in which one member argued that the proposal was '. . . totally subversive of the last remains of English liberty', but lapsed after a second reading in the Lords, as did a Bill proposing 'Proper Registers of Births, Deaths and Marriages' presented in 1758.[20] By the time of Rickman's memorandum on 'a general enumeration of the people of the British Empire' in 1796[21] the situation had changed considerably. There was a growing awareness of population growth, increasing dependence on imported food and, in the view of some — including the Reverend Thomas Malthus whose first 'Essay on Population' was published in 1798 — of population pressure. A Bill was introduced on 19th November 1800, the Population Act, passed speedily and without opposition, received Royal Assent on 31st December and the census was conducted on 10th March 1801. John Rickman was in charge of the taking of the census and the preparation of the abstracts and reports and the organisation devised by him, under the Act, was essentially that which operated in the first four censuses. There were two objectives in the censuses of 1801 and 1831: first the enumeration of the population; secondly an estimation of vital population trends from parish register abstracts called for from the clergy and involving a special schedule on which were returned totals of burials and baptisms for each tenth year from 1700 to 1780 and annually from 1780 to 1800, and of marriages in each year from 1754 to 1800.

The enumeration was conducted by Overseers of the Poor or 'other fit persons'. The 1801—31 Acts laid down the

general framework of reference but did not directly supervise
the execution of the census. Information was collected by the
enumerator's personal enquiry, no schedules being issued to
the householders themselves. The enumerator's schedule was
limited, in 1801, to a few questions on inhabited and uninhabited houses, families, persons (male and female) and
persons in three broad occupational categories (agriculture;
trade, manufactures and handicraft; others). Though suggestions for a wider-ranging census had been discussed, Rickman
himself doubted the ability of the overseers to handle more.

The returns were made on a prescribed schedule issued by
and returned to Clerks of the Peace or Town Clerks by whom
they were transmitted to the Home Department. A few copies
of these enumerators' and clergy schedules have survived and
show that, despite justifiable misgivings, the work was generally honestly done and often included helpful comments
on population trends.[22]

But, in addition, local records of early nineteenth century
censuses have survived which often add considerable detail
to the bare totals of the official returns. These include some
locally printed household schedules, forms with more detailed
information than that brought together in the final returns
(for example of ages under question 7 of the 1821 census, or
occupations under 'Formula No. 2' of the 1831 census) and
manuscript notes kept by enumerators, as well as correspon-
dence relating to the taking of the censuses.[23]

The Bolton reference library has local material relating to
the 1811, 1821 and 1831 censuses.[24] In the 1811 lists, in
addition to the 'tally' of items required by the census, the
names and addresses of household heads are given as in the
example on p. 14.

In other cases enumerators listed all individuals at each
address. In addition there are summaries for 21 enumeration
districts under the various specified heads contained in a
'General Account of Population of Great Bolton' from which
a general picture of the population geography of the town
may be reconstructed. In the 1821 schedules the limits of
the enumeration districts are described and the additional
information required in that census on ages shows signs of
having been collected with care and precision.

NAMES	STREET Back Rothwell St.	Inhabited Houses	By how many Families inhabited	Houses now Building	Empty Houses	Families employed chiefly by Agric.	Families in manufactures and Handicraft	Others not in the preceding categories	Males	Females	TOTAL
Joseph Todd	1	1	1				2*		3	2	5
John Devenport	2	1	1				4*		3	2	5
William Hilton	3	1	1					1	4	4	8
Thomas Brown	4	1	1					1	1	1	2
William Heckeril	5	1	1					1	2	2	4
Mary Sothern	6	1	1					1	1	2	3
Subtotals (carried over)		82	103		7		228	14	292	311	603

*Clearly the reference here must be to persons, not families.

The range of information gathered, the procedures for both enumeration and collection of parish register abstracts and the process of coordinating these with abstracts and reports remained under Rickman's supervision and were essentially unchanged in the early censuses. In 1831, the 1821 experiment of a question on age was dropped, apart from the specification of males over 20 years, and a seven-fold classification of occupations was introduced (see below, Chapter 5). On the basis of parish register returns, population trends were estimated for the intercensal periods and summarised for Hundreds and counties in tables published in a volume of *Parish Register Abstracts,* which also included a statement on the availability of parish registers in each Hundred from the sixteenth century.

2. THE ESTABLISHMENT OF THE REGISTRAR GENERAL'S OFFICE AND THE 1841 CENSUS

The beginning of the Victorian era marked the establishing

of permanent government machinery for both the recording
of vital statistics and the organisation and taking of the census.
Despite attempts to reform the regulation and practice of the
keeping of parish registers in the eighteenth and early nineteenth centuries they remained unsatisfactory.[25] Official,
medical and statistical opinion were, by the 1830s, in favour
of civil registration and a Select Committee was appointed in
1833 to enquire into the state of parochial registration. Two
Bills were introduced in February 1836 — one amending laws
regulating marriages of Dissenters and the second proposing a
general registration of births, deaths and marriages: considerably amended, these were passed on 17th August 1836
and came into operation on 1st March 1837.[26]

The administrative pattern of the new system of registration
grew out of the framework of Poor Law Unions set up under
the Poor Law Act of 1834. The 624 Unions were adopted as
registration districts within which 2,190 registrar's sub-districts
(in 1851) were created.[27] The new office of the Registrar
General was responsible for the conduct of registration and
the coordination of the returns into quarterly and annual
reports. Although registration was at first incomplete, especially for births, and legal penalties for failure to notify were
not introduced until 1874, the information is invaluable for
population studies in two ways. First, and so far little used in
research, there is a vast amount of information on the certificates of births, marriages and deaths[28] which, by nominal
record linkage,[29] could provide the individual demographic
histories which are the essential basis of cohort studies, one
of the most fruitful techniques of demographic analysis.
Secondly, much of this demographic data is summarised in
the quarterly and annual reports of the Registrar General.
The reports themselves contain summary tables of marriage,
births, deaths and emigration for England and Wales, with
particular reference to public health and epidemics in urban
areas. The tables include abstracts of marriages, by counties
and registration districts, while births and deaths are also given
for sub-districts, with summary tables of age of death by
county and district and cause of death for registration
divisions.[30]

Responsibility for taking the census also passed to the

General Register Office, and the 1841 census may thus be seen as the first modern census both in the range of information collected and in the procedures followed in the enumeration and processing of the results. Rickman may have been involved in the first Bill for the 1841 census which was brought before Parliament on 1st June 1840 and which envisaged a similar procedure and range of questions to previous censuses. But this was withdrawn in favour of a more wide-ranging enquiry, under the supervision of R.G. Lister, the first Registrar General, and the Census Commissioners, incorporating many — though not all — of the proposals made by a Committee of the Statistical Society of London.[31] Parish register abstracts were compiled for the last time, though the introduction of general civil registration had made them redundant from 1837. The registrars were responsible for dividing their sub-districts into enumeration districts of 100 households on average, though there was considerable variation in this (see below, Chapter 3). For each household a schedule was issued on which the head was required to enter particulars of each individual present on census night, their name, age and sex, occupation and birthplace. This established the nominative procedure for the taking of the census, which is of such fundamental value in enabling studies to be pursued at individual level and in relating the census to other personal information. The household schedules were collected, checked and transcribed by the enumerators into enumerators' books, together with a summary of houses and persons in the district, and estimates of persons temporarily present or absent from the district. These were checked and revised by the registrar and sent to the Census Office, together with a summary of the accounts of all enumerators, for final revision before the preparation of the abstracts. The original household schedules were destroyed on the authority of a Departmental Committee presided over by Sir H.C. Maxwell Lyte in 1904. In addition to the *Parish Register Abstracts*, three volumes of abstracts were produced in the 1841 census: these were the totals and birthplaces of population; ages; and occupations. The administrative areas for which these were given were mainly traditional — ancient counties, boroughs and parliamentary boroughs, Hundreds and Wapentakes, ancient parishes and their sub-divisions — though population and houses were also given for the new registration districts.[32] In this sense also the 1841 census marked a transition to those of the latter half of the nineteenth century.

3. THE CENSUS 1851—1891

The enumeration and processing of the census remained essentially the same from 1841 to 1901, though the new procedures were more fully developed and systematised by 1851.[33] The scope of the census questions and the detail in which the subjects of enquiry were treated were extended during the later nineteenth century (see Chapters 3—6 below), though the focus remained essentially as established in 1851: the names of members of households dwelling at specified addresses,[34] and particulars for each individual of relation to the head of the household, marital condition, age and sex, occupation, birthplace and infirmity (blind, deaf or dumb).

One fundamental change in the 1851 census was the full adoption of the new administrative framework under the Civil Registration Act of 1837 in the preparation of tables in the report. Each parish or place in England and Wales was arranged under the registration district and sub-district in which it was located, and these in turn were grouped into registration counties and eleven registration divisions.[35] Within this framework two sets of population tables were compiled: *Population Tables I* give population and houses at all census dates from 1801 to 1851; *Population Tables II*, for 1851 alone, include ages, civil condition, occupations, birthplaces and infirmities. The special censuses of religion and education, which were never to be repeated, were organised and conducted separately (see Chapters 7 and 8 below).

In 1861 the Census of Scotland was conducted separately, though on parallel lines to that in England and Wales, under the new registration procedures established in January 1855, a system which remains and has caused some difficulties in comparative studies.[36] A notable feature of the English census of 1861 was the bringing together in a *General Report* summary tables and a commentary on the results of the census. Much of the analysis of the results of the census and the remarkably detailed commentaries on population was the work of Dr William Farr, who had been appointed Compiler of Abstracts in the General Register Office in 1839 and was Assistant Commissioner at the 1851, 1861 and 1871 censuses. Farr, a distinguished statistician, who made notable contributions to demography, in particular to the study of mortality,[37] retired in 1880 after a long and distinguished career in the General Register Office.

The 1861 census also confirmed the pattern for the publication of the tables and reports which remained essentially the same for the 1871–1891 censuses. In addition to the *General Report* there were two volumes which presented tables of population and houses, first for a variety of administrative divisions — the ancient and geographical counties, together with the new administrative counties and county boroughs in 1891, and their divisions including the parliamentary divisions — and, secondly, for civil parishes in the various registration sub-districts and districts. A third volume gave tables of ages, civil condition, occupations and birthplaces for registration districts and principal towns.

Although the subject matter of the census schedules remained essentially the same between 1851 and 1891, numerous proposals for widening the scope of the enquiry were made from time to time. The turmoil of change in mid-Victorian times involved growth and redistribution of population, especially between country and town, unprecedented geographical, occupational and social mobility, vast problems of housing and health, particularly in the large towns and industrial districts, and the problems of personal, administrative and territorial adjustment to these new forces. There was widespread interest and concern over such matters in parliament, in local government and among the various statistical, medical, charitable and social organisations concerned with aspects of population. Various formal and informal links existed within and outside government circles relating such problems to the questions asked in the census: in 1851 proposals for collecting some information on wages, on health and on agriculture were made; in 1860 the Statistical Society again proposed an agricultural census. Attempts were made to include questions in the census on education, and details of accommodation, on industrial establishments and, in 1861, 1871 and 1881, a compulsory question on religion.[38] But all were rejected, partly due to opposition, partly for fear of making the schedule over-complex.

One of the most fundamental proposals, for a quinquennial census, was made by the National Association for the Promotion of Social Science in 1880. There was much evidence from errors in the Registrar General's estimates of population between censuses to indicate the need for more frequent censuses, and the case was pressed by the first departmental committee on the census, a Treasury Committee set up in 1890 of which Charles Booth was a member.[39] In the end little came of these representations, not least because of the cost involved: the first quinquennial census had to await the ten per cent sample census taken in 1966. Changes in the range of information gathered were meagre before 1911. In 1891 the enquiry on the Welsh language was introduced, there were some changes in occupational classification (see below, Chapter 5) and a division into 'employers, employed and working on own account' was introduced. Finally, a limited enquiry on housing, requiring the number of rooms in tenements of less than five rooms, was made, though proposals for much fuller details of housing had been made thirty years earlier.

4. THE EARLY TWENTIETH CENTURY CENSUSES

In organisation, content and tabulation the 1901 census is essentially nineteenth century in character, though in two important aspects it differed considerably from its predecessors. First, the considerable changes in organisation resulting from the Local Government Acts of 1888 and 1894 and the division of London into 28 metropolitan boroughs in 1899 are reflected in the increased complexity of the tabulations. Secondly, the report was published in separate volumes for each administrative county in England and Wales, which included tables of all the information gathered in the census — population, houses, tenements, age and sex, occupation, birthplaces and, for Wales, language. In addition an index to these county tables was provided, together with

summary tables and a *General Report*. Although tables of
population change, births, deaths and marriages for registration
districts were included in the county reports and summary
tables the emphasis had swung heavily away from the framework which had dominated the censuses of 1851—91.

The 1901 census was also the last to follow the procedure
whereby householders' schedules were copied into enumerators' books from which the results of the census were tabulated
by hand. The possibility of using Hollerith punched cards to
store and process census data had been first discussed by the
Departmental Committee on the Census in 1890,[40] and it
was adopted in 1911. Machine processing involved preliminary
coding, which was done direct from the household schedules.[41]
A second major change in the 1911 census was the advance
preparation of maps used in the drawing up of enumeration
districts,[42] which were later coordinated into a special set of
maps of each registration sub-district showing a variety of
administrative boundaries to ward and parish level.

The 1911 census also saw a number of important additions
to the enumeration. The most significant were the questions
relating to the first British survey of the fertility of marriage,
namely the duration of existing marriages and the numbers of
children born to each marriage and those alive at the time of
the census. Secondly, a question was asked on the industry in
which people worked, as well as their occupation (see below,
Chapter 5). Finally, the information on housing was considerably extended by a question on the number of rooms in all
dwellings.

The additional information and the much greater flexibility
of processing data by the punched card method permitted
much more detailed analysis of results than ever before and
produced a large number of very valuable cross-tabulations.
The county volumes of 1901 were abandoned and the table
for each subject, together with a report outlining the treatment of that subject in censuses since 1801, were published
in separate volumes.[43] Together with the *General Report,*
these provided an invaluable basic source for the student of
census history and the user of census statistics which is often
the readiest means of resolving difficulties in the use of

particular types of census information for the period 1801–1911.

Conclusion

While the reports in the 1911 census looked back over the information gathered on population trends and structure since 1801 and described the developments during the first three quarters of a century of the General Register Office, in its scope, its method of enquiry and compilation it looked forward to present-day methods of census-taking. Moreover many of the population changes between 1901 and 1911 anticipated later demographic trends: although the actual intercensal increase of population and the natural increase were the biggest ever recorded in England and Wales, the fertility enquiry indicated a decline in fertility and family size from the late nineteenth century.[44] Most of the larger cities had reached their population peak and suburbs were reaching out into the surrounding countryside; many of the major industrial and coalfield regions of Victorian Britain were losing population by migration to the South-east and Midlands of England. All these trends were to find their full expression in the years after the first world war.

The many environmental, social and economic problems of the nineteenth century — health and disease, housing and sanitation, employment and unemployment, deprivation and poverty — gave rise to an abundance of Royal Commissions and Committees of Enquiry and local government investigations and committee reports. But, in these and related matters, the census of population must often be the starting point of investigation, whether at the national or local scale.

The studies which follow are selective in their range of topics and their approach. They focus on practical problems in the utilisation of census material for England and Wales between 1801 and 1911 rather than on statistical methods of analysis or analytical techniques particular to individual disciplines. We have tried to provide a broadly-based practical introduction to the use of nineteenth century censuses which complements the factual information contained in the *Guide,* and which we hope will be of assistance to students and researchers in many disciplines — including local and regional history, economic and social history, sociology and geography — in which census material is being increasingly used. Studies involving census data must, of course, begin with the census reports themselves. Fortunately a selection of the volumes of the nineteenth century censuses, many of which were scarce, has been recently reprinted,[45] while many public libraries and county and city archives have copies of the enumerators' books for their locality on micro-film.

Users of the census should always approach the statistics carefully and critically. Errors in census data could arise through incorrect information supplied by the householder or enumerator, or through incorrect processing. The census-takers themselves believed that it was '... impossible ... to enumerate every individual ... so that the population is always somewhat understated; but there is reason to believe that the numbers that escape are few ... The errors in the revised figures are not likely to be of any magnitude'. However, the census-takers were well aware of the many possible sources of inaccuracy and confusion in their statistics and took great pains to guide their readers through the difficulties presented by changes in questions or units of tabulations or methods of analysis. Users of published censuses and of the enumerators' books should always study carefully the statements in reports and tabulations concerning the methods of collection and analysis of the data. In the end the census records and reports themselves are usually the best guide to their proper utilisation.

NOTES

1. D.V. Glass, *Numbering the people. The eighteenth-century population controversy and the development of census and vital statistics in Britain* (Saxon House, 1973).
2. Chapter 1 of E.A. Wrigley (ed.), *Nineteenth-century Society. Essays in the use of quantitative methods for the study of social data* (Cambridge University Press, 1972).
3. C. Booth, 'Occupations of the People of the United Kingdom, 1801—81', *Journal of the Statistical Society, 49* (1886).
4. See J.M. Goldstrom, *The Social Content of Education 1808—1870* (Irish University Press, 1972).

5. For a study of English family and household structure based on enumerators' books see M. Anderson, *Family Structure (1970)* summarised in chapter 2, 'The Study of Family Structure' in Wrigley, *op. cit.* A comparative international study is P. Laslett (ed.), *Household and Family in Past Time* (Cambridge University Press, 1972).

6. For a general study see R.Lawton, 'Population changes in England and Wales in the later nineteenth century: an analysis of trends by Registration Districts' *Transactions, Institute of British Geographers 44* (1968), pp. 55–74 and T.A. Welton, *England's Recent Progress* (Chapman and Hall, 1911).

7. The literature is voluminous and for official reports at national level the list of British Parliamentary Papers should be consulted. A useful introduction is provided by *English Historical Documents*, Vol. XI, 1783–1832 (ed. A.Aspinall and E.A. Smith, 1959), Vol. XII (1), 1833–1874 (ed. G.M. Young and W.D. Handcock, 1956), Vol. XII (2), 1874–1914 (ed. W.D. Handcock, 1977). For local studies, the local record office or library should be consulted. The only original census records likely to be found are the enumerators' lists for the 1801–1831 censuses, but local listings, population and social surveys were often carried out and there is usually a wealth of material on local health, housing and social problems which contain much population data.

8. See chapters 4–6 of E.A. Wrigley (ed.), *Identifying People in the Past* (Edward Arnold, 1973).

9. T.W. Freeman, *Pre-famine Ireland: A Study in historical geography* (Manchester University Press, 1951). Mr. Freeman shows that the Irish census was much fuller, in many ways, than the Census of Britain of 1841: for example, it gathered information on literacy (ability to read and write, and ability only to read), a much fuller account of housing and accommodation; from 1861 a question on religious allegiance was included in all censuses and, in addition to abundant statistical material on occupations, there is more information on farm sizes and agriculture than in the British censuses. Although there was no full civil registration of births and deaths (and causes of death) in Ireland until 1864, a notable study of the prevalence of disease was made in the 1851 Irish Census (*Report on the Status of Disease*) and was repeated in each census to 1911.

10. D.V. Glass, *op. cit.*

11. A.J. Taylor, 'The taking of the Census, 1801–1951', *British Medical Journal* April, 1951, pp. 715–22.

12. M. Drake, 'The Census, 1801–1891', Chapter 1 of E.A. Wrigley (ed.) *Nineteenth-century Society.*

13. *Guides to Official Sources: No. 2. Census Reports of Great Britain 1801–1931* (HMSO, 1951). See also *Guide to Census Reports Great Britain 1801–1966* (HMSO, 1977).

14. These are often widely scattered in historical and population journals, but there are numerous useful studies in the journal

Local Population Studies (1965 — continuing) and a number of classic papers are reprinted in D.V. Glass and D.E.C. Eversley (eds.) *Population in History. Essays in Historical Demography* (Edward Arnold, 1965). A recent short introduction to sources, methods and problems of study is N.L. Tranter, *Population since the industrial revolution. The case of England and Wales* (Croom Helm, 1973).

15. See, for example, E.A. Wrigley (ed.), *An Introduction to English Historical Demography* (Weidenfeld and Nicolson, 1966) and E.A. Wrigley (ed.) *Nineteenth-century Society.*

16. W. Farr's estimates suggest that '... in the period 1841—50 birth registration was about 93 per cent complete': (D.V. Glass, *op. cit.*, p. 131): for an earlier discussion see D.V. Glass, 'A note on the under-registration of births in Britain in the nineteenth century', *Population Studies 5* (1951—2), pp. 70—88.

17. For an account of this controversy see G.T. Griffith, *Population Problems of the Age of Malthus* (Cambridge University Press, 1926), D.V. Glass, 'Population and populations movements in England and Wales, 1700—1850', Chapter 9 of Glass and Eversley (eds.) *op. cit.* and D.V. Glass, *Numbering the people.* For a discussion of population trends in the eighteenth century see E.C.K. Gonner, 'The population of England in the eighteenth century', *Journal of the Royal Statistical Society*, 76 (1913), pp. 261—303, H.J. Habakkuk, 'English population in the eighteenth century', *Econ. Hist. Rev.* 2nd series, *vol. 6* (1953), pp. 117—33 and, for a recent brief review, M.W. Flinn, *British Population Growth, 1700—1850* (Macmillan, 1970).

18. For a review see C.M. Law, 'Local censuses in the eighteenth century', *Population Studies*, 23 (1969), pp. 87—100.

19. A pioneer study using aggregative and family reconstitution methods is E.A. Wrigley's study of Colyton, Devon, for which records are complete from the initiation of the system of parochial registration in 1538 to 1837. See his *Introduction to English Historical Demography*, Chapter 4, and his papers 'Family limitation in pre-industrial England, *Econ. Hist. Rev.* 2nd series, *vol. 19* (1966), pp. 82—109 and 'Mortality in pre-industrial England: the example of Colyton, Devon over three centuries', *Daedalus*, Spring 1968 (Historical Population Studies), pp. 546—80. There are a considerable number of local studies using parish registers: for two examples on Nottingham by J.D. Chambers and on Worcestershire by D.E.C. Eversley see Glass and Eversley, *op. cit.*

20. See Glass, *Numbering the People*, pp. 17—21.

21. Glass, *op. cit.*, p. 90 and, for a later version of Rickman's memorandum, pp. 106—13.

22. For example a number of forms for places in Bedfordshire survive in the library of the Office of Population Censuses and Surveys. I am indebted to Mrs. M. Havord of that Office for drawing my attention to these.

23. I am indebted to Mr. Paul Laxton of the Department of Geography, University of Liverpool for this information and for the Bolton example which follows. Mr Laxton has made a preliminary survey of local records of early nineteenth century censuses in England. Glass (*Numbering the People*) gives examples of some surviving local material for Braintree (Essex) and Croydon (Surrey) (*op. cit.* note 20, pp. 100—1). Similar documents survive in parts of Wales. Dr. W.T. Rees Pryce has traced manuscript census material for 1811 for Hawarden parish in the Bell Jones Collection of the Flintshire Record Office (see W.T.R. Pryce, unpublished Ph.D. thesis, CNAA, Lanchester Polytechnic, Coventry, 'The Social and Economic Structure of Northeast Wales, 1750—1850,' p. 59).

24. Bolton Reference Library, Census Returns for 1811 (MS 1), 1821 (MS 2) and 1831 (MS 3).

25. The Hardwicke Act of 1753 which instituted Banns of Marriage and required that weddings were solemnised in churches or chapels improved marriage registration, but Rose's Act of 1812 aimed at improving the keeping of parish registers was ineffectual: indeed, the quality of many registers deteriorated in the early nineteenth century.

26. An Act for Marriages in England and an Act for Registering Births, Deaths and Marriages in England (6 and 7/Gul. IV (cap. 85 and 86), 1836): these were implemented by an Act of 1 Vic. (cap. 22), 1837. A general account is Chap. 4 of Glass, *Numbering the People*). Civil registration in Scotland came later from 1st Jan 1855, under an Act of 1854, and led to a separate General Register Office.

27. For an account of the setting up of the machinery of civil registration (by R.G. Lister, the first Registrar General) see the *First Report of the Registrar General* (1839).

28. Births had to be registered within 42 days and the certificate contained the sex of the child, name and surname, rank or profession of the father and the name and maiden surname of the mother. Marriage registers were signed in church and the certificates included age, marital status and rank or profession of the bride and bridegroom and the occupations of the respective fathers. Death registration was required within five days of death and the certificate gave name, age, sex and rank of the deceased, and the cause of death, though this was not included as a legal requirement of registration until the 1874 Amending Act which also introduced legal penalties for failure to notify a birth, marriage or death.

29. An account of some of the techniques and problems of nominative record linkage is given in E.A. Wrigley (ed.), *Identifying People in the Past.*

30. The 13th (for 1850), 23rd (1860) and 33rd (1870) Annual Reports contain valuable summary tables for the preceding decade of marriages (for registration districts), births and deaths (for

districts and sub-districts). In combination with the population totals from the censuses of 1851, 1861 and 1871 it is possible to calculate population change due to natural trends (that is the balance of births and deaths) and net migration. From 1871, these may be calculated by summing from the annual reports.

31. In addition to the census questions eventually included on the Schedule (for which see Chapter 2 below), questions were proposed on marital status, religion and health, with more detail than was eventually obtained on birthplace and occupation (*Jnl. Stat. Soc., Vol. 3* (1840), pp. 72–101 and 204–5 and *Vol. 4* (1841), pp. 69–70).

32. See below, Appendix XI. A very useful table of areas for which census information was tabulated is given in Appendix 2 to M. Drake 'The Census, 1801–1891', pp. 7–46 of E.A. Wrigley (ed.) *Nineteenth-century Society*.

33. These procedures are fully described in the *Report* to the 1851 Census, pp. xi–xvii. For the instructions to registrars concerning enumerators and enumeration districts see the *Report*, p. cxxxv.

34. For a discussion of the methods of distinguishing separate households on the schedules see below, chapter 2.

35. The registration counties were amalgamations of registration districts covering much of the same territory but not exactly co-extensive with the ancient or geographical counties; this is confusing where — as in the birthplace tables — both types of unit are used, in this case to show the geographical county of birth of those enumerated in the 624 registration districts of England and Wales (see Baines, chapter 4, below). For a description of the topographical organisation of the census tables see the Report to the 1851 Census, section II, 1 (Plan of the publication), pp. xix *seq.* The 11 Registration divisions were London, South Eastern, South Midland, Eastern, South Western, West Midland, North Midland, North Western, Yorkshire, Northern and Welsh.

36. For example, the administrative areas used in tabulation are different in character; in birthplace statistics no details of the county of birth of Scots living in England, and vice-versa, are given; and the form of the schedule and tabulations differ in detail. For an outline of these differences see *The Guide*.

37. For his classic study of occupational mortality see the *35th Annual Report of the Registrar General* (1875). A collection of his work is contained in N.A. Humphreys (ed.), *Vital Statistics* (1885).

38. For an account of these various representations see M. Drake, *op. cit.*, pp. 10–19.

39. Drake, *op. cit.*, p. 14.

40. Drake, *op. cit.*, p. 15.

41. For a full account see *1911 Census of England and Wales. General Report, Appendix B.* Three sets of cards were used; one for information relating to individuals; a second for the fertility

enquiry; and a third for population and buildings in enumeration districts.

42. See Census 1911, *Preliminary Report*, pp. iii–iv.
43. For a list of the volumes of the 1911 census see below Appendix XI pp. 298–9; they include a *Preliminary Report, Summary Tables,* a *General Report* and volumes covering area, families and population, buildings, tenements, marriage, birthplaces, occupations and industries, the Welsh language and fertility.
44. For a modern analysis see D.V. Glass and E. Grebenik, *The Trend and Pattern of Fertility in Britain* (HMSO, 1954).
45. Irish University Press series of *British Parliamentary Papers*; Population (25 volumes) (1968–70).

CHAPTER 2

The Census Enumerators' Books: a Commentary

W.A. ARMSTRONG

No commentary on nineteenth century English censuses would be complete without a chapter on the nature, utility and limitations of the original enumerators' books — a source virtually untapped until a few years ago, but which is now attracting legions of historians and social scientists seeking a long-term historical perspective for their studies. In what is believed to be the first general description of the source, M.W. Beresford confined himself to observations on the utility of the material to biographers, genealogists, and local historians.[1] Other scholars had also made limited use of the source, but it is probably fair to say that no methodology designed for its *systematic* exploitation was published until 1966, the by-product of my thesis on the social structure of mid-nineteenth century York.[2]

My study of York used 1 in 10 samples drawn on a household basis from the enumerators' books for 1841 and 1851. Thus details of 628 and 781 for 1841 and 1851 respectively were recorded in notebooks and subsequently codified for processing on standard 80-column Hollerith punched cards, each with up to 12 punching positions, details of which are given in Wrigley (1966), pp. 220—1. From these cards it was possible to produce tables relating the several variables efficiently and quickly. The main findings of this study of York and a similar piece of work in Nottingham have already appeared, and we may anticipate a spate of publications of a similar nature during the next few years.[3]

The method of analysis painfully thrashed out by an inexperienced research student could not aspire to be definitive and now requires amplification and modification in the light of the work of others and of my own experience. In recent years, advances have been made on almost all fronts: investigators have now examined many more of the enumerators' books; weaknesses and areas of confusion in my original methodology have been exposed, leading to a good deal of highly fruitful discussion on standardisation; the aid of the computer has been enlisted by several researchers; and novel methods of analysing the data to answer ever more specific and more carefully defined questions are constantly being proposed. This activity suggests that the census enumerators' books have become common ground for at least three categories of scholars.

1. Practitioners of what Dr Eversley has called the 'new social history', who are less concerned with the domestic manners of the various classes or their sports and pastimes than with tracing the development of social structure and popular culture.[4] Historical demography and the evolution of household and family structure are obviously central here, though these are by no means to be treated in isolation from related cultural, economic, or political trends.

2. Local historians working either individually or increasingly in groups with professional tutors. Though primarily interested in local developments, such researchers cannot avoid methodological debates if they are to make full use of the data. As it happens, familiarity with topography and terrain may give the local historian special advantages in interpreting census data.

3. Social scientists seeking the dynamics of long-term change, for an historical perspective or for opportunities to apply empirical tests to accepted generalisations: such scholars are likely to tend to give their work a more consciously theoretical orientation though in practice their methods may not differ greatly from investigators in the first two groups.

Against this background of activity, the time seems ripe to survey the enumerators' books of the mid-nineteenth century from the following selective standpoints:

1. the administration of the censuses of 1841–71;
2. the nature and quality of the data in the enumerators' books;
3. the range of uses to which they can be put from the point of view of the social historian; and
4. the much-debated issues of the best procedures for ordering the data into households and families; of sampling; of the classification of occupations and of the use of computers.

The administration of the census

The census of 1841 was the first carried out by officials of the recently created General Register Office. When the system of civil registration came into operation in 1837, 624 registration districts were created in England and Wales, co-extensive with the new Poor Law Unions of 1834,[5] each having a superintendant registrar. These in turn were divided into 2,190 sub-districts, each with its local registrar of births, deaths and marriages. For the purpose of the census, the 2,190 registrars were directed to divide their sub-districts into enumeration districts, numbering, in 1841, over 30,000. By these means the services of the Overseers of the Poor, who had conducted the 1801–31 censuses, were dispensed with[6] and it was found possible to number the people 'in one day', in order to obviate the chance of inaccuracy from omissions or double entry.[7] Even if, as one suspects, some overseers were in fact appointed as enumerators, a degree of guidance at the local level could now have been expected from local registrars. Householders' schedules and enumerators' summary books were used for the first time and distributed a few days before census day to allow familiarisation with the contents. Their use, it was reported, had 'contributed in no small degree to the accuracy of the returns . . . while they greatly lightened the labours of the enumerators on the day on which the census was taken'.[8] These schedules, after having been examined by the several registrars and countersigned by the superintendent registrars, were returned to the census commissioners in London. At the census office, upwards of 100 million separate facts were reduced into tabular statements by clerks who, we are told, worked for months with ready willingness for 12 hours a day, despite the fact that they were 'an establishment . . collected together for the express purpose, remunerated with the lowest salaries, and without prospect of employment from Government beyond the continuance of the office'.[9]

In 1851 the procedure was similar. Householders' schedules were delivered in the week preceding 31st March, as well as the special forms used for places of religious worship and schools.[10] The forms were all collected on one day, and, the enumerators were required to fill up any incomplete schedules after verbal enquiry, as well as to correct any 'manifestly false particulars'. The enumerators then transcribed particulars from the schedules into the 'enumerator's book', according to a set of instructions set out below (see Appendix I) and completed some first stage summary tables of houses and persons enumerated. A week was allowed for this, after which the books and schedules were passed to the local registrar who was required to examine and revise them, paying special attention to the correctness of the place-headings (parish, township, etc.), the observance of the correct boundaries of the enumeration district, the possibility of omission, the correct use of the 'lines for the purpose of distinguishing houses and separate occupiers', the accuracy of summary totals, and the consistent use of the proper columns for each question. The registrar then forwarded the original schedules to the census office, and the enumeration books to the superintendent registrar, who was to revise them again, but less minutely.[11] Further revision was carried out at the census office, special attention being paid to inconsistent entries under age and sex, relation to head of family and marital condition, and to the correctness of the totals at the foot of each page and at the end of each book.[12]

On any account, the census of 1851 was a great improvement on its predecessor although it actually cost less to administer.[13] More care had been taken with the form of the questionnaire, which now called for further precision in the recording of birthplaces (parish and county of birth) and ages (which were no longer, as with over-15s in 1841, to be given merely to the lowest term of 5). Above all, the relationship of each individual to the household head and his or her marital condition had to be recorded, this being accordingly the first English census which can be used for the precise study of family and household structure. The census authorities pronounced themselves much gratified with the results. Not once, in ensuring the completion of over four million schedules, had the penalties of the law been enforced. 'The information was cheerfully furnished, and on the whole, we believe, with a nearer approach to accuracy than has before been attained, here or elsewhere. The working classes often took much trouble to get their schedules filled up, and to facilitate the enquiry'.[14]

The forms and procedures used at the next two censuses were closely similar to those of 1851. It is possible that the quality of enumeration was slightly higher, since in 1861 'several of the enumerators who had acted in the same capacity ten years before remarked that a more intelligent appreciation of the objects and uses of the inquiry, combined with the utmost willingness to furnish the returns, was evinced by the poorer population; a result which may be fairly ascribed to the co-operation of the educated and influential classes of society, particularly of the clergy of all denominations and of public writers in the press', whilst that of 1871 was 'fully as correct as any census that has ever been taken'.[15]

To summarise, it will be appreciated that there were three distinct stages in each census:

1. distribution and collection of householders' schedules;
2. compilation of the enumerators' books (specimen pages are illustrated in Appendix I);
3. preparation and publication of the printed abstracts or reports (see Appendix XI).

Nature and quality of the information in the enumerators' books

The original householders' schedules used in these censuses (stage 1) have been destroyed and there survive only the enumerators' books and the printed abstracts (i.e. Stages 2 and 3 in the census process). Errors in census material can be identified only in the two surviving sources, though many such errors would originate at Stage 1.[16] Broadly speaking, errors in census data may be classified under two headings:

1. errors of coverage, that is under- or (much less commonly) over-enumeration;
2. errors of content, that is mistakes in reporting or recording or in further processing of the data.

ERRORS OF COVERAGE

The direct procedure of checking for omission used today is to compare the census results with other independent data such as civil registers, electoral lists, tax records, etc. Another method is to reveal the omission rate by promptly following up the main enquiry with a sample census, under more rigorously controlled conditions. A third approach is to compare census results with population estimates generally based on the results of the previous census, making due allowance for births, deaths, and migration. On the basis of the last method it has been suggested that modern British censuses are only very slightly defective in overall numbers (by one part in 1,000 in 1921, one-half a part per 1,000 in 1931 and three per 1,000 in 1951),[17] but it is clear that this method has little applicability in a situation where every census may be expected to be a considerable improvement on its predecessor, whether in underdeveloped countries today or in early attempts at census-taking in Europe.

Whatever the overall rate of omission, it is recognised that deficiencies are liable to be most marked in respect of infants and very young children. By comparing the results of the enumerations of 1921, 1931 and 1951 with the relevant registration records, it has been found that deficiencies in the totals recorded for the first two years of life were 46,000, 33,000 and 23,000 (2.9 per cent, 2.8 per cent and 1.2 per cent respectively).[18]

In the nineteenth century there were no follow-up sample censuses and, since the independent sources needed for checking are either themselves open to question (for example, registration particulars) or of very doubtful reliability (for example, migration statistics), the actual amount of omission in these censuses must remain a matter for conjecture. The introduction of the householders' schedule in 1841 and the dropping of the old tally-sheet methods may have produced some improvement,[19] but one cannot say how much. A number of scholars have pointed to improbable irregularities in age-distribution which suggest omission,[20] but the only serious attempt to calculate the probable level of omission is that of D.V. Glass.[21] Glass aimed primarily at calculating the under-registration of births, which he approached by constructing estimates of child populations from the relevant statistics of births and deaths, then comparing these with the corresponding census statistics covering children in the 2—4 age group (i.e. omitting children aged 0—1 in the census, assumed to be particularly deficient). He was thus able to calculate a series of correction factors of great interest which showed that birth registration became virtually complete by 1881.[22] Once registration was complete, an accurate ratio of the estimated population aged 0—4 to the enumerated population could be calculated. Then, by backward extrapolation, Glass estimated child (0—4) populations for 1871, 1861 and 1851 and compared these with the actual enumerated populations. The ratios between enumerated and estimated populations were as follows:

1871	1.027 (m)	1.026 (f);
1861	1.033 (m)	1.030 (f);
1851	1.048 (m)	1.042 (f);

Thus omissions within the 0—4 age group varied between 4.5 per cent (1851) and 2.5 per cent (1871). There are no better estimates of omission from the censuses and no one can be sure about the dispersion of local omission rates around these national means.

ERRORS OF CONTENT

The question of *mis-statement of ages* overlaps with the problems of omission discussed above, since a proportion of the under-representation in the 0—2, or 0—4 age groups could be simply the result of rounding up young children's ages. Various census reports have published the results of inquiries into mis-statements of age, but for Britain there is nothing of much value before Dunlop's analysis of the age returns of the Scottish census of 1911, which was confined to children's ages.[23] Dunlop attempted to match census records relating to 14,400 children under 5 in two registration districts to the corresponding birth records. Only 11,981 could actually be matched. The comparison showed that ages 0 and 1 were 4.8 per cent and 2.9 per cent deficient respectively, but ages 2, 3 and 4 were slightly inflated in the census. The errors arose out of age overstatement by one year only, in the vast majority of cases.

It would not be unreasonable to suspect the censuses of the mid-nineteenth century of containing errors at least as large. Krause has inferred omission in the child age groups by comparing the sex ratios for 1841 with those implied by the English Life Table No. 3. Males per 1,000 females in age groups 0–4 and 5–9 in the census were 991 and 1001 respectively, while the corresponding ratios from the life table were 1014 and 1010. This suggests omission, but it must be remembered that the method depends upon the accuracy of the data on mortality from which the life table was drawn up.

With infants and young children, deficiencies probably arose mainly from the upward rounding of the ages of children who were 'near enough' 1, 2, 3 etc. – and probably from an erroneous impression that newly born children who were unchristened or unnamed need not be included. How far adults were fully knowledgeable of their own ages and, even more, how frankly they were prepared to disclose them, is another question. Krause has noted that 'simple inspection of the female age groups (of 1841) reveals apparent inaccuracy'. The 20–4 age group in 1841 was larger than that of 15–19; the 40–4 age group larger than the 35–9, and the 60–4 group larger than that of 55–9. With males, these peculiarities were not evident to the same extent, since only the 60–4 age group was larger than the preceding one.[24] Very approximate age data were perhaps the best that could be expected from the 1841 census, since the age question was novel and since only an indication to the lowest term of 5 was required from adult persons over 15.

The data for 1851 exhibit no such crude irregularities, which would accordingly lead one to expect that the age data (now required precisely) were more exact, at least for young persons and adults. But the compilers of the abstracts themselves noted some evident mis-statements,[25] and it is now possible to bring to bear various revealing pieces of evidence, from recent studies based on the census enumerators' books. Professor Tillott's study group has compared the ages of persons found in both the 1851 and 1861 enumerators' books for Hathersage (Derbyshire) and 157 persons in the village of Braithwell (Yorkshire) and his results are shown in Table 2.1.

TABLE 2.1
Accuracy of age statements, 1851 and 1861

	Percentage of cases with 10 year interval	Percentage of cases with 9 or 11 year interval	Percentage of cases with a larger error
Hathersage	60.6	28.0	11.4
Braithwell	67.5	22.4	10.1

Dr M. Anderson has traced 475 inhabitants of Preston recorded both in 1851 and 1861, and found that no fewer than 47 per cent are credited with an age in 1861 more or less than 10 years older than that given in 1851. However, only 4 per cent were more than two years out and under 1 per cent more than five years in error.[26] Essentially this method tests consistency and, since it to some extent compounds the errors of both censuses, the true errors in any one census will be considerably less than those given above.

Another test of the quality of age data is designed to measure the extent to which there is an over-concentration by respondents on ages which end with the digits '0' or '5'. One sums the age returns between 23 and 62 years (inclusive) and calculates the ratio of the sum of the returns of years ending with 5 and 0 to one-fifth of the total sum of returns.[27] The method requires detailed knowledge of the age distribution; quinquennial groups, such as were printed in the census abstract, will not do. However, it proved possible to apply it to detailed-age data drawn from York in 1851, consisting of 635 household heads and 484 wives.[28] For the household heads, the Whipple coefficient was 120.4, and for their wives, 129.0. Conventionally, scores of 100–104.9 are taken to indicate 'highly accurate' age enumeration, 105–109.9 'fairly accurate', 110–124.9 'approximate', 125–174.9 'rough', and 175 and over 'very rough'. If the York data were representative of the country as a whole, the English census of 1851 would fall into the approximate or rough category.

Birthplace data are obviously much more difficult to check, though it would presumably be possible (if exceedingly laborious) to check individual statements against parochial or civil registration data. Anderson provides an indication of the level of reliability for Preston by using a test again based on the principle of consistency. Of the 475 persons traced in two successive censuses, a minimum of 14 per cent had a discrepancy between the two years. Some of these were not of great importance, 'but in half of these cases migrants became non-migrants and *vice versa*'.[29] Apart from the occurrence of obvious clerical errors, Anderson's data represent the sum total of what is known about the reliability of the birthplace returns.

Altogether more attention has been paid to the reliability of the *occupational data*. Tillott suggests that when census data are compared with the corresponding information given in directories 'on the whole the directory entry tends to be more detailed but rarely differs from the census about the main occupation followed ... generally speaking the tendency is to upgrade the status implied by the census occupation but this is a characteristic that should be regarded with suspicion since it is most probably a reflection of the advertising nature of the directories'.[30] It is well known that, in 1851, farmers sometimes failed to specify their acreage, and, frequently, the number of men they employed.[31] Tradesmen neglected to state whether they were masters-in-trade or journeymen, or how many workers they employed.[32] Apart from these general deficiencies, the census authorities criticised the 'extremely inaccurate and inadequate manner' in which respondents persisted in describing their callings, in census after census. It was claimed that characteristic faults included a tendency to state, in very general terms, only the industry within which the respondent worked (e.g. 'cotton hand'), or his personal position without reference to the industry ('foreman', 'weaver', etc.); purely local or colloquial terms ('all-rounder', 'baubler', 'crowder', 'dasher', 'fluker', etc.) were used; and probably the returns were affected by 'the foolish but very common desire of persons to magnify the importance of their occupational condition'.[33]

Such deficiencies in the occupational return were in part caused by a paucity of relevant instructions on the householder's schedule. Although there were thirteen short paragraphs of instructions on this point on the reverse of the 1851 schedule,[34] no less than six were devoted to laying down in detail the procedure to be adopted in recording the occupations, titles and degrees of landed and professional respondents, and two or three more were concerned with how to record people outside the labour market (young children, persons with no specific calling, etc.). Not until 1911 was an extra question introduced into the schedule designed to distinguish between personal occupation and industry of employment.

It was clearly impossible to produce summary tabulations more accurate than the data from which they were drawn, and the shifting systems of classification employed in successive censuses make comparisons across the years somewhat hazardous. Moreover, retired persons were included in their original occupations prior to 1881; students and apprentices with the trades or professions for which they were training;

TABLE 2.2
Proportion of wives and husbands temporarily away from home, 1851

Age	Proportion of wives absent to 100 husbands	Proportion of husbands absent to every 100 wives
15	86.7	50.4
16	89.5	31.8
17	66.5	19.3
18	38.6	14.2
19	19.5	11.6

Census 1851, *Population Tables II* (I), p. xxix

and, there is good reason to suspect, labourers with crafts-men.[35]

On the other hand, data on the *civil or conjugal condition* of the people was probably complete. The census report commented that overall about 1 in 13 of husbands and wives were temporarily separated on census night, but such separation was particularly marked in the 15–19 age group (Table 2.2): the probability is that a proportion of those persons under the age of 20 who were returned as married were not.

Use of the census enumerators' books

The uses to which this comprehensive body of material may be put are very varied, as are the levels of sophistication of methods of analysis which can be employed. They will yield information on individuals,[36] they can be brought to bear to illustrate the history of institutions, communities, particular social groups, streets or areas. For example, a simple count of railway workers in York in 1851 revealed to E.M. Sigsworth that, out of 513, 390 were immigrants, and these had brought with them 537 dependents. For St Helens, T.C. Barker and J.R. Harris concluded from the evidence of the enumerators' books that the Irish element was overwhelmingly concentrated in three districts of the town.[37] This kind of approach simply seeks to amplify what can be derived from the printed census reports, since the census authorities did not, on the whole, attempt to do much more than provide printed summary tables relating to total population, total of houses, age and sex structure, marital conditions, and occupations. Even this aggregative information is available in the printed volumes only for larger towns and registration districts, so that comparable data for smaller units such as parishes and town-ships has to be wrested from the original returns.[38] (See below pp. 121–27 for a discussion of this problem in urban areas.)

Many local historians will of course require to work with units of this size. One can surmise that students will find the appeal of looking at their community on a 'then and now' basis irresistible, and that the significance of local studies could bear on some of the most interesting issues in social history, such as rural depopulation, decline in the birth rate, the changing size and distribution of units of production and the like.

In recent years, there have been a number of attempts to handle the data systematically on a larger scale, with a view to *measuring the relationships between variables.* An early case in point is Professor Lawton's study of Liverpool, which surveys the population in 1851 by means of 17 samples drawn from different districts within the Liverpool area.[39] This study was successful in drawing attention to the distinctiveness of various districts or zones in the area, but the analysis was conducted only in terms of occupations, migratory groups, and age—sex structure, and with certain exceptions, such as his attempt to relate birthplaces to occupations, we are left to form impressions about the relationships of these variables to one another. Subsequent work, while by no means ignoring spatial variables, has paid increasing attention to household and family composition and the factors governing these parameters, which social historians and sociologists tend to view as an undeservedly neglected and uncharted field. Whilst it would be futile to try to indicate here all the uses to which the census enumerators' books can be put, an idea of the possibilities can be gained from briefly considering a selection of results from some of the studies which are already completed, especially in respect of household and family structure, and immigration patterns.

The analysis of household and family size and composition is not yet free from ambiguities,[40] but a few statistics at present available, when viewed comparatively, are beginning to fall into a meaningful pattern. Comparing York, a community which had urbanised quite rapidly, with Preston (a true factory town, characterised both by rapid population growth and industrialisation), and both in turn with modern data and with the 100 pre-industrial communities which have been studied by Laslett,[41] the following similarities and differences are evident:

1. Mean household size in York was the same as in the pre-industrial communities (4.7), while in Preston it was higher (5.4). All are substantially higher than in modern England and Wales.

2. Contrary to what one might imagine, households with kin were twice as prominent in 1851 as in Laslett's pre-industrial parishes (Preston 23 per cent, York 22 per cent, Laslett 10 per cent). By 1966, the national proportion had reverted to the pre-industrial level.

3. The proportion of households with lodgers was much higher in Preston (23 per cent) and in York than in Laslett's communities (less than 1 per cent, outside London) or in modern Swansea (less than 4 per cent).

4. The proportion of households with servants was markedly lower in Preston (10 per cent) than in Laslett's communities (28 per cent). The York figure is over 21 per cent, perhaps attributed to the fact that York was still almost wholly pre-industrial in 1851.

Obviously such comparisons are very crude and pose further questions before their significance can be finally assessed. Analysis of the communities in question is pushed much further than is possible here in the various studies from which these statistics have been drawn.[42]

The census enumerators' books also throw new light on migration problems, as the following selection of findings for York[43] shows:

1. Irish-born household heads were significantly over-represented in social classes IV and V (56.0 per cent), by comparison with those born in York itself (21.6 per cent), the West Riding (25.7 per cent), contiguous northern counties (16.1 per cent), or the rest of England (12.8 per cent).

2. York-born household heads were distributed among the social classes very closely in accordance with overall community proportions, but immigrants tended to be clustered towards the upper and lower extremes. Long-distance immigrants (except the Irish) tended to bunch towards the top (for example 35.9 per cent of heads born in the rest of England were in social classes I and II as against 20.8 per cent of the York-born): whilst local immigrants from the agricultural East and North Ridings were over-represented at the bottom (33.0 per cent in classes IV and V, as against 21.6 per cent York-born).

3. Whilst each York registration sub-district had a very high proportion of immigrant heads and wives (63 to 72.5 per cent), significantly more heads born in the West Riding were found south of the river; but in absolute terms heads born in the East and North Riding predominated across the whole city, probably reflecting the fact that West Riding towns had a stronger pull than did York.

4. 65.4 per cent of household heads were immigrants, but as many as 72.0 per cent of their wives, giving some support to the view that females were more migratory than males over short distances.[44]

5. 67.5 per cent of York's predominantly female domestic servants were immigrants from the surrounding Ridings and only 21.2 per cent were actually born in the City of York.

Furthermore, the York sub-district (Walmgate) most noted for its unwholesome public health conditions, both in 1841 and 1851, contained proportionately more class III — V and fewer class I — II residents than the healthier sub-districts. However, the sample suggested that the mean number of children aged 0—4 per 100 married women was about as high in the most unwholesome sub-district (852 as against 804 and 838 — no assertion of difference was possible with these figures), implying that the known higher fertility of that sub-district made up for its higher losses from infant mortality. Such a conclusion was strengthened by the ratios of children 0—15 to the toal population in the census which worked out at 41.7, 41.2, and 42.5 per cent respectively, for the three York sub-districts. Yet, as other reports show,[45] Walmgate was the least effectively schooled and churched area of the city. Thus, by relating census data, both from the enumerators' books and the printed volumes, to other statistical sources, notably the annual reports of the Registrar General and private enquiries, and to the literary or qualitative evidence, a mosaic of patterns begins to emerge.

Considerable interest has been shown by geographers in the value of enumerators' books for the study of spatial distribution. In addition to Lawton's study,[46] Dr June

Shepherd has examined ratios of acreage per agricultural worker and mapped out the regional distribution of agricultural labourers, farm servants and family workers under varying soil conditions in the East Riding of Yorkshire.[47] An interesting paper by P.J. Taylor primarily intended as a theoretical contribution to the methodology of using the locational variable as a differentiating element in the construction of regional systems, uses as an illustration of 'location-based nodal clustering' eight discrete and compact social regions based on the social status scores of 302 enumeration districts of Liverpool in 1851.[48] (See also Chapter 3, below, pp. 126–7).

These examples serve to indicate the sort of conclusions which may be drawn from manipulation of the data in the census enumerators' books. No complete conspectus of their uses can be drawn up at this stage, for it is certain that ingenious researchers will go on adding to the methodology for years to come. These developments are likely to involve more sophisticated statistical techniques and a more consciously theoretical orientation.

The basic statistical tools used by most researchers have been and may well continue to be simple measures of averages, dispersion, and proportions — which might be termed descriptive statistics — or, where samples have been used, elementary procedures based on the normal distribution which must be brought to bear to test the reliability of resultant estimates (inferential statistics). The extent to which historians will be impelled towards using more advanced statistical techniques, such as multiple correlation, factor and principal components analysis, remains to be seen and this is not the place to expound on them.[49] Two examples of imaginative statistical estimation may be cited here however, one an ingenious but purely arithmetical operation, the other relying on orthodox statistical procedures of a more sophisticated kind than historians usually use.

Dr M. Anderson found that 65 per cent of his sample of the population of Preston aged over 65 resided with children, married or unmarried. This figure is immeasurably more significant when it is appreciated that only about two-thirds of the age group in question would have had a child alive at all.[50] In fact the outcome of his calculations is an estimate that 30 per cent of the aged population of Preston would have had no surviving children in 1851, and that 70 per cent or thereabouts had only one child alive. Compared with the 65 per cent who were in fact living with a child, the striking conclusion emerged that nearly all old people with a child alive were in fact living with that child. As Anderson remarks, such estimates are necessary to provide a yardstick against which to measure one's findings and they will no doubt be developed much further.

A similar statistical yardstick, used by J.O. Foster,[51] is based on matching actual data with predicted random patterns. Foster was seeking indirect indications of the extent to which a sense of common *class* consciousness would be found among skilled workers and labourers in Oldham by looking at the incidence of intermarriage between these groups (using the Registrar General's marriage certificates) and also at incidence of craft-labour neighbouring (from addresses in the enumerators' books). In both cases the essence of the technique is to compare actual incidences with postulated random incidences derived from contingency tables. Deviations from random behaviour can then be assessed by the usual tests of significance of difference.[52]

Another likely development in census studies is the adoption of a more consciously theoretical approach. Unfortunately, many historians tend to confuse the term 'theory' with grandiose cosmic explanations of complex phenomena, exemplified in the nineteenth century by Marx and Malthus and in the twentieth by Toynbee and Spengler. They do not always appreciate the extent to which social scientists have withdrawn from the search for universal and comprehensive laws governing human society and have narrowed their sights on more modest targets, progressively advancing from one fragmentary hypothesis to another, isolating facts through the medium of their interpretation and testing their interpretations by the facts. Theory is often seen merely in terms of the dictionary definition — that is 'supposition explaining something' — as opposed to hypothesis — 'supposition made as a basis for reasoning'. There seems to be no reason why historians should not theorise more logically and systematically by reference to the scientific procedures appropriate to the social sciences. Theory helps to define the questions to which the historian can most fruitfully address himself while at the same time it can help to form analytical categories which permit cross-comparison over time and as between different social situations. The conscious application of theory has perhaps been hitherto most consistently advocated and attained in the field of economic history,[53] but there also appears to be a powerful trend in the area of political history away from character biographies towards the analysis of past patterns of mass political behaviour, an emphasis which may have started with Namier and which, for a later period and at grass-roots level, has been termed 'electoral sociology'.[54] In the analysis of census data, economic and sociological theories are likely to be most relevant, especially those relating to the factors governing family and household structure, population change, occupational distribution and migration. The historian should approach such sources with an awareness that sound theory will contribute to logical interpretation of data and that his findings, if ordered aright, can contribute to the enrichment of social theory through its study in the time dimension. No doubt such considerations led one of our leading historians to write that 'the more sociological history becomes, and the more historical sociology becomes, the better for both'.[55]

Some special methodological problems

Since 1964, when my contribution to Wrigley (1966) was prepared, a great deal of methodological discussion concerning the use of the census enumerators' books has taken place. Four leading issues are commented on in the following pages: sampling procedures; definitions of households and families; the classification of occupations; and the potentialities of computers in this field.

SAMPLING

The method of sampling used in my study of York involved taking every tenth household and, where that household turned out to be institutional or 'quasi-institutional', replacing it by the next normally acceptable household (see below); the next household sampled would then be the ninth, retaining the original sequence. This procedure has been censured by Floud and Schofield,[56] who point out that this sampling proportion is not in fact one in 10, but an unknown proportion of 'normal' households (less than 10 per cent in fact). Moreover, a sample so drawn must be biased since:

1. some households (those appearing in the source immediately after institutions or quasi-institutions) have a double chance of selection ('one might for instance, have an overweighting of schoolmasters living next to their schools');
2. there will be an over-representation of normal households in those areas of the community where the institutions and quasi-institutions are thick on the ground. ('If these areas happen to be where a particular set of economic or social conditions prevail — if for example they happen to be the poorer areas, the slums clustered round Irish boarding houses — then the results of the sample will be biased.'

I have shown that only overall community results could be significantly biased in the manner suggested and that for York the replacement procedure objected to was only used 11 times in drawing a sample of 781 households in 1851.[57] Nor would the replacement procedure be used often in studies of other communities, for many institutions are separately treated outside the main body of schedules, and quasi-institutions (in the sense in which they were defined for this purpose)[58] are unlikely to be common.

However, Floud and Schofield's alternative sampling method is likely to produce a marginally more representative sample. Their disarmingly simple solution is to sample 'the whole population' which must then yield a sample representative of the whole population.[59] This is easy to envisage if every n'th individual *person* was being sampled; one would then take every n'th name, whether in an ordinary household, in a lodging or boarding house, or in a large-scale institution, such as a hospital or workhouse. But it might not be so easy to operate where the household is being used as the sampling unit. It might be found more practicable to *begin* the analysis by excluding institutions and quasi-institutions, renumbering and sampling on the basis of every n'th household in the remainder, which would be greatly facilitated if a Xerox copy of the returns was in use.

All are agreed that while the institutions and quasi-institutions referred to are certainly part of the total social structure of a given community and that their analysis should never be neglected, it would be misleading to incorporate institutional data into the main sample of households as these would almost certainly distort conclusions concerning household size and composition. In their calculations of household composition modern census-takers similarly exclude persons enumerated in hotels, boarding houses, defence establishments and institutions generally,[60] with the same object in view, that is to focus attention on the private household as such.

Turning to the broader issues, it is obvious that other forms of sampling can be used in connection with the census enumerators' books. Systematic samples may reveal the broad parameters of a community's social structure but as analyses become increasingly sophisticated and explicit, the more evident do their disadvantages become. Thus Anderson remarks that a 10 per cent household sample of Preston (population 69,542 in 1851), produced only 93 persons over the age of 65, only 158 childless couples where the wife was under 45, only 38 upper middle class and only 32 'families definitely migrant from purely agricultural areas.'[61] Should such specific groups be of special interest to the researcher, all these totals are too small to obtain significant statistical results. Similar drawbacks appeared in my York (1851) sample of 781 households which yielded only 39 household heads in class I, and only 25 Irish-born household heads, etc. Some of the drawbacks of working with small sub-groups may be seen from the following examples from York. In a table of the mean number of children aged 0—4 per 1,000 married women aged 15—49 by class (York, 1851) the results were 783 (classes I—II), 862 (class III) and 814 (classes IV—V).[62] Though there was no statistically significant difference between the three ratios, I surmised that these statistics gave some grounds for suspicion that the higher classes were limiting their fertility to a certain extent. Since infant mortality bore more hardly on the lower classes than on the upper, the ratios pertaining to the upper classes ought (if fertility was equal in all classes) to have been considerably higher than those of the lower classes. It is easy to see why the conclusion had to be so tentative and speculative. Combinations of classes I and II and IV and V would not have been required if the number of class I wives aged 15—49 had not been as low as 14. But even if the absolute number of cases had been considerably larger for each individual class, it is doubtful whether they would have been adequate for demonstrating significant differences on an *age-specific* basis, which would be the essential further step in the exploration of apparent differences revealed by such gross comparisons.

The possibility of taking larger samples, if necessary up to 100 per cent, needs to be kept in mind where specific problems of interest arise: for example, in my study of York special attention was paid to two streets of railway housing (Oxford and Cambridge Streets) and the Bedern, with its many Irish households. Similarly, in an attempt to push the analysis of fertility further than was possible from his systematic sample, R.J. Smith computed the fertility ratio for *all* Nottingham wives with husbands in a selection of upperclass occupations.[63] Thus, the method of relying mainly on a simple proportional sample covering the whole community, coupled with subsidiary samples, has a good deal to recommend it,[64] but as the questions asked become more precise, other types of sampling will no doubt be employed. Possible alternatives would mainly lie in the use of stratified samples (for example, all the Irish, all immigrant households, all 'professional' households) according to the focus of the study.

HOUSEHOLDS AND FAMILIES

Two grave difficulties impede such analysis in the 1801—41 censuses. First, no consistent definition of a house was in use, the matter being left to the discretion of enumerators. Yet the national ratio of persons per inhabited house remained remarkably stable in the first four censuses, (at 5.6; 5.7; 5.7;

and 5.6) and when, in 1841, the ratio fell to 5.4 the conclusion of falling density was hotly contested by Chadwick who suggested that this result merely arose from a shift of definition.[65] Secondly, not even the more detailed 1841 census asked for 'relationship to head of family' and such relationships have to be inferred from the enumerators' books. A set of conventions for this purpose have been set out elsewhere,[66] but the 1841 data do not seem to have attracted much attention.

Much more elaborate instructions were issued to enumerators for distinguishing houses and households in 1851 and 1861, but certain difficulties remained. Indeed Tillott, with a dash of exaggeration, writes that 'in its attempts to analyse the way in which houses were occupied by households, the census of 1851 met its Waterloo, and the battle was hardly reversed ten years later'.[67]

The 1851 *General Report* drew attention to some of the ambiguities of the word 'family', the 'social unit' to which earlier censuses had referred. 'The family, in the sense which it has acquired in England, consists of the occupier of the house (his other roles — householder, master, husband, father), his wife, children, servants, relatives, visitors, and persons constantly or accidently in the house'.[68] This is, broadly, the kind of usage which Laslett encountered in his study of pre-industrial communities,[69] whereas in modern sociological studies the term 'family' is likely to be qualified by the adjective 'nuclear', and taken to mean head, wife and children only.

Accustomed as they were to the more traditional usage, we must assume that many enumerators would have entertained doubts as to whether, say, a single woman in a cottage or some other incomplete complement of components could constitute a 'family'. Additionally, the difficulties of deciding when a lodger was part of a family, and when he was separately accountable, had already been mentioned by Rickman.[70] This may have been an increasing problem;[71] at all events the 1851 decision to go over to the principle of *occupation units* appears to have been a consequence of the recognition of the complexity of the lodger/boarder/family question. In the act for taking the census of 1851, occupier is substituted for 'family', and the occupier, with whom the enumerator was to leave a separate schedule, is defined in the instructions to be (1) a resident owner, or (2) person who paid rent, whether, as a tenant, for the whole of a house, or (3) as a *lodger*, for any distinct floor or apartment.[72] Similarly, while in the past the definition of what constituted a distinct house had been 'considered insuperable' by Mr Rickman, who had therefore left the matter to those who made the return, the rubric for a house was now stated as 'a distinct building, separated from others by party walls'. Flats and sets of chambers therefore, must 'not be reckoned as houses'.[73]

In the censal process, the enumerator was to leave a separate schedule with every 'occupier', in the sense defined above. The enumerator was instructed to recover the schedule on March 31st, and enjoined to pin or tie together the schedules from any house in multiple occupation. On copying up the details into the enumeration book, his instructions were as follows:

> Under the last name in any *house* (i.e. a separate and distinct building and not a mere story or flat), he should draw a line *across the page as far as the fifth column*. Where there is more than one occupier in the same house, he should draw a similar line under the last name of the family of each occupier; making the line however, in this case, commence a little on the left hand side of the third column.[74]

These definitions and instructions certainly gave more guidance than ever before to enumerators, but they are obviously full of loopholes and ambiguities. Data collected in the manner described should, in theory, have permitted calculation of the average number of persons per occupier (i.e. per schedule), as well as of the average number of persons per house. The census authorities noted that the average number of persons per house in 1851 (5.5 in England and Wales), was not substantially different from that in preceding censuses (see above pp. 48–49), while the number of persons per occupier (4.8), was closely similar to previous figures of persons per 'family' (4.7, 4.7, 4.8, 4.8, in 1801–31; no statistics for 1841). Hence it was concluded that 'family and occupier have been used in nearly the same sense'.[75] While this was probably true of a great many enumeration districts, especially in rural areas where well-defined houses succeeded one another regularly and complications over lodgers, shared dwellings and apartments etc. were infrequent, it was nevertheless evident that there had been a good deal of variation in implementing the instructions, which it would have been futile to attempt to correct at the Census Office.[76]

Tillott has catalogued some characteristic difficulties in correctly identifying separate houses and occupiers in the enumerators' books:

1. omission of lines, especially at the foot of a page;
2. a fairly high percentage of 'head equivalents' (for example, 'traveller's wife');
3. lack of consistency in giving the address;
4. sub-groups, often consisting of nuclear families, sometimes appearing designated as 'lodgers' when they should probably have been separately enumerated;
5. lodgers who were probably boarders in every sense sometimes designated as separate occupiers (the converse of 4);
6. failure of the appearance of 'head' in column to coincide with a new schedule number, or be preceded by either a long or short line.[77]

It has become increasingly apparent that there is a need for careful definition and standardisation of terminology in respect of 'household' and 'family', and of the meaning of the terms 'lodger' and 'sharing'. The set of rules used in the York and Nottingham studies rested on one consistent set of definitions and conventions: 'household' was taken to cover all persons listed between the *long* lines in the enumerators' books, the 'family' was defined in the nuclear sense, not in the original census or 'old English' sense. Relatives, visitors and domestic servants were separately distinguished, and all others were labelled 'lodgers' (which category, however, could be sub-divided between head's trade assistants, and lodgers in the normal sense of the word, and their dependents). Where, among the lodgers so defined, *either* a married couple *or* a male or female person having one or more children could be discerned, this was deemed to indicate 'sharing'.[78]

These conventions served their purpose well enough, but

ought now to be discarded in favour of those evolved, after painstaking enquiry, by Anderson, who has laid down the following general principles.[79]

1. Analysis of the composition of and relationships within residential units should be carried out in terms of what the census authorities somewhat misleadingly called 'the family', that is the group who, in the words of the 1851 instruction to enumerators, co-resided with an occupier. This will also be, presumably, the nearest possible equivalent to the 'household' in the modern sense of the term, usually defined in terms of commensality.[80] This group should henceforth be described as the *co-residing* group.

2. The co-residing group should, in 1851, be defined as comprising all names from one entry 'head' in the 'relation to head of family' column to the last name preceding the next entry 'head', *except* that,

    (a) a head equivalent ('widow', 'traveller's wife', 'husband away', 'spinster' etc.) will be acceptable in place of head where the entry is preceded by either a long or a short line: *lodger* must never be taken to be a head equivalent;

    (b) where two successive individuals are both listed as head, but no line separates them and there is no other indication of a new 'census family', both should be included in the same co-residing group, it being assumed that they shared the headship.

3. In 1851 a new *house* should be counted after each long line, rather than relying on patchy address data; where it is required to refer to all the inhabitants of a house, the preferred terminology is the *dwelling* group (or houseful).

4. A shared house would be one in which there were two or more co-residing groups.

5. The head's nuclear family should be referred to as the *primary* family and any other nuclear families within the co-residing group as *secondary* families (secondary lodger families, and secondary kin families are distinguishable sub-groups here); 'family' in the census or 'old English' meaning is dropped.

The rationale behind this plan of classification and the reasons for rejecting certain alternatives are fully considered by Anderson, whose argument in favour of the co-residential unit as the basic unit of analysis is convincing. It is, he suggests, the unit least likely to be subject to discrepancies both within the same enumerator's book and between different enumerators' books; it is the unit most likely to give comparability between successive censuses; it is probably the nearest unit to the household defined in its modern sense (commensality); and it is 'the smallest unit that can be successfully and regularly identified', so that in using it, 'the maximum freedom to cross-classify and combine data is preserved'. Finally, Anderson has pointed out that sociologically the co-residing group (like the 'census family' or 'household' with which it may roughly be equated) is a meaningful unit — a group 'interacting together on a reasonably regular basis' — whereas the occupants of a house clearly might not be. This is easily appreciated if one recalls that in Scotland, especially, large tenement buildings were often treated as one house.[81]

In 1861 the instructions to enumerators were worded somewhat differently and a revised set of examples issued to assist them. Ambiguities in the instructions were not, however, ironed out; on the contrary they were worse.[82]. Broadly speaking, the underlying definitions for 1861 remained the same as for 1851, i.e. the occupation of separate apartments. But greater emphasis was now placed on the point that each occupier (or lodger) must make a return for his portion of the house on a separate paper; the upshot of this was that in 1861 (and thereafter), many more schedules were issued to single lodgers and small families than had previously been the case. There was, of course, much variation in practice as between different enumerators. Anderson points out that in cases where there were half a dozen lodgers, some enumerators would group all of them together as 'lodgers'; some would do the same but arbitrarily defining one as 'head'; some would make each a separate 'head'; and some would (as in 1851) simply include most lodgers — especially if single — in the same 'census family' as the head.

Furthermore, reverting to the practice of 1841, long and

short lines to divide houses and households were replaced by double and single oblique strokes respectively.[83] Such divergencies of practice may make it difficult to make precise comparisons with 1851, especially in urban areas; it may well be that there was less homogeneity of practice among enumerators in 1861 than in the previous census.[84] Pending further research into these questions, the researcher would be well advised to follow Anderson's advice and continue to use the word 'head' as the appropriate cut-off point in 1861 for the household or co-residing group. This may mean that a small number of lodgers designated as heads may be included in one's survey as independent co-residing groups when there might be grounds for thinking they were merely boarders; on the other hand this procedure would quite properly exclude lodgers (so designated) from the status of independent co-residing units. Relying on some criterion other than 'head' entries as the dividing line (oblique lines, or schedule numbers) might lead to considerable over-counting of 'co-residing groups' (or households).

OCCUPATIONAL GROUPINGS

The occupational data in the enumerators' books can be used as a basis for social classification, or can be aggregated into industrial categories.[85] I shall discuss the two approaches separately.

A. Social class

In my study of York, a system of social classification was used based on the Registrar General's scheme which refers to five classes, 'homogeneous in relation to the basic criterion of the general standing within the community of the occupations concerned'.

Class I	Professional, etc. occupations
Class II	Intermediate occupations
Class III	Skilled occupations
Class IV	Partly skilled occupations
Class V	Unskilled occupations

In the York and Nottingham studies the 1951 attribution lists were used[86] to give a classification for each household head, with the modifications listed below.

1. All employers of 25 or more persons were raised to class I, whatever their occupational classification in the Registrar General's lists.

2. All 'dealers', 'merchants' (except those distinctively described as brokers or agents — class II — or hawkers — class V) and persons engaged in retail board, lodging and catering were initially classed as III, despite the fact that the Registrar General's lists placed them variously.

3. From class III (or in some cases class IV) *upon considera- tion of individual cases* those who employed at least one person (other than own family), were then raised to class II. In catering etc., the employment of one or more servants counted for this purpose which had the effect of raising all those whose undertakings or dealings were at all substantial, for (at a minimum) the employment of an apprentice is an obvious indication of self-employed status.[87]

4. House and land proprietors were placed in class I (along with those 'living off interest', 'of independent means'); class II (annuitants); and class V (paupers). Other less informative entries ('husband away', 'spinster' etc.), were placed in a residual class X. Retired persons were classified on the basis of previous occupations.

Two objections might be brought forward against this scheme. First, the Registrar General's scheme of classification has an inherent tendency to produce a large and swollen class III. Secondly, it is anachronistic to apply a scheme devised for 1951 to data for 1851 in view of the major social changes that have taken place over the last hundred years.

That one will usually get a very large class III seems virtually certain,[88] because in the source itself the information is insufficiently detailed to facilitate the drawing of more precise distinctions which would enable the investigator to use more detailed categorisations which are commonly used today, such as the Hall-Jones scale or the socio-economic groupings used in the 1961 census.[89] In this connection it might be argued that there were and are a large number of persons whose occupations are not the final guide to their social status among those included in class III. For example, we might expect to find distinctions in a number of individual factors — the person with a college education who did not succeed for some reason: the fact that one iron-moulder enjoyed a small legacy while another did not; that one railwayman had married a virtuous wife devoted to keeping up appearances, while another had married a slattern; or that one bricklayer was a temperate and sober individual, while another bricklayer drank to excess; in terms of occupation persons grouped under class III might very well be on much the same baseline, but the accidents of human life could well determine the social standing of given individuals or individual families.

Clearly there is no basis in the evidence for weighing such factors; yet it is urged that class III needs to be broken down, since to a greater extent than any other class it mingles own account (non-employer) shopkeepers and workers, traditional craftsmen, employees in the new industries of the industrial revolution, and workers in transport, building and services. There are various ways in which class III may be functionally sub-divided in practice; some researchers might find it helpful to distinguish between manual and non-manual workers in class III, or between petty entrepreneurs, clerks and skilled workers, as Dyos has been able to do with reasonable accuracy.[90] If the industrial classification to be discussed below is operated in parallel, the need for subdivision of class III would be reduced. By sorting punched cards (or processing computer tape, or manual sorting) it would be possible to distribute class III cases among a wide range of industrial groups. Thus the common criticism that class III is too large, unwieldy and undifferentiated may be dealt with by sub-division, without any implication that the social ranking of one sub-section is in any way superior to that of another.

As for the criticism that it is anachronistic to apply a modern classification to mid-nineteenth century data, many arguments can be cited on both sides. But while there have been large changes in the class structure over the last hundred years, it is at least arguable that most of the changes have been structural, i.e. have occurred as a result of the shifting distribution of the occupied population among the various groups (notably the great rise in the proportion of managerial and white-collar workers, and decline in the proportion of self-employed and unskilled) rather than in the socially accepted hierarchial ordering of the occupations themselves.

The Registrar General's scheme, however modified, can only be a crude tool of analysis, but it is necessary to remember that the essential aim is to arrange empirical data so as to further understanding and facilitate analysis. There are numerous practical advantages in using the scheme and, until something better is devised it will no doubt continue to be used. That the scheme outlined above, has a certain rationale and is meaningful in relation to 1851 data is suggested by Table 2.3

TABLE 2.3
Distribution of domestic servants, 1851[91]
(Percentage of household heads having one or more domestic servants)

	Social Class				
	I	II	III	IV	V
York	81.4	57.9	9.1	5.8	–
Nottingham	58.5	42.9	7.0	3.0	1.7
Radford	45.4	34.0	6.5	3.5	1.1

B. Industrial groups

I have suggested elsewhere that it is possible to arrange census data along these lines with the aid of Charles Booth's article of 1886.[92] His calculations yielded national results which have subsequently been heavily relied upon by scholars wrestling with the changing economic structure of England and Wales,[93] but their utility does not end at that point. For thanks to his thoughtfulness in preserving his worksheets, Booth's study is also of great value to the local researcher who can, without much risk of significant misallocation, arrange the printed census data for his community along Booth's lines, so securing comparability with the national figures and approximate long-run comparability across the years down to 1881 (see Appendix VI, Chapter 6).

Booth's original analysis was based on the occupational data laid out in the *printed* census volumes;[94] from census to census the number of individual occupational sub-headings varied remarkably, and he effectively reduced these to 346 standard headings. From his working calculations, it has been possible to trace Booth's steps and publish his detailed attribution lists for 1861 and 1881. By employing these lists, local printed census data may be ordered along Booth's lines, though no attempt has yet been made to apply the scheme to the enumerators' books. The allocation list for 1861 covers over 1,000 designations, and the vast majority of respondents in any area will certainly have used terms contained in the list. The great advantage of the scheme is its flexibility, in that it is open to the researcher to try alternative combinations among the 79 industrial sub-groups and, at the same time, to make systematic comparisons with the work of other scholars.[95]

*   *   *   *   *

The tools of analysis discussed in this section are crude and elementary in character. Yet without some grouping one cannot work effectively and most researchers would agree that attainment of comparability between studies is worth the loss of a little finesse in individual methodology. Actually, there is little need to sacrifice anything; local researchers can align their work with others by using the schemes described and, *at the same time,* are free to run alternative schemes of their own or to focus on individual occupations which might be of particular interest in their areas (e.g. tin-miners in Cornwall). The best way to advance is by a judicious combination of controlled experimentation coupled with due attention to comparability.

DATA COMPUTING

Early studies of the census enumerators' books mainly employed either manual methods of analysis or punched cards. *Manual methods of analysis* may be preferable for co-operative group projects where it is essential to give all those involved a sense of participation. Professor Tillott has successfully employed such methods with extra-mural classes at Sheffield in a large-scale survey which commenced with the market town of Tickhill and was planned to cover at least 14 villages in Yorkshire, Lincolnshire and Nottinghamshire, and diverse urban populations in Skipton, Grimsby, Doncaster and Sheffield (the last on a 10 per cent sample basis):[96] the combined populations of these areas in 1851 total more than 60,000. Basically, Tillott's classes work with 'data collection slips' of his own devising, each consisting of 38 boxes where information may be filed. Each individual has one slip and, where possible, the entire slip is filled for household heads, yielding similar information to one of the 'household' cards used in my York study. Additionally, the data collection slips are also used to amplify the information on individual members of the head's family and for all others (lodgers, servants, etc.). At a later stage a further series of forms is brought into use, to collate the information on these slips.

On the other hand, most individual researchers will require mechanical assistance for routine operations: the first aid deserving mention is electric card-punch and sorting equipment.[97] Recourse to 80-column punched cards was fairly novel in the 1960s, though it has recently been criticised as restrictive.[98] Some of the obvious advantages of employing a computer will be considered below, but it is perhaps worth affirming that punched cards are not so inflexible and archaic as some appear to think. Perhaps the use of only one card per household in the York study was insufficient, even with some double-punching, but Anderson has shown how two, three or more packs may be employed. He grouped data on co-residing groups (households) on series A cards; series B cards contained details of individuals, while the first 25 columns overlapped with those of series A to allow cross-tabulation of the characteristics of those individuals with those of the head and his wife, and with details of the co-residing group as a whole. Finally, series C cards contained data on 'supplementary nuclear families', that is, nuclear families whose members were listed in the census as kin of the head or as lodgers.[99] Imaginative manipulation of punched cards — a cheap and readily understood tool of analysis — will obviously take a good many investigators as far as they will want to go, especially if the analysis in question is unlikely to be repeated and perhaps is incidental to the researcher's main preoccupations. P.H. Smith Jr, a representative of the IBM Corporation, has written:

> It is advisable at this point to put in a word for the punched card, which has been all but forgotten in this decade of the rise of the computer. Fifteen years ago there was essentially nothing but punched cards to work with, and for many jobs they may still be the best mechanical tool ... the advantages of punched card equipment are several. The primary one is that it is cheap and available. Any computer installation is bound to have a group of punched card machines acting as satellites to the big computer and these machines are usually less busy than the computer itself. Then too, it is *easier to see what one is doing on punched card machines and to feel one's way along through the various stages of work* [my italics]. Furthermore, anything that goes into a computer will have to pass through one or more punched card machines first anyway, and if a scholar has a great deal of data to prepare for the computer, the punched card machines can be an enormous help in doing some of the repetitive chores connected with getting the data ready, with the preliminary organizing of the data, and with checking it.[100]

Therefore, depending on their individual aims and objectives and the resources open to them, researchers will want to consider using both manual and punched card methods, which are certainly not yet outdated. Computers can only rearrange quantifiable data according to pre-set instructions into a more intelligible pattern and make further statistical calculations such as means, correlations, standard deviations, etc. These functions the computer may perform more efficiently (i.e. more rapidly, more accurately, more cheaply) than either manual or punched card methods. Yet it is important to keep in mind the limitations of computers, which can neither spontaneously develop new hypotheses nor interpret results, and which are still apt to confront the historian with various unforeseen practical difficulties.[101] It may be that in the future the scholar will simply be able to write down his problem in very much the language he would ordinarily use, and the computer, backed by a very powerful language, will develop its own programme.[102] Yet this development is still a distant prospect and for years to come users will have to grapple with the complexities of adapting existing languages to their ends, entailing the diversion of a considerable amount of time and effort, perhaps too much for those whose problems can be tackled by established methods.

On the other hand, it is evident that the balance of advantage and disadvantage is constantly changing and, on the whole, in such a way as to make use of computers an increasingly practicable proposition for historical research.[103] It would be idle to pretend that the computer does not offer great advantages. First, it tolerates much more complexity than the human mind can cope with or than the standard punched card has space for. Using a computer one could avoid 'premature' reduction of the basic data to general categories which might turn out to obscure as much as they illuminate. For example, exact ages and precise occupations could be retained to a late stage in processing, an advantage when it is remembered that all general categorisations necessarily involve some loss of information. [104] Secondly, because the computer is tireless and in terms of costs is increasingly efficient, the larger the project, it clearly offers one way round sampling difficulties. One might not need to sample at all, if, for example, to cover an entire population were only 50 per cent more costly than taking a 10 per cent sample, though much would depend on the ratio between the costs of assembling and coding the data and the actual computing costs. Thirdly, certain techniques of statistical manipulation which are inherently difficult using punched card equipment, and almost impossible by hand, can be programmed for the computer to handle. For example, in a multiple correlation analysis measuring the relationship between a given variable and other variables the arithmetical procedures and the numbers of runs on punched cards would be quite easy to envisage if only two or three variables were being considered, but this would be a very different matter if the number of variables were larger.[105]

Apart from these valuable properties, the computer may be used for quite mundane listing operations. In nominative analysis of the census enumerators' books, pioneering work is being carried out by Professor K.M. Drake and Mrs C.G. Pearce at the Open University in a study of Ashford conceived of as a three-stage project. The first stage involves the transfer to cards of information (including names) from the enumerators' returns for Ashford (Kent) in 1841, 1851 and 1861. The second stage will be to transfer to cards nominative information drawn from such sources as poor law records, poll books, school registration, directories, pay sheets, registers of births, marriages, deaths etc. The third stage, at which the computer will become quite indispensable, will be to merge the information taken from these different sources. The project is at once more ambitious than anything yet tried and yet partly exploratory; it is evident that research at this level of detail and sophistication is expensive, even for a small community (Ashford's population was 5,522 in 1861).

Conclusion

Much stress has been laid here and elsewhere on the deficiencies of the census enumerators' books, but it is hoped that the prospective ·researcher will not be deterred. One must remember that all categories of historical evidence are more or less liable to inaccuracy and in many instances the chance survival of this or that piece of evidence necessarily raises queries regarding its typicality or representativeness. In fact, in two important respects the census enumerators' books are of well above average quality as historical evidence. First, they are universal and comprehensive, and secondly they contain information 'in a standardised format capable of being treated in a uniform manner'.[106]

Recent endeavours to utilise census books have been made in other countries where similar material has survived, and offer the prospect that 'whole dimensions of the past that had either been neglected entirely or treated superficially may be brought into clearer focus'.[107] This will entail the juxtaposition of such quantitative evidence with more or less well-known 'literacy' sources, and will enable us to delineate Victorian social structure, urban history and social history generally with increasing sensitivity in the years to come. In short, the promise for research in this field is far more impressive than the various pitfalls.

NOTES

1. 'The Unprinted Census Returns of 1841, 1851 and 1861 for England and Wales', *Amateur Historian*, V, (1963), pp. 260—9.
2. W.A. Armstrong, 'Social Structure from the early Census returns' in E.A. Wrigley (ed.), *An Introduction to English Historical Demography* (1966), hereinafter referred to as Armstrong (1966). *Ibid*, 'The Social Structure of York, 1841—51' (University of Birmingham, Ph.D. thesis, 1967).
3. W.A. Armstrong, 'The Interpretation of the Census Enumerators' Books for Victorian Towns' in H.J. Dyos (ed.), *The Study of Urban History*, (1968): *Ibid, Stability and Change in an English County Town: a social study of York, 1801—51*, (Cambridge, 1974): R.J. Smith, 'Early Victorian household structure; a case study of Nottinghamshire', *International Review of Social History*, XV, (1970), Pt. I, pp. 69—84, based on his thesis 'The Social Structure of Nottingham and adjacent districts in the mid-nineteenth century', (Nottingham University Ph. D, 1968). These studies are referred to subsequently as Armstrong (1968): Armstrong (1974); Smith (1970) and Smith (thesis). Other recent studies include those of Dr Anderson cited frequently elsewhere in this chapter; C. Thomas, 'Rural Society in Nineteenth Century Wales: South Cardiganshire in 1851', *Ceredigion*, VI, (1971), 388—414; N.L. Tranter, 'The Social Structure of a Bedfordshire parish in the mid-nineteenth century', *International Review of Social History*, XVIII (1973), Pt. I, pp. 90—106.
4. D.V. Glass and D.E.C. Eversley, *Population in History* (1965), p.24.
5. The exceptions being cases where two or more unions were combined to form one registration district and, in some instances, where the administration of poor law relief continued to be administered under local acts.
6. While these had been 'a body of men, in many parts of the country, fully competent to the task thus imposed upon them . . . in some districts, from want of education, or habits of business, and from ignorance of the importance and real object of the enquiry they were conducting, essentially unfitted for it'. 1841 Census, *Enumeration Abstract*, p. 1. See also above, pp. 14—17.
7. The overseers had been allowed to go on 'day after day' until answers to all their queries were obtained. *Ibid*.
8. *Ibid.*, p. 4.
9. *Ibid.*, p. 38.
10. These unique censuses are discussed by Dr D.M. Thompson and Dr J.M. Goldstrom in chapters 7 and 8.
11. Census, 1851, *Population Tables, I* (II) pp. xiii—xvi.
12. On the whole, such revisions appear to have been carried out only cursorily. See P.M. Tillott, 'Sources of inaccuracy in the 1851 and 1861 censuses' in E.A. Wrigley (ed.), *Nineteenth Century Society* (Cambridge, 1972), hereafter referred to as Tillott (1972).

13. The cost was reduced from £5.9s. to £5.4s. per 1000 enumerated, mainly, it would seem, by a reduction in the number of enumerators from 32,353 to 30,610. *Returns of the expense of the Census in 1841 and 1851, etc.* 1854 XXXIX pp. 333—5. The cost per 1000 was reduced still further to £4.15s.5d, in 1861, but subsequently began to rise again. See *Return of the expenses incurred in taking the Census in 1871, etc*, 1875 XLII, p. 155.

14. Census, 1851, *Population Tables, II* (I), p. cxix. However, such comments may not tell the whole story. In the overcrowded Irish district known as the Bedern in York, the inhabitants at first refused to give any information, 'and it was not until the influence of the Roman Catholic priest was brought to bear upon them that they would heed the applications of the enumerator'. *Yorkshire Gazette*, 5th April, 1851.

15. Census, 1861, III, *General Report* pp. 1—4; 1871 Census, IV, *General Report*, p. x, and *Appendix B*, pp. 169—72.

16. For a fuller exposition of this subject, see Tillott (1972).

17. B. Benjamin, *Demographic Analysis* (1968), p. 50.

18. *Ibid.*

19. See pages 12—14 above.

20. e.g. J.T. Krause, 'Changes in English fertility and mortality, 1780—1850', *Economic History Review*, Second series, 11 (1958—9), pp. 52—70, whose comments on this subject are alluded to below.

21. 'A note on the under-registration of births in Britain, in the nineteenth century', *Population Studies*, 5, (1951—2), pp. 70—88.

22. In 1874 responsibility for registering a birth was firmly placed on the *parent*, and failure to notify was subject to a 40s. penalty.

23. J.C.D. Dunlop, 'Note as to errors of statement of ages of young children in a census', *Journal of the Royal Statistical Society*, *89* (1916), pp. 309—17.

24. Krause, *op. cit.*, p. 61.

25. When the number of girls aged 10—15 in 1841 was compared with the number of young women aged 20—25 in 1851, there was a *rise* of 27,000! Similarly if the 20—5s of 1841 were compared with the 30—5s of 1851, an unduly large fall of 205,000 was indicated. Making due allowances for mortality and migration, it seemed almost certain that both in 1841 and 1851 a proportion of older women were returned as 20—5. Census, 1851, *Population Tables II* (I), p. xxiv.

26. Tillott (1972); and M. Anderson, 'The study of family structure' in E.A. Wrigley (ed.). *Nineteenth Century Society*, (1972), subsequently referred to as Anderson, 'Family Structure', (1972).

27. The method described in U.N.O. *Demographic Yearbook* (New York, 1962), pp. 16—17 is known as 'Whipple's index'. First devised by the official in charge of the 1931 Indian census, it assumes that digital preferences are closely correlated with other sources of error in age statements.

28. These are the heads and wives appearing in the 1 in 10 household sample referred to on p. 28. Since it is a large sample there is no reason for thinking the Whipple method is inappropriate.
29. Anderson, 'Family Structure', (1972), p. 75.
30. Tillott (1972), p. 85.
31. 249,431 persons in England and Wales described themselves as farmers; 225,318 returned themselves as occupying land, and in only 2,047 cases was the acreage unstated. But 91,698 farmers appeared to have no labourers, and among those who did, 'some uncertainty prevails as to whether the farmers returned all their indoor farm servants; and women and boys were included in some cases and not in others'. Census, 1851, *Population Tables, II* (II), pp. lxxviii–lxxx.
32. 'The return of masters in trade is imperfect; all the masters have not so returned themselves'. In fact 129,002 only in England Wales so returned themselves, and of these 41,732 either employed no men, or made no return of the number of men in their employ. *Ibid*, pp. lxxvii – lxxviii.
33. Census, 1891, IV, *General Report*, pp. 35–36. See also below, Chapter 5.
34. Census, 1851, *Population Tables, I* (I), p. cxxxviii.
35. Charles Booth, 'Occupations of the People of the United Kingdom, 1801–81', *Journal of the Statistical Society, 49*, (1886), p. 336, observes that in the census returns 'skilled and common labour are inextricably mixed'. And few historians would be prepared to credit the 1851 finding that only 5.7 per cent of the male occupied population were general labourers (4.8 per cent for 1861, and 7.2 per cent for 1871, according to Booth's figures). See below, Chapter 6 and Appendix VI.
36. Beresford, *op. cit.*
37. *Victoria County History, City of York* ed. P.M. Tillott, (1961), p. 269; T.C. Barker and J.R. Harris, *A Merseyside Town in the Industrial Revolution: St. Helens 1751–1900* (1959), p. 281. For further examples see W.H. Chaloner, *Social and Economic History of Crewe* (Manchester, 1950), pp. 38, 59; and J.F. Ede, *History of Wednesbury* (Wednesbury Corporation, 1962), pp. 414–5).
38. For an exemplary study on these lines reporting the findings of a local history research group see P.M. Tillott and G.S. Stevenson, *North-West Lindsey in 1851* (University of Sheffield, Department of Extra-mural Studies, 1970).
39. R. Lawton, 'The population of Liverpool in the mid-nineteenth century', *Transactions of the Historical Society of Lancashire and Cheshire*, 107 (1955), pp. 89–120.
40. See below, pp. 48–54.
41. P. Laslett, 'Mean household size in England since the sixteenth century', *Population Studies*, XXIII, (1969), 199–223. Data on York, Preston and Swansea are from W.A. Armstrong, 'A note on the household structure of mid-nineteenth century York in

comparative perspective', and M. Anderson, 'Household structure and the Industrial Revolution; mid-nineteenth century Preston in comparative perspective', both in P. Laslett, (ed.) *Household and Family in Past Time*, (Cambridge, 1972), which also includes its editor's article in *Population Studies*. Note that the Preston and York data are based on samples.

42. Especially in Dr Anderson's study of Preston, now published as *Family Structure in Nineteenth Century Lancashire*, (Cambridge, 1971). He maintained from the outset distinctions within the component groups — servants, lodgers, and especially kin — which could only be painstakingly recovered from the first stage notebooks used in my own work and that of Dr Smith. This is a good example of progressive design improvement in work of this kind.

43. Armstrong (1974), chapters 4, 5 and 6, where the data are set out more fully. The social classification scheme mentioned in the following paragraphs is discussed on pp. 54—7 and in ch. 6. All differences quoted are significant at the 95 per cent confidence level.

44. E.G. Ravenstein, 'The Laws of Migration', *Journal of the Statistical Society*, 48, (1885), pp. 196—7.

45. Particularly the Educational and Religious Reports of the 1851 census, discussed elsewhere in this volume; T. Laycock, *Report on the Sanitary State of York; Royal Commission on the State of Large Towns and Populous Districts*, 1844: Manchester Statistical Society, *Report on the State of Education in York*, (1837).

46. See above, note 39.

47. June A. Shepherd, 'East Yorkshire's Agricultural Labour Force in the mid-nineteenth Century', *Agricultural History Review*, 9, (1961), pp. 437—54.

48. P.J. Taylor, 'The Locational variable in Taxonomy', *Geographical Analysis*, 1, (1969), pp. 181—95.

49. R. Floud, *An Introduction to Quantitative Methods for Historians*, (1973) is a useful guide to statistical methodology, which may be supplemented by one or more of a number of texts written with the problems of behavioural scientists in mind, e.g. H.M. Blalock, *Social Statistics*, (New York, 1960) or N.M. Downie and R.W. Heath, *Basic Statistical Methods*, (New York, 1965).

50. The steps involved in this calculation included:
    (i)   the construction of a local life table, using national data adjusted for local variations to give life chances for any individual over any period of years:
    (ii) from the census figures of proportions ever-married, making estimates of the proportions of over 65, who had not married at an age where they would have had children:
    (iii) estimating the likely number of children born to those who did marry from data gathered for the Fertility Census of 1911.

Anderson, 'Family Structure', (1972), pp. 63—9 should be consulted for further details.

51. J.O. Foster, 'Nineteenth century towns — a class dimension', in H.J. Dyos, (ed.) *The Study of Urban History*, (1968), pp.281—300.

52. Dr Anderson 'Family Structure', (1972), pp. 73—4, has used the same technique in comparing actual and random distances between residences of related pairs of kin, which enables him to say that whereas, randomly, one would expect 27 per cent of his sample pairs to live within 399 yards of one another, in fact 87 per cent of the pairs were so situated.

53. T.S. Ashton, *An Economic History of England: the Eighteenth Century*, (1955), advises economic historians to find answers to the questions economists ask (or should ask) of the past. See also W.W. Rostow, *British Economy of the Nineteenth Century*, (1948), pp. 3—4 and, for useful surveys of recent literature, R.W. Fogel, 'The New Economic History; its Findings and Methods', *Economic History Review*, Second series, 19, (1966) pp. 642—656, and E.H. Hunt, The New Economic History: Professor Fogel's study of American Railways', *History*, 53, (1968), pp. 3—18.

54. L.B. Namier, *The Structure of Politics at the Accession of George III* (1929): J.R. Vincent, *Pollbooks: How Victorians Voted* (Cambridge, 1967): H. Pelling, *Social Geography of British Elections, 1885—1910* (1967). Many of the studies described in the *Historical Methods Newsletter* published by the University of Pittsburgh are concerned with the quantitative analysis of political behaviour.

55. E.H. Carr, *What is History?* (Pelican edn., 1968), p. 66.

56. R.C. Floud and R.S. Schofield, 'Social Structure from the early census returns', *Economic History Review*, Second series, 21 (1968), pp. 607—9.

57. *Ibid.*, pp. 609—13. Dr Schofield has subsequently contributed a valuable chapter entitled 'Sampling in Historical Research' to E.A. Wrigley (ed.) *Nineteenth Century Society* (1972), hereafter referred to as Schofield (1972).

58. A household containing more than ten non-members of the head's family.

59. *op. cit.*, p. 608.

60. Census, 1961, *Household Composition Tables* (HMSO, 1966), p. xi.

61. Anderson, 'Family Structure' (1972), p. 55.

62. Armstrong, (1968), p. 62.

63. Armstrong, (1974), pp. 98, 125—6; Smith (thesis), pp. 237—8, where the ratio again comes out lower for the higher social classes than for the community as a whole.

64. Not necessarily 1 in 10 though it is worth keeping in mind that it is necessary to *quadruple* the size of a sample in order to double its accuracy i.e. halve the 'standard error'. Broadly, the larger the

population, the smaller the sample need be to yield results at a given level of significance. For national data, 1 per cent samples were used in the 1951 census to give rapid general results. On this and related matters see Schofield, (1972).

65. E. Chadwick, *Report on the Sanitary Conditions of the Labouring Population of Great Britain*, 1842, ed. M.W. Flinn, (Edinburgh, 1965), pp. 5, 188—9.

66. Armstrong, (1966), p. 229.

67. Tillott, (1972), p. 90.

68. Census, 1851, *Population Tables, I* (I), p. xxiv.

69. P. Laslett, *The World We Have Lost*, (1965), p. 2. The same author in the article referred to in footnote 41 discusses this point further, reserving the term 'family' for the conjugal or nuclear group, and using 'household' to describe the co-residential unit (i.e. including servants, kin etc.).

70. Census, 1831, *Enumeration Abstract*, I, p. ix. In general, the overseers and schoolmasters who took the first four censuses had been instructed to deem boarders (using the same kitchen and eating together) to be members of the family, but lodgers who did not board in the house in which they lived, were separate 'families': Census, 1851, *Population Tables, I* (I) p. xxiv.

71. See contributions by W.A. Armstrong and M. Anderson to P. Laslett (ed.), *Household and Family in Past Time* (1972), mentioned in footnote 41.

72. Census 1851, *Population Tables, I* (I), p. xxxv.

73. *Ibid.*, p. xxxvii—xxxviii.

74. *Ibid.*, p. cxiv. See Appendix I.

75. Census, 1851, *Population Tables, I* (I), p. xxxvi.

76. *Ibid.*, p. xxxv.

77. Tillott, (1972), pp. 90—105.

78. Armstrong, (1968), pp. 77—8; *ibid*, (1974), p. 12.

79. In a further contribution to E.A. Wrigley (ed.) *Nineteenth Century Society*, entitled 'Standard Tabulation Procedures for the census enumerators' books 1851—91', subsequently referred to as Anderson *Standard Tabulation Procedures*, (1972).

80. Census, 1951, *Housing Report*, p. xvi.

81. Anderson, 'Standard Tabulation Procedures' (1972), pp. 135—6.

82. *Ibid*, pp. 141—2.

83. *Ibid;* see also the specimen pages in Appendix I.

84. This applies also to the 1871 returns, in which the practice of enumerators was close to that of 1861, leaving 1851 out of line with both preceding and subsequent practice. In the 1871 Census, IV, *General Report*, xx—xxi, we read that, respecting families, 'the general results appear to agree with those of the earlier censuses ... the number of families was in proportion of 119 families to 100 houses, and in 1801 the proportion was nearly the same — it was 120 to 100 houses. There was little fluctuation in

any intermediate census, except in 1851 when the proportion was lower'.

85. Some scholars prefer systems of occupational classification which merge the two principles, for example Tillott and Stevenson in the publication referred to in footnote 38. The whole question is examined at greater length in W.A. Armstrong, 'The Use of information about occupation' in E.A. Wrigley (ed.) *Nineteenth Century Society* (1972), subsequently referred to as Armstrong (1972). See also Chapters 5 and 6 below.

86. i.e. General Register Office, *Classification of Occupations* (HMSO, 1950). Corresponding lists for 1911 could have been used, but investigation has shown that there would be no clear advantage in doing so, and later lists are obviously more widely available. See also the discussion by Professor Banks of this problem as it relates to the published census reports in Chapter 6, below.

87. Perhaps this procedure would have been unnecessary if householders had consistently stated whether or not they were masters or journeymen: but they did not (see p. 37 above).

88. As indeed is the case in the mid-twentieth century use of the scheme. See D.C. Marsh, *Changing Social Structure of England and Wales* (1958), p. 194, who shows that in 1951, 3 per cent of the occupied population were in class I, and 14, 52, 16 and 15 per cent in classes II—V, respectively.

89. J. Hall and D.C. Jones, 'Social Grading of Occupations', *British Journal of Sociology*, I (1950), pp. 31—55; Census, 1961, *Socio-Economic Group Tables*, pp. vii—viii.

90. See *The Study of Urban History*, (1968), pp. 103—6.

91. Data from Armstrong (1974), p. 179, and Dr R.J. Smith (personal communication). Differences between York, Nottingham and Radford are probably attributable to wider employment opportunities for single females in the East Midlands. See also below, Chapter 5, p. 169.

92. Armstrong, (1972), pp. 226—52; see also below, Chapter 6, pp. 191—3.

93. e.g. P. Deane and W.A. Cole, *British Economic Growth, 1688—1959*, (Cambridge, 1962), p. 140.

94. At that stage, of course, there had already been much rendering down of the multiplicity of original occupational statements given by householders. The Census authorities published no details of their conventions until 1911, although internal codebooks were in use. See Armstrong, (1972), pp. 230, 425, for further details and also Banks, Chapter 6 below.

95. All the points made here are further developed in Armstrong, (1972), where the 1861 and 1881 attributions are to be found on pp. 255—310. See, in relation to standardisation as it applies to the published censuses, J.A. Banks, below Chapter 6.

96. Tillott's work is described in his article, 'The Analysis of Census

Returns', *Local Historian*, 8, (1968), pp. 2–10, as well as in a series of cyclostyled progress reports emanating from the Department of Extra-Mural Studies at Sheffield University.

97. A basic card layout, with illustrations, as used in the York Study, is given in Armstrong (1966), pp. 220–228.

98. Floud and Schofield, *op. cit.*, p. 609.

99. Anderson, 'Family Structure', (1972), pp. 56–7.

100. 'The computer and the humanist', in E.A. Bowles (ed.), *Computers in humanistic research*, (Englewood Cliffs, N.J., 1967), pp. 16–28.

101. As is evidenced by H.J. Dyos and A.B.M. Baker in their account of problems arising in drawing up a suitable programme for computer analysis of the census books. See *The Study of Urban History*, (1968), pp. 87–112.

102. S.D. Conte, Chairman of the Computer Sciences Department at Purdue University, writing in Bowles, *op. cit*, p. 255.

103. New languages becoming available for research in the humanities and social sciences include DATA-TEXT (based on FORTRAN), and PL/I.

104. Just how far this can be carried in practice is a matter for judgment and experimentation; without some categorisation the resultant output from the machine could consist of miles of printed particles of related information of which only a further major computing exercise could make sense.

105. For a simple worked out example see Downie and Heath, *op. cit.*, pp. 205–6. Standard programmes such as the SPSS (Statistical Package for the Social Sciences) permit speedy production of basic statistical tests and correlations, including complex procedures involving many variables in large data sets.

106. Dyos, in *The Study of Urban History*, (1968), p. 92.

107. S. Thernstrom and R. Sennett, eds., *Nineteenth Century Cities: Essays in the New Urban History* (New Haven and London, 1969), p. x. See also J.P. Viennot, 'La population de Dijon d'après le recensement de 1851', *Annales de démographie historique*, (1969), pp. 241–60.

APPENDIX I

Instructions to enumerators, 1841—71, together
with examples of enumeration schedules.

	Pages
1841	73—4
1851	75—7
1861	78—9
1871	80—1

Respecting the manner in which Entries may be made in the Enumeration Schedule.

After "*City or Borough of*" write the name, if the District is in a City or Borough; if not, draw a line through those words, or through whichever of the two the District does not belong to. After "*Parish or Township of*" write the name; if there is no Township in the Parish, draw a line through "*Township;*" if it is a Township, write the name of the Township, and draw a line through "*Parish.*" If it is Extra-Parochial, draw a line through "*Parish or Township of,*" and write "*Extra-Parochial*" over those words, and after it the name.

In the column headed "*Place,*" write the name of the house (if it has a name), or of the street or other part of the town, or of the village, hamlet, or extra-parochial place in which it stands, opposite to the mark denoting each house, or the first house in the street, &c., and write "*do.*" opposite to every other in the same street, &c.

"*Houses.*"—Insert houses uninhabited or building in the manner shewn in the Example, writing "1 U" or "1 B," as the case may be, in the proper column, opposite to the inhabited house to which each stands nearest. Every house which is unoccupied at the time of your visit and is believed not to have been slept in the night before, may be inserted as uninhabited. New houses, not yet inhabited, may be inserted as "*Building.*" Where there is a row of such houses the total number may be inserted before the letter *B.* instead of the separate insertion of each.

By "*House*" is meant *Dwelling-House;* and every building in which any person habitually sleeps must be considered as a dwelling-house; but buildings, such as churches or warehouses, or any others, which were never used or intended to be used as dwelling-houses, must not be inserted.

"*Names of each Person who abode therein the preceding night.*"—Insert, without distinction or omission, *every* living person who abode or slept in each house. Leave no blank spaces between the names, but enter each immediately after the one preceding it, so that each page may contain 25. Set down one after the other those who have the same surname, beginning with the heads of the family, and put no others between them. As long as the surname is the same do not repeat it, but write "*do.*" Where there are more christian names than one, as "John William," or "Maria Louisa," write down only the first.

When the person is a Peer or Peeress, the title may be written instead of the name. The words "Lord," "Lady," "Sir," "Rt. Hon." "Hon." may be put before the names of those to whom they belong.

If no christian name has been given to an infant write "*n. k.*" for *not known*, as in the Example.

If, as may happen in a lodging-house or inn, a person who slept there the night before, has gone away early and the name is not known, write "*n. k.*" where the name should have been.

At the end of the names of each family draw a line thus ⁄ as in the Example. At the end of the names of the inmates in each house draw a double line thus ⫽

"*Age and Sex.*"—Write the age of each person opposite to the name in one of the two columns headed "Males" and "Females," according to the sex.

Write the age of every person under 15 years of age as it is stated to you. For persons aged 15 years and upwards, write the lowest of the term of 5 years within which the age is.

Thus—for Persons aged 15 years and under 20 write 15 | 35 years and under 40 write 35 | 55 years and under 60 write 55
20 years and under 25 write 20 | 40 years and under 45 write 40 | 60 years and under 65 write 60
25 years and under 30 write 25 | 45 years and under 50 write 45 | 65 years and under 70 write 65
30 years and under 35 write 30 | 50 years and under 55 write 50 | 70 years and under 75 write 70
and so on up to the greatest ages.

If no more can be ascertained respecting the age of any person than that the person is a child or is grown up, write "*under 20,*" or "*above 20,*" as the case may be.

"*Profession, Trade, Employment, or of Independent Means.*"—Men, or widows, or single women, having no profession or calling, but living on their means, may be inserted as *independent,* which may be written shortly, thus "*Ind.*"

The profession, &c., of wives, or of sons or daughters living with their husbands or parents, and assisting them, but not apprenticed or receiving wages, need not be set down.

All persons serving in Her Majesty's *Land* service as officers or privates in the Line, Cavalry, Engineers, or Artillery, may be entered as "*Army,*" without any statement of their rank, adding "*H.P.*" for *Half-Pay,* and "*P.*" for *Pensioner.*

All persons belonging to Her Majesty's *Sea* service, including Marines, may be entered as "*Navy,*" adding "*H.P.*" for *Half-Pay,* and "*P.*" for *Pensioner.*

All domestic servants may be entered as "*M.S.*" for *Male Servant,* or "*F.S.*" for *Female Servant,* without statement of their particular duties, as whether butler, groom, gardener, housekeeper, cook, &c., &c.

Insert all other professions, trades, or employments, as they are described by the parties, or by others on their behalf, writing "*J.*" for *Journeyman,* "*Ap.*" for *Apprentice,* and "*Sh.*" for *Shopman,* after the statement of the trade of those who are such. "*Master*" need not be inserted; every one will be so considered who is not entered as journeyman or apprentice.

Time may be saved by writing the following words, shortly thus, "*M.*" for *Manufacturer,* "*m.*" for *Maker,* as "*Shoe m.*" for *Shoemaker,* "*Cl.*" for *Clerk,* "*Ag. lab.*" for *Agricultural labourer,* which may include all farming servants and labourers in husbandry. Use no other marks or abbreviations but those herein allowed.

Rank, or any such term as "*Esq.*" or "*Gentleman,*" must *not* be entered in this column.

"*Where born.—Whether in the same County.*"—Write opposite to each name (except those of Irish, Scotch, or Foreigners,) "*Y.*" or "*N.*" for *Yes* or *No,* as the case may be.

Whether in Scotland, Ireland, or Foreign Parts.—Write in this column, "*S.*" for those who were born in *Scotland;* "*I.*" for those born in *Ireland;* and "*F.*" for *Foreigners.* This latter mark is to be used only for those who are subjects of some Foreign State, and not for British subjects who happen to have been born abroad.

Enter the Totals at the bottom of each page as in the Example, and enter and add up all the Totals in the summary in the last page. This may be done at home, and must be written with *ink.*

The entries in the pages of the Enumeration Schedule (except the Totals) may be written with a pencil, which will be furnished for that purpose. All that is written in the 3 pages following them must be with *ink.*

City or Borough of *Southwark*

Parish or Township of *St Saviour*

PLACE.	HOUSES		NAMES of each Person who abode therein the preceding Night.	AGE and SEX.		PROFESSION, TRADE, EMPLOYMENT, or of INDEPENDENT MEANS.	Where Born	
	Uninhabited or Building.	Inhabited.		Males.	Females.		Whether Born in same County.	Whether Born in Scotland, Ireland, or Foreign Parts.
George Street		1	James Johnson	40		Chemist	Y.	
			Jane do.		35		N.	
			William do.	15		Shcem. Ap.	Y.	
			Anne do.		13		Y.	
			Edward Smith	30		Chemist's Sh.	N.	
			Sarah Roolins		45	F. S.		I.
do.	26	1	John Cox	60		Publican	N.	
do.	1 B		Mary do.		45		Y.	
do.	1 B		Ellen do.		20		N.	
			James Macpherson	25		M. S.		S.
			Henry Wilson	35		Army	N.	
			n. k.	above 20				
Extra Parochial Place, named The Close.		1	William Jones	50		Farmer	Y.	
			Elizabeth do.		40		Y.	
			William do.	15		Navy	Y.	
			Charlotte do.		8		Y.	
			n. k. do.		5 months		Y.	
			Richard Clerk	20		Ag. Lab.	N.	
do.	26	1	Robert Hall	45		Tailor	Y.	
			Martha do.		30		Y.	
			John Muller	25		Tailor J.		F.
			Ann Williams		20	F. S.	N.	
Chapel Row.		1	Edward Jackson	35		Ind.	N.	
			Charles do.	30		Cl.	N.	
			James Leary	20		M. S.		I.
TOTAL in Page	226 2 B	5		15	10			

DIRECTIONS.

Respecting the manner in which Entries should be made in this Book.

The process of entering the Householder's Schedules in this Book should be as follows:—

The Enumerator should first insert, in the spaces at the top of the page, the name of the Parish or Township, Ecclesiastical District, City or Borough, Town or Village, to which the contents of that page will apply, drawing his pen through all the headings which are inappropriate. If the place be extra parochial, he should draw his pen through the words "Parish or Township," in the first column, and write "Extra Parochial" after the name of the place.

He should then, in the first column write the No. of the Schedule he is about to copy, and in the second column the name of the Street, Square, &c. where the house is situate, and the No. of the house, if it has a No., or, if the house be situate in the country, any distinctive Name by which it may be known.

He should then copy from the Schedule into the other columns, all the other particulars concerning the members of the family (making use if he please of any of the authorized contractions); and proceed to deal in the same manner with the next Schedule.

Under the last name in any *house* he should draw a line across the page as far as the fifth column. Where there is more than one Occupier in the same house, he should draw a similar line under the last name of the family of each Occupier; making the line, however, in this case, commence a little on the left hand side of the third column, as in the example on page vi.

Where he has to insert an uninhabited house, or a house building, this may be done, as in the example, by writing in the second column on the line under the last name of the last house

inserted, "One house uninhabited," "Three houses building," as the case may be; drawing a line underneath, as in the example.

At the bottom of each page, on the line for that purpose, he must enter the total *number of HOUSES* in that page, separating those *inhabited* from those *uninhabited* or *building*. If the statement regarding any inhabited house is continued from one page to another, that house must be reckoned in the total of the page on which the *first* name is entered. He must, also enter on the same line the total number of males and of females included in that page.

When he has completely entered all the Schedules belonging to any one *Parish* or *Township*, he should make no more entries on the LEAF on which the last name is written, but should write across the page, "End of the Parish [or Township] of ——;" beginning the entry of the next Schedule on the next subsequent LEAF of his book. The same course must be adopted with respect to any isolated or detached portion of a distant parish; which portion, for the sake of convenience, may have been included in his District. When he has entered all the Schedules belonging to any *Borough, Ward, Tything, Hamlet, Village, Ecclesiastical District*, &c., he should make no more entries on that PAGE, but write underneath the line after the last name, "End of the Borough, [or Ecclesiastical District Hamlet, Tything, Ward, Village, &c.] of ——;" making his next entry on the first line of the following PAGE.

In this way he will proceed until all his Householders' Schedules are correctly copied into his Book; and he must then make up the statement of totals, at page ii of his Book, in the form there specified. He must also, on page iii, make up the summaries there mentioned, in the form and according to the instructions there given.

[Example of the manner in which Entries should be made in the Schedule Book.]

vi

No. of Householder's Schedule	Name of Street, Place, or Road, and Name or No. of House	Name and Surname of each Person who abode in the house, on the Night of the 30th March, 1851	Relation to Head of Family	Condition	Age of Males	Age of Females	Rank, Profession, or Occupation	Where Born	Whether Blind, or Deaf-and-Dumb
4	7, Charlotte Street	Michael Morgan	Head	Mar.	50		Victualler	Ireland.	
		Mary Do.	Wife	Mar.		30		Ireland.	
		Ellen Do.	Dam.			7m.		Middlesex ; St. Jas. Westmr.	
		Catherine Fox	Serv.	U.		30	General Serv.	Hants ; Andover	
		Catherine Doyle	Serv.	U.		25	Servant	Ireland.	
5	8, Charlotte Street	Lambert Foster	Head	Mar.	50		Tea-dealer ; (master, employing one man.)	Cumberland ; Wigton.	
		Emma Do.	Wife	Mar.		30		Cumberland ; Longtown.	
		William Do.	Son		9			Middlesex ; St. Jas. Westmr.	Deaf
		Henrietta Do.	Dam.			4 m.		Do. ; Do.	
		George Betts	Shopman	U.	19		Tea-dealer's Shopman	Do. ; Shoreditch	
		Jane Cook	Serv.	U.		22	General Serv.	Do. ; Marybone.	
6		James Phillips	Head	Mar.	40		Plumber	Yorkshire ; Leeds.	
		Harriet Do.	Wife	Mar.		30		Do. ; Do.	
		Sophia White	Serv.	U.		11	General Serv.	Middlesex ; St. Jas. Westmr.	
	Three Houses uninhabited								
7	2, Bird Lane	William Hampton	Head	U.	72		Coach Trimmer	Stafford. ; Bilston.	
		Ann Do.	Wife	Mar.		77		Do. ; Do.	
8	3, Bird Lane	Thomas Johnson	Head	Wid.	10		Retired Grocer	Devonshire ; Honiton.	
		Emma Do.	Niece	U.		11		Middlesex ; St. Pancras.	
		Jane Turner	Apprentice	U.		14	Corset Maker (App.)	Middlesex ; Putney.	
		Total of Males and Females			7	12			

Total of Houses 1 4 ; U 3 ; B —

Parish or Township of St. James, Westminster. Ecclesiastical District of City or Borough of Westminster Town of Village of vii

[Example of the manner in which Entries should be made in the Schedule Book.]

Parish or Township of *Enfield*	Ecclesiastical District of *St. James.*	City or Borough of	Town of	Village of *Banford*							
Name of Street, Place, or Road, and Name or No. of House	Name and Surname of each Person who abode in the house, on the Night of the 30th March, 1851	Relation to Head of Family	Condition	Age of (Males)	Age of (Females)	Rank, Profession, or Occupation	Where Born	Whether Blind, or Deaf-and-Dumb
---	---	---	---	---	---	---	---	---
Mayfield Lane	William Johnson	Head	Mar.	61		Bricklayer's Labourer	Bucks; Aylesbury	
	Sarah Do.	Wife	Mar.		30		Surrey; Walton	
	Eliza J. Do.	Daur.	U.		19		Do. ; Do.	
	William T. Do.	Son		10			Do. ; Do.	
	Caroline Do.	Daur.			8	Scholar	Do. ; Do.	
One House building								
Banford Lane	John S. King	Head	Mar.	55		Agricultural Labourer	Surrey; Dorking.	
	Mary Do.	Wife	Mar.		53		Do. ; Walton.	
	Mary Do.	Daur.			1 m.		Do. ; Do.	
	George Newman	Head	Mar.	54		Basket Maker	Kent; Chislehurst.	
	Susannah Do.	Wife	Mar.		47		Surrey; Mitcham.	
	John G. Do.	Son	U.	23		Basket Maker	Surrey; Walton.	
	Frances Do.	Daur.	U.		19		Do. ; Do.	
	End of the Ecclesiastical District of St. James; and also of the village of Banford							
	Total of Males and Females...			5	7			

GENERAL INSTRUCTION TO THE ENUMERATOR.

As soon as possible after the completion of the Enumeration—

(1.) *Arrange the Householders' Schedules in order* so that all those relating to one Parish or Township, Hamlet, Ecclesiastical District, &c., are together.

NOTE.—This order will be indicated by the Schedule Numbers entered in your "Memorandum Book," prepared in conformity with the instructions.

(2.) COPY VERY LEGIBLY *in ink* the Householders' Schedules into this *Enumeration Book*, in accordance with the following directions :—

Directions respecting the manner of entering the Householders' Schedules.

1. Insert first, in the spaces at the top of the page, the name of the Parish or Township, City or Municipal Borough, Ward (if in a City or Municipal Borough), Parliamentary Borough, Town, Hamlet, &c., or Ecclesiastical District, in which the houses of that page are situate, drawing your pen through such of the words as are inappropriate.

2. In the first column, write the *No. of the Householder's Schedule* you are about to copy, commencing with No. 1 ; in the second column write the name of the Road, Street, Square, &c, where the house is situate, and the No. of the *house*, or any distinctive Name by which it is known ; then insert in the third column the figure 1 for an Inhabited House, and Copy from the Schedule into the other columns all the particulars concerning the persons mentioned therein, making use of any of the authorised contractions (see below), and taking especial care to class the *ages* of MALES and FEMALES *under their* PROPER COLUMNS.

Proceed to enter in the same manner the other Schedules, up to the last, in strict numerical order.

3. Under the name of the last entered person in each *house*, draw a DOUBLE line, as in the example on the opposite page, to separate the inmates from those of the house next following ; and where there is *more than one Occupier* in the same house, draw a *single line* to distinguish each Family, as in the example. [NOTE.—*A Lodger, with or without a family, is to be considered an Occupier*].

4. Where you have to insert an uninhabited house, or a house building, do this by writing in the fourth column, "1 U," or "1 B," on a distinct line, following the order in which the houses occur in the Road, Street, &c. When two or more houses, uninhabited or building, occur together, insert the total number, thus :—"3 U," "2 B," as the case may be.

5. At the bottom of each page, on the line for that purpose, enter the total *number of* houses in that page, as in the example. If the statement respecting any inhabited house is continued from one page to another, that house will be reckoned in the total of the houses in the page on which the *first* name is entered. Enter also, on the line at the foot of the page, the total number of MALES and FEMALES in that page.

6. When all the Schedules belonging to any one *Parish or Township, Borough, Ward, Town, Hamlet, &c., or Ecclesiastical District*, have been entered, write across the page, "*End of the Parish [or Township] of——,*" "*End of the Borough, Ward, Town, Hamlet, &c,*" or *Ecclesiastical District, of ——,*" following this order of preference where the boundaries are conflicting. Make the next entry on the first line of the following PAGE.

Persons not in HOUSES ; and Completion of the Enumeration Book.

After having completed the entry of all the HOUSEHOLDERS' SCHEDULES, according to the above directions, commence a fresh page, and writing over the top "*List of Persons not in Houses,*" proceed to copy from your "Memorandum Book" the particulars contained in the List of Persons who slept in Barns, Sheds, &c.; but in making up the totals at the foot of that page, the columns headed "Houses" must be left blank, as Barns, Sheds, &c., are not to be reckoned as *Houses*. Then, having satisfied yourself of the correctness of your book, fill up the tables on pages iv. and v., and sign the Declaration on page vi.

CONTRACTIONS TO BE USED BY THE ENUMERATOR.

ROAD, STREET, &c.—Write "*Rd.*" for Road ; "*St.*" for Street ; "*Pl.*" for Place ; "*Sq.*" for Square ; "*Ter.*" for Terrace.

NAMES.—Write the *First Christian Name* in full : *initials* or first letters of the other Christian names of a person who has more than one, may be inserted. When the same *surnames occur several times* in succession, write "do." for all such surnames except the *first*, which should be written in full. Where the *name* or *any particular is not known*, "*n. k.*" should be entered in its place.

In the column "RELATION TO HEAD OF FAMILY," write "*Head,*" for head of family ; "*Daur.*" for daughter ; "*Serv.*" for servant.

In the column "CONDITION," write "*Mar.*" for married ; "*Un.*" for unmarried ; "*W.*" for widow ; "*Widr.*" for widower.

In the columns for AGE write the number of *years* carefully and distinctly in the proper column for "Males" or "Females," as the case may be ; in the case of Children under One Year of age, as the age is expressed in months, write "*Mo.*" distinctly after the figures.

In the column for "RANK, PROFESSION, OR OCCUPATION," the following contractions may be used : "*Ag. Lab.*" for agricultural labourer ; "*Ap.*" for apprentice ; "*Cl.*" for clerk ; "*Serv.*" for servant.

[Example]

iii

The undermentioned Houses are situate within the Boundaries of the

Parish [or Township] of	Municipal Borough of	Municipal Ward of	Parliamentary Borough of	Hamlet or Tything, &c., of	Ecclesiastical District of
St. Saviour	Southwark	High Street	Southwark		Christchurch

No. of Schedule	Road, Street, &c., and No. or Name of House	HOUSES Inhabited	HOUSES Uninhabited or Building	Name and Surname of each Person	Relation to Head of Family	Condition	Age Males	Age Females	Rank, Profession, or Occupation	Where Born	Whether Blind, or Deaf-and-Dumb
4	7, Claylands R. "Queen's Arms"	1		Michael Mannion	Head	Mar.	31		Victualler	Middlesex; Islington	
				Mary F. Do.	Wife	Mar.		29		Surrey; Camberwell	
				Ellen Do.	Dau.			7 mo		Surrey; St. Saviour, Southwark	
				Ann Fox	Serv.	Un.		28	General Serv.	Herts; Amwell	
				Catherine Pugh	Serv.	Un.		24	Barmaid	Ireland	
5	8, Claylands R.	1		Lambert Nesbit	Head	Mar.	39		Grocer; (master, employing 2 men)	Cumberland; Wigton	
				Joanna Do.	Wife	Mar.		36		Cumberland; Langtown	
				William Do.	Son		12		Scholar	Surrey; St. Saviour, Southwark	
				Henrietta Do.	Dau.			9	Do.	Do. Do.	
				George Bacon	Shopman	Un.	19		Grocer's Shopman	Middlesex; Shoreditch	
				Jane Cook	Serv.	Un.		22	General Serv.	Marylebone	
6				James F. Phillips	Head	Mar.	41		Binder's Cl.	Yorkshire; Leeds	
				Harriet Do.	Wife	Mar.		29		Do.; Bradford	
				Sophia Wild	Serv.	Un.		16	General Serv.	Middlesex; St. Ives, Westminster	
7	9, 10, 11, Do.	3		William Frampton	Head	Mar.	72		Coal Porter	Suffolk; Bilston	
	1, Bird Lane			Ann Do.	Wife	Mar.		69		Do.; Exmouth	
8	2, Bird Lane	1		Thomas Salmon	Head	Wid.	68		Retired Grocer	Devon; Honiton	
				Emma Do.	Niece	Un.		41	Vessel Maker	Middlesex; St. Pancras	
				Jane Palmer	Apprentice	Un.		18	Vessel Maker (Ap.)	Middlesex; Stepney	
9	Do.	2		Wallis Johnson	Lodger	Un.		27	Ship Carpenter	Durham; Sunderland	
									End of Christchurch Ecclesiastical District		

| | Total of Houses... | 4 3 2 | | | | Total of Males and Females... | 8 | 12 | | | |

ii.

GENERAL INSTRUCTION TO THE ENUMERATOR.

As soon as possible after the completion of the Enumeration—

   (1) *Arrange the Householders' Schedules and other Schedules in order* so that all those relating to one Parish or Township, Hamlet, or other Local Sub-division, are together.

   (2) COPY VERY LEGIBLY in *ink* the Schedules into this *Enumeration Book*, in accordance with the following directions:—

Directions respecting the manner of entering the Schedules.

1. Insert first, in the spaces at the top of the page, the name of the Civil Parish or Township, City or Municipal Borough, Ward (if in a City or Municipal Borough), Parliamentary Borough, Town, Village, &c., Local Board or Improvement Commissioners' District, or Ecclesiastical District, in which the houses of that page are situate.

2. In the first column, write the *No. of the Schedule* you are about to copy, commencing with No. 1; in the second column the name of the Road, Street, Square, &c., where the house is situate, and the No. of the *house*, or any distinctive name by which it is known; then insert in the third column the figure *I* for an Inhabited House, and Copy from the Schedule into the other columns all the particulars concerning the persons mentioned therein, making use of any of the authorized contractions (see below), and taking especial care to class the *ages* of MALES and FEMALES *under their* PROPER COLUMNS.

   Enter in the same manner the other Schedules, up to the last, in strict numerical order.

3. Under the name of the last entered person in each *house* draw a strong DOUBLE line, as in the example on the opposite page, to separate the inmates from those of the house next following; and where there is *more than one Occupier* in the same house, draw a *single line* to distinguish each Family, as in the example. [NOTE.—*A Lodger, with or without a family, is to be considered an Occupier.*]

4. If you have enumerated any persons in Canal Boats or Barges, enter the *Schedules for Vessels* in the same manner as the Householders' Schedules, stating in col. 2 the locality in which the boats, &c., were met with.

5. Where you have to insert an uninhabited house, enter a cipher in the fourth column, "1 U," or "1 B," on a distinct line, taking care to omit in the fourth column none which are noted in your Memorandum Book. When two or more houses uninhabited or building, occur together, insert the total number, thus:—"3 U," "2 B," as the case may be.

6. At the bottom of each page, on the line for that purpose, enter the total *number of* HOUSES in that page, as in the example. If the statement respecting any inhabited house is continued from one page to another, that house will be reckoned in the total of the houses in the page on which the *first* name is entered. Enter also, on the line at the foot of the page, the total number of MALES and FEMALES in that page.

7. When all the Schedules belonging to any one *Parish or Township, Borough, Ward, Town, Village, Hamlet, Local Board or Improvement Commissioners' District,* or *Ecclesiastical District,* have been entered, write across the page, "*End of the Parish* [*or Township*] *of*——," "*End of the Borough, Ward, Town, Hamlet,* &c., *Local Board or Improvement Commissioners' District, or Ecclesiastical District, of*——" following this order of preference where the boundaries are conflicting. *Make the next entry on the first line of the following PAGE.*

————

Persons not dwelling in HOUSES; and Completion of the Enumeration Book.

   Enter under the proper Road, Lane, or other locality, any particulars you have obtained respecting persons not dwelling in houses but in Barns, Sheds, Caravans, &c.; in making up the totals at the foot of that page, however, the Barns, Sheds, &c., are not to be reckoned as Houses.

   Having satisfied yourself of the correctness of your book, fill up the tables on pages iv and v, and sign the Declaration on page vi.

CONTRACTIONS TO BE USED BY THE ENUMERATOR.

ROAD, STREET, &c.—Write "Rd." for Road ; "St." for Street ; "Sq." for Square ; "Pl." for Place ; "Ter." for Terrace.

NAMES.—Write the *First Christian Name* in full ; *initials* or first letters of the other Christian names may be inserted

   When the same surnames occur *several times* in succession, write "do." for all such surnames except the *first,* which should be written in full.

   Where the *name or any particular is not known,* "n. k.," should be entered in its place.

   In the column "RELATION TO HEAD OF FAMILY," write "*Head,*" for head of family ; "*Dau.*" for daughter ; "*Serv.*" for Servant.

   In the column "CONDITION," write "*Mar.*" for married ; "*Unm.*" for unmarried ; "*W.*" for widow ; "*Widr.*" for widower.

   In the columns for AGE write the number of years carefully and distinctly in the proper column for "Males" or "Females," as the case may be ; in the case of Children under One Year of *age,* as the age is expressed in months, write "*Mo.*" distinctly after the figures.

   In the column for " BLANK, PROFESSION, OR OCCUPATION," the following contractions may be used ; "*Ag. Lab.*" for agricultural labourer.

[Example]

iii

The undermentioned Houses are situate within the Boundaries of the

No. of Schedule	Road, Street, &c. and No. or Name of House	HOUSES In-habited / Un-inhabited (U.) or Building (B.)	Name and Surname of each Person	Relation to Head of Family	Condition	Age of (Males | Females)	Rank, Profession, or Occupation	Where Born	Whether 1. Deaf-and-Dumb 2. Blind 3. Imbecile or Idiot 4. Lunatic
4	2, Charlotte St. ("President's Arms")	1	Michael Morrison	Head	Mar.	31	Licensed Victualler	Middlesex; Islington.	
			Mary J. Do.	Wife	Mar.	29		Salop; Condover.	
			Ellen Do.	Daur.		June		Salop; Shrewsbury.	
			Elizabeth Morrison	Mother	W.	55	Accountant	Salop; Shrewsbury.	Lunatic.
			Ann Fox	Visitor	Unm.	28	General Serv.	Hants; Andover.	
			Catherine Doyle	Serv.	Unm.	24	Servant	Ireland.	
5	3, Charlotte St.	1	Lambert Newton	Head	Mar.	31	Grocer; [master, employing 3 men]	Cumberland; Wigton.	
			Emma Do.	Wife	Mar.	30		Do.; Longtown.	
			William Do.	Son		12	Scholar	Salop; Pulton.	Deaf-and-Dumb from Birth.
			Henrietta Do.	Daur.		9	Do.	Do.	
			George Mason	Shopman	Unm.	19	Grocer's Shopman	Middlesex; Shoreditch.	
			Jane Cook	Serv.	Unm.	23	General Serv.	Scotland; Leeds.	
6	Do.		James T. Phillips	Head	Mar.	24	Painter's Clerk	Yorkshire; Bradford.	
			Harriet Do.	Wife	Mar.	20		Do.; Bridgenorth.	
			Sophia White	Serv.	Unm.	16	General Serv.	Salop; Shrewsbury.	
7	9, Do.	1	William Thompson	Head	Mar.	72	Coach Trimmer	Staffordshire; Bilston.	
			Jane Do.	Wife	Mar.	67		Do.; Tamworth.	
8	1, Bird Lane	1	Thomas Johnson	Head	Wed.	68	Retired Grocer	Devon; Honiton.	
			Henry Robinson	Son	Unm.	31	Organist	Salop; Shrewsbury.	
			Emma Do.	Niece	Unm.	41	Const. Maker	Middlesex; St. Pancras.	
			Jane Turner	Apprentice	Apprentice	18	Const. Maker [Apprentice]	Salop; Ludlow.	
	Do.		Walter Campbell	Lodger	Unm.	23	Ship Carpenter [out of employ]	Durham; Sunderland.	Blind from Sixth Year.
	Total of Houses... 4	1 1B / 2 2B				End of St. Michael Ecclesiastical District			
			Total of Males and Females...			9 13			

Civil Parish (or Township) of St. Mary. — City or Municipal Borough of Shrewsbury. — Municipal Ward of High Street. — Parliamentary Borough of Shrewsbury. — Town (not being a City or Borough) of — Village or Hamlet, &c., of — Local Board (or Improvement Commissioners District) of Shrewsbury. — Ecclesiastical District of St. Michael.

CHAPTER 3

Census Data for Urban Areas

RICHARD LAWTON

Urbanisation in nineteenth century England

Many of the most striking of the nineteenth century population changes were associated with the rapid growth of towns. In urbanisation — as in industrialisation — Britain led the world and was the first to experience the many associated economic and social problems. In 1801, even using the conservative census estimate of 'places over 5,000 population', one quarter of the population of England and Wales was urban, but R. Price Williams[1] argued that the true figure was perhaps as much as two-fifths (see Table 3.1). Recently, C.M. Law.[2] taking account of previous studies, has estimated that one third of the population of England and Wales was urban at the time of the first census of 1801. By the 1840s the impact of railways and the concentration of industrial and commercial activity was leading to the rapid growth of large towns and industrial regions and a marked out-migration from the countryside which set the seal on the demographic differentiation between an older, rural England and the newer, urban England. Indeed, a significant turning point was reached in the early Victorian era when the population of England ceased to be predominantly rural.

In 1843 Robert Vaughan justifiably claimed, 'Ours is the age of great cities'.[3] Even by the conservative definition of the 1851 Census, over half the population of England and Wales lived in towns and, as compared with only 15 'cities' with over 20,000 population in 1801, there were 63 by mid-century in which lived 6,265,011 people — 34.9 per cent of the total population.[4] The continuing rapid concentration in

TABLE 3.1

Estimates of Urban Population in England and Wales 1801–1911

	Total Enumerated Population (000)	Estimated urban population							
		Census[1]		R.Price-Williams[2]		T.A.Welton[3]		C.M.Law[5]	
		No.	%	No.	%	No.	%	No.	%
1801	8,893	2,154	24.2	3,615	40.1	3,978	39.1	3,009	33.8
1811	10,164	2,603	25.6	4,248	42.8	4,710	46.3	3,722	36.6
1821	12,000	3,245	27.1	5,212	43.4	5,789	48.2	4,805	40.0
1831	13,897	4,106	29.5	6,394	46.0	7,143	51.5	6,153	44.3
1841	15,914	5,074	31.9	7,680	48.3	8,594	54.0	7,693	48.3
1851	17,928	8,991	50.2	9,214	51.4	10,291	57.4	9,688	54.0
1861	20,066	10,961	54.6	10,717	51.9	12,185	60.7	11,784	58.7
1871	22,712	14,041	61.8	12,577	55.6	14,406	65.0	14,802	65.2
1881	25,794	17,637	67.9			17,295	67.1	18,180	70.0
1891	29,003	20,896	72.0			19,939	68.8	21,601	74.5
1901	32,528	25,058	77.0			{25,925}[4]	79.4	25,372	78.0
1911	36,070	28,163	78.1			{28,154}	80.7	28,467	78.9

1. Estimates for 1811–41 taken from figures for 62 Principal Towns plus London, Census, 1851, Appendix to Report Table 42, cxxvi; for 1851–1911 from Census, 1911, Vol. I, Report, p. xvi. (HMSO, 1912)

2. Jnl. Roy. Stat. Soc. 43 (1880), pp. 462–508.

3. Jnl. Roy. Stat. Soc. 63 (1900), pp. 526–95 (Table D) for towns over 1,000 and (4) Jnl. Roy. Stat. Soc. 76 (1913), pp. 304–17 (for towns and 'populous districts').

5. Trans. Inst. Brit. Geogr. 41 (1967), pp. 125–43.

A.K. Cairncross (op. cit.) gives the population in London, 8 large towns and 118 other towns together with 9 colliery districts in England only as 9,743,290 (61.2 per cent 'urban') in 1841 and 29,109,688 (80.7 per cent 'urban') in 1911.

the towns of people and jobs during Victorian and Edwardian times reflected complementary phenomena of urbanisation and rural depopulation and left its mark upon both the population map and the townscapes of England. (See Figs 2, 4, 6, 8 and 10.) By the end of the nineteenth century nearly four-fifths of the population were town-dwellers and the proportion of those dependent upon towns for a living but living in suburbs outside the administrative boundaries of Boroughs and Urban Districts may have formed a further 10 per cent of the total population.[5]

The impact of such numbers in such concentration was profound whether in physical terms — expressed in such problems as water supply, sanitation and housing, in social terms — through the impact on family and the changing structure of society, or in economic terms — through the problems attendant upon new systems of commercial and industrial organisation. The political and administrative problems of creating a new framework of organisation for local government were reflected in the complexities of the changing map of administrative areas. Yet despite the significance of the process of urbanisation it is not easy to analyse the basic elements of population and socio-economic change from census sources alone. Although contemporaries stressed the importance of urban growth in census reports and tabulations, especially from 1841, they did not find the task of defining and analysing urban population an easy one.

There are many imperfections in census data for towns, some of which still persist. The basic problems are threefold. First, the lack of precise definitions of urban — and rural — areas bedevils any attempt at spatial or structural delimitation of urban population. One must deal with various formal definitions — all more or less unsatisfactory — which change from time to time, thus making it difficult to obtain exact and comparative information even about total population numbers (see below pp. 86—109).

Secondly, published censuses can only deal with a selection of the possible tabulations of the original individual data. Although during the later nineteenth century an increasing amount of information was processed for urban areas, individually and collectively, it is difficult to match this with other statistical information for towns. Moreover, the lack of a sufficiently small and consistent unit of enumeration from which comparable urban areas may be .aggregated to study changes over time, creates great difficulty in studies at both regional and local level. Indeed, this problem is only approaching solution with the adoption, in the 1971 census, of a geo-coded grid system as a basic component in storage and tabulation of data.[6] The enumeration districts under which individual schedules were grouped, and for which summaries of population and houses are available (see below, pp. 121—7), were redrawn at every census to take account of changes in population distribution. Moreover, these are available to the public only after a 100-year period of confidentiality has elapsed.

Thirdly, the data collected for urban areas varied with the questions asked in successive censuses and were not necessarily consistent from one census to another. Thus, precise comparisons of essentially similar subjects is often difficult. For example, public concern with housing in the nineteenth century led to an increase in the amount of information gathered and published in the census especially in the late nineteenth and early twentieth century (see Appendix XI), but operational definitions of basic terms such as house and dwelling, family and household also changed making comparative statistical analysis difficult. Population mobility, of crucial significance to the growth and characteristics of urban populations,[7] is difficult to analyse comparatively for urban areas. Indeed it was only in 1911 that the census permitted analysis both of the birthplaces of those enumerated in the large towns and of the place of enumeration of those born in cities, though there were tables of birthplace for boroughs and large towns and for counties from 1841 (see D.E. Baines, below, Chapter 4).

This brief review focuses on three major problems in the study of nineteenth century towns from census sources: first, the question of urban definition in relation to the urban areas for which census data are published; secondly, the range of information available for urban areas; thirdly, the problems and potentialities for internal analysis of urban population at regional and local level.

Urban definition

Although nineteenth century censuses all collected and tabulated information for urban areas, the units of enumeration
changed from census to census (see Appendix II). It is thus
difficult to precisely delimit and compare the numbers and
characteristics of urban population. Not surprisingly there
has been considerable discussion over the precise degree of
urbanisation and the nature and extent of such processes as
migration to the towns; nor is it easy to examine the exact
demographic, social and economic impact of the rapid urbanisation of the period.

The difficulties are two-fold. First, the legal definition of
towns often excluded settlements which were functionally
and physically urban in character, while including some whose
urban functions were dead or moribund. Secondly, the rapidly
changing situation led to rapid out-dating of both the structure
and the boundaries of local government areas. Dr William Farr,
chief statistician to the Registrar General from 1839—79,
frequently stressed the problems caused by the complex and
changing administrative structure in the compiling and analysis
of population data. Since the legally constituted and defined
urban areas were — at any one time — out of touch with
reality it is difficult both to estimate the precise numbers and
distribution of urban population and even more difficult to
analyse their characteristics since, at best, these are given in
censuses for *de jure* urban areas.

This long-standing problem in population studies has been
tackled in some countries by adopting definitions of urban
population based on population numbers, or on function, or
on degree of concentration or size and degree of clustering of
the settlement unit.[8]

While the urban units used by the Registrar General vary
from census to census, the period 1801—1911 falls into four
distinct phases: the pre-Reform Act period, 1801—31; the
mid-nineteenth century (1841—61), during which population
figures for unincorporated towns of over 2,000 were added
to those for the reformed boroughs; a transitional phase
between 1871—81 when, as a solution was being sought to
the problem of local government, information was available

for municipal boroughs and places with local boards or Improvement Commissioners (the urban sanitary districts of 1881); finally the era from 1891 when a more up-to-date — though not precise — definition of urban and rural was achieved under the Local Government Acts of 1888 and 1894.

Each of these census phases will be examined in turn, relating changes in local government structure to changes in the tabulation and analysis of urban population data.

1801–1831

Prior to the Municipal Corporations Act of 1835[9] the legal structure of local government can be properly described as archaic. Though the development of the English burghal system, extending back into Saxon and Norman times, does not directly concern us here,[10] its legacy confronted the census-takers of the early nineteenth century with a wholly unsatisfactory framework for urban population analysis. In the 1801–31 censuses the overseers (in charge of local enumeration) and the clergy (who provided parish register abstracts)[11] were required to locate their populations by County, Hundred, *City, Town, etc.* [my italics] and Parish. The High Constables' 'form of Indorsement' of these returns (required under the Population Act of 1800) refers to urban areas under the heads of City, Borough, Town *or* County Corporate.[12]

The *Abstract of Answers and Returns* from the 1801 census noted that the Act required returns of the houses, persons and occupations (in three very broad groups) for 'every Parish, Township and Place'. Although no specific mention of urban areas was made in the instructions, information was given in the main tabulations for boroughs and towns, and in summary tables for Hundreds and towns. These summaries pick out 119 'Cities' and 'Towns' in England and a further 17 in Wales, and Monmouth, ranging in population from 545 to 818, 129 for 'Greater' London. However, in addition the returning officers described many of their 'Places' as a 'Town'. Thus, in Lancashire, while only 6 centres were specifically identified as towns in all tables (Salford being included as a suburb of Manchester), a further 8 places were described by the enumeration as 'towns', including such ancient towns as Preston and Warrington and such sizeable industrial centres as Oldham, Bury, Bolton and Blackburn. But there is no precise indication of how urban status was determined in such cases nor of the accuracy of definition of the urban area and population.

The censuses from 1811–31 gave similar information for towns, but specifically distinguished three types of urban centre — boroughs, cities and towns, giving population totals for the principal towns '... in conformity with the Population Abstracts of 1801, 1811 and 1821'.[13] In all 129 urban places were distinguished in the 1831 census: 68 boroughs, 26 cities, 33 towns and 2 Liberties (Appendix II).[14] The boroughs listed in this census misrepresented the urban population in two ways. First, they included boroughs which were only nominal: for example, Over (Cheshire) elected a Mayor annually but had no municipal functions; Cornwall had many boroughs — such as Bossiney — which had a Corporation but exercised no function; in Kent, Romney Marsh had a Corporation but was essentially rural in character; while Wales was rich in examples of moribund or extinct Corporations.[15] Secondly, many important urban centres were omitted because they had neither legal status as towns nor recognition by the census as 'principal towns': thus, in Lancashire, apart from the boroughs of Lancaster, Liverpool and Wigan, only Manchester was additionally listed, in Durham only Durham City and Sunderland were recognised; while in the west Midlands none of the Black Country towns were separately distinguished, though many of the industrial villages of 1801 had become towns by the 1830s[16] including such places as West Bromwich, Tipton, Darlaston, Willenhall, Wolverhampton and Stourbridge. The maps of urban administrative areas and urban population both understate the situation (figs 1 and 2).

Throughout the nineteenth century, as always, London was a special case. By far the largest urban centre in 1801, with a population of 864,845, the metropolitan area had grown to some one and a half millions by 1831 though a wider definition of 'an area some 8 miles around St. Pauls' gave a population of 1,776,556.[17] Clearly London already presented conurban characteristics and a wider definition of its

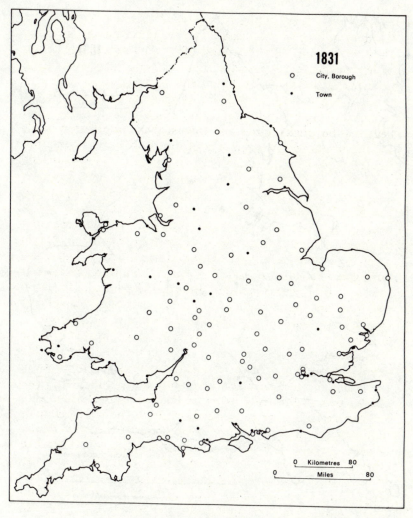

1831

○ City, Borough

• Town

Figure 1 – URBAN AREAS, 1831

The categories of boroughs, cities and towns are as given in the *Census of Great Britain, 1831*, Population Abstract, pp. 410–6.

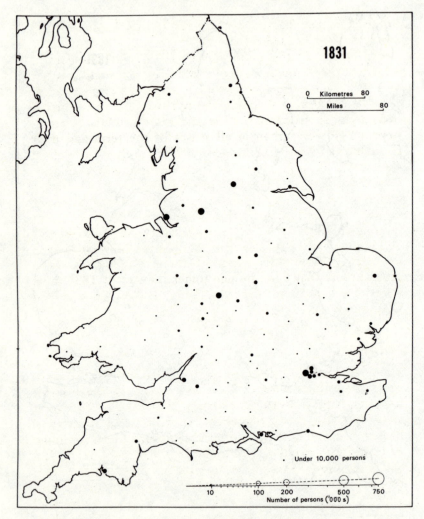

Figure 2 — URBAN POPULATION, 1831

The size of population of 'principal towns' is shown by proportionate circles on a logarithmic scale which is directly
comparable with figs. 4, 6, 8 and 10.

population than that covered by the strictly legally defined urban area was needed.

On the eve of the Reform Act of 1832 and the parallel reform of the boroughs under the Municipal Corporations Act of 1835, the situation was therefore one in which *de jure* and *de facto* definitions of towns were not in accord. Nevertheless, of 285 places visited by the Municipal Corporations Commissioners 246 were urban in all senses of the term and their population of 2,085,513 formed one sixth of that for England and Wales, though in many of these the population overflowed the borough boundary and it is difficult to reckon the numbers of these 'suburban' populations. Moreover, many big urban areas had not borough status and developed their powers and government under local Acts, under which some 300 improvement bodies of various sorts had been established by 1834. [18] Such places were not all consistently regarded as urban before that date, though under the Act of 1835 these were empowered to transfer these powers to reformed Corporations.

1841–1861

The Municipal Corporations Act of 1835 is a landmark in local government history [19] and also marks the beginning of an improvement in the tabulation of census data. Moreover it coincides with the development of much fuller population data in England and Wales with the adoption of civil recording of births and deaths under the Acts of 1836 and 1837 [20] and the revision of recording of marriages,[21] together with the reorganisation of the census and the institution of continuous vital registration within the office of the Registrar General all contributed to this general improvement in population data. However, the local units of census organisation and registration, the registration districts, did not themselves distinguish between urban and rural in tabulations, though they were a more rational and consistent framework of analysis of population data and remained one of the main units of tabulation until the First World War.

Although the census of 1841 did not benefit fully from the administrative reforms of the 1830s either in respect of

the method of taking and tabulating the census or in terms of
its tabulation of urban populations, the changed urban
administrative structure initiated by the Acts of 1835 led to
a more realistic definition of urban areas in the period 1834–
70. The 1841 Enumeration Abstract gave the populations for
the reformed cities, parliamentary boroughs and districts
of boroughs and listed altogether some 216 towns together
with no less than 753 other urban townships (see Appendix
II, note 2). In all the 1835 Act had created 178 reformed
boroughs and, in addition at this time, there were 88 'un-
reformed Corporate Towns' and the City of London.
Furthermore, in the 1830s and '40s an additional 18 boroughs
were granted Charters of Incorporation.

But by 1851 the basis of definition of urban areas had
been realistically widened under the 1848 Public Health Act
which gave administrative powers to local Improvement
Boards as well as to boroughs (fig. 3). Thus the census for
that year was able to make the first adequate estimate of
urban population (see table 3.1) and to draw up a useful
table of 'Comparative Population of Principal Towns ...
1801-51'[22] for places of over 20,000 population in 1851.
It tabulated 534 '... Cities, Boroughs and Principal Towns in
England and Wales'[23] and included 196 boroughs and 89
corporate towns, distinguishing populations within the municipal and parliamentary limits,[24] and 248 'towns' (ranging in
size from 45 at Cefnllys, Radnorshire, to 375,955 in
Liverpool). By 1851 most large towns had both parliamentary
and municipal status, though many populous areas were still
without municipal organisation. Thus many parts of London
were parliamentary boroughs but had no *civic* status, including
Tower Hamlets — with over half a million people —
Marylebone, Finsbury, Lambeth and Westminster — all a
quarter of a million or over — and Greenwich (105,784).
Moreover many industrial towns of over 20,000 had either
only parliamentary borough status (Brighton, Stoke and
Merthyr Tydfil are notable examples) or, like Birkenhead,
Burnley and Stalybridge, had no urban status at all. Yet very
small units were still described as boroughs, including the
tiny constituent parts of 13 Welsh 'Parliamentary Districts of
Boroughs'.[25]

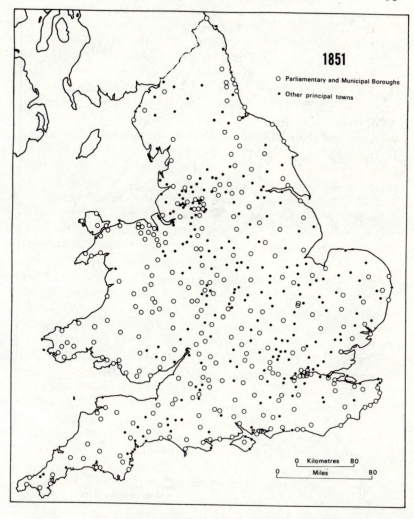

Figure 3 – URBAN AREAS, 1851

The categories of boroughs (municipal and parliamentary) and other principal towns are as given in the *Census of Great Britain, 1851,* Summary Tables, Table VII, pp. cciv–ccvii.

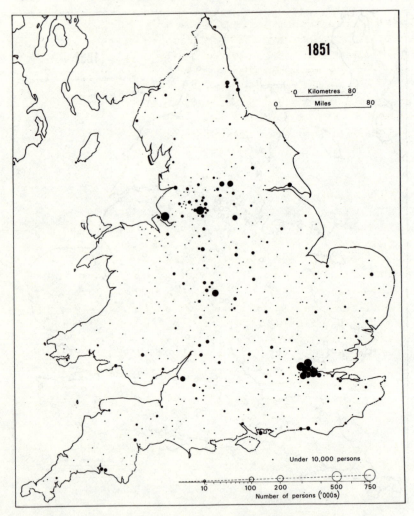

Figure 4 — URBAN POPULATION, 1851

The size of population of all urban places in fig. 3 is shown on the logarithmic scale used in figures 2, 6, 8 and 10.

Based on *Census of Great Britain, 1851,* Summary Tables, Table VII, pp. cciv–ccvii.

Despite the more realistic definition of urban places in the 1851 census many of the urban limits defined under the 1835 and 1848 Acts were outdated, and definition and control of essentially unitary urban areas was divided. Even after its 1835 boundary extensions[26] parts of the continuous built-up area of Liverpool and suburban 'out-townships' in West Derby Registration District were outside the borough. On the other hand some borough boundaries were more generously drawn, as for example in Leeds, where the parish — one of the largest in the north of England — included out-townships, especially in the north, which were rural rather than suburban in character and which, in the mid-nineteenth century, contrasted markedly with the industrial townships of Hunslet, Holbeck and Bramley to the south of the river Aire.

Many emerging industrial areas were however still without formal urban status. Parts of the textile areas of east Lancashire and west Yorkshire, the mining areas of north-east England and much of the Black Country, formerly areas of industrial villages, were by the mid-nineteenth century as much urban as rural. The recognition of their status was largely an outcome of their problems of health, sanitation and water supply. The 1848 Public Health Act gave administrative powers in such matters to 276 towns of over 5,000. The cholera epidemics of 1849 and 1854 gave urgency to further urban administrative reforms, though not always in the direction of a coordinated structure. Whereas a central Department of Health emerged in 1855, the 1858 Local Government Acts abolished the existing Boards and split their powers, giving legal control to the Home Office and medical control to the Privy Council. Moreover the principle of *ad hoc* administrative areas, each dealing with a separate function of local administration separately, often within different boundaries, led to a proliferation of local administration units which inevitably complicated organisation of statistical data. The Registrar General was driven to remark that:

The inconveniences and perplexities which the variety of ecclesiastical, military and civil, fiscal and judicial, ancient and modern, municipal and parliamentary, subdivisions of the country occasion, have been sensibly felt by us, as they were brought under our notice in the enumeration of the population. It is not within our province to reduce them to simplicity and harmony; but we call your attention to their existence; and venture humbly to suggest that the task of taking any future census, the comparision of statistical facts of every kind, and probably all administrative arrangements, would be greatly facilitated by the adoption of a uniform system of territorial divisions in Great Britain.[27]

In London some progress was made, for the essential unity of the Metropolitan area was recognised by the Metropolis Management Act of 1855. Excluded from the Royal Commision on Municipal Corporations of 1835, London had a separate report issued in 1837.[28] The 1855 Act was the outcome of another Royal Commission of 1854 which led to a reorganisation of the previously haphazard administrative structure under a Metropolitan Board of Works controlling sewerage, highways, lighting and health. In terms of population statistics this gave a unit which accorded with the 36 districts of the Registration County of London (Group I of the registration counties developed as the statistical framework of the Registrar General's Office and the basis of enumeration from the 1851 census). Thus, in 1861 the Metropolitan Board of Works area controlled a range of services in 99 parishes with a combined population of 2,803,000: as T.W. Freeman observes, 'In a sense it was a single community and many communities at one and the same time'.[29] Hence, while for many purposes a single co-ordinating authority was necessary, it was also necessary to have within the greater London area more local administrative bodies providing for the varying community of interest of the different parts of the city.

Between 1848 and 1868, therefore, the rapid development of the urban administrative districts added 554 towns to the Municipal Corporations which took powers under Local Board procedures.[30] But the position remained unsatisfactory in two ways. First, there remained a complex of large and small boroughs — some operating under Local Government Acts, some not — and a similar confusion of non-corporate towns. Secondly, despite the development of more logical boundaries between 1834 and 1870, the definition of urban areas followed by the census understated the urban popula-

TABLE 3.2

Changes in Total and Urban Populations in England and Wales, 1801–1911

Population: 000s	England & Wales Total	% change	All Urban Total	% change	Towns Over 100,000 Total	% change	Towns of 50–100,000 Total	% change	Towns of 20–50,000 Total	% change	Towns of 10–20,000 Total	% change	Towns of 2,500–10,000 Total	% change
1801	8,893	—	3,009	—	982.2	—	309.2	—	423.0	—	418.0	—	876.9	—
1811	10,164	14.0	3,722	23.7	1,393.2	41.9	378.6	22.4	415.1	−1.9	435.6	4.2	1,099.5	25.4
1821	12,000	18.1	4,805	29.1	1,869.1	34.2	512.0	35.2	616.9	48.6	492.4	13.0	1,314.2	19.5
1831	13,897	15.8	6,153	28.0	2,589.4	38.5	552.8	8.0	940.6	52.5	599.3	21.7	1,471.1	11.9
1841	15,914	14.3	7,693	25.0	3,301.1	27.5	879.7	59.2	1,079.8	14.8	841.1	40.3	1,591.4	8.2
1851	17,928	12.6	9,688	25.9	4,450.7	34.8	1,037.3	17.9	1,262.9	17.0	1,154.7	37.4	1,782.4	12.0
1861	20,066	11.9	11,784	21.6	5,774.5	29.7	1,225.5	15.4	1,503.9	18.9	1,320.5	14.4	1,959.7	9.9
1871	22,712	13.2	14,802	25.6	7,404.1	28.2	1,260.5	2.8	2,173.0	44.4	1,501.6	13.7	2,462.8	25.6
1881	25,794	14.7	18,180	22.8	9,394.4	26.9	1,903.6	51.0	2,440.8	12.3	1,710.8	13.9	2,730.6	10.9
1891	29,003	11.6	21,601	18.8	11,433.3	21.7	2,487.9	30.7	2,647.4	8.4	2,062.1	20.5	2,970.4	8.8
1901	32,528	12.2	25,372	17.5	14,201.8	24.2	2,409.6	−3.1	3,235.7	22.2	2,641.7	28.1	2,883.1	−2.9
1911	36,070	10.9	28,467	12.2	15,811.9	11.3	2,887.1	19.8	3,750.2	15.9	2,840.2	7.5	3,178.1	10.2

Based on Law (1967); Appendix, Table XI (p. 141).

tion to a more marked extent than in the late nineteenth century (see tables 3.1 and 3.2).

1871–1881

By the late 1860s urban administration reform was under way but, despite improvements in regulation of urban health,[31] sanitation and housing[32] and the rationalisation under the Local Government Act of 1858 of various public services for the towns under local boards,[33] the administration of local government was still unsatisfactory. A Royal Commission, appointed in 1869 to investigate local government, initiated in its second report in 1871[34] a phase of transition during which a start was made on reshaping the complex and unsatisfactory local administration of mid-Victorian times. This structure was described by G.J. Goschen in 1871 as '... a chaos as regards authorities, a chaos as regards rates and a worse chaos as regards areas',[35] while William Farr, discussing the statistical difficulties caused by the state of affairs of the 1870s, described the administrative map as '... a curiously confusing reticulation of mutually intrusive and intersecting jurisdictions'.[36]

Nevertheless the development of local administration through the local government boards, especially for health and physical improvement in towns, had led to a fuller definition of the urban component of the population.[37] The urban areas listed in the 1871 Census included in addition to 308 boroughs and 92 towns — most of them well established by the mid-nineteenth century — a further 576 local boards (Appendix II and fig. 5).[38] Many small towns of historic borough status had been carried forward into the post-Reform Act period, especially in Wales, south-west, southern and south-east England. In contrast, the local boards were most numerous in the rapidly urbanising areas around the great cities and in the major industrial regions: the Metropolis, the west Midlands, the Potteries, south Wales and north-east England all had many such urban districts. But the major concentration of small local board areas lay in the textile districts of east Lancashire and west Yorkshire, laying the foundation for the fragmented local authority map of the present day.

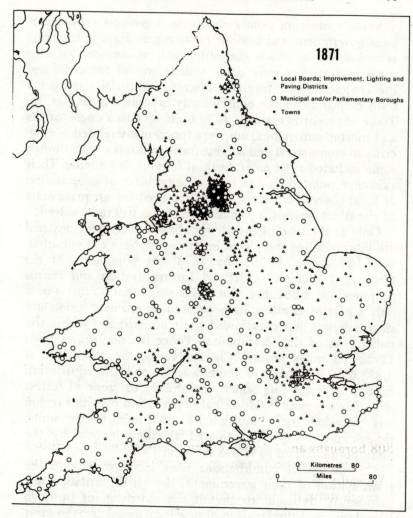

Figure 5 — URBAN AREAS, 1871

The categories of boroughs (municipal and parliamentary), local boards or districts and other towns are as given in the *Census of England and Wales, 1871*, Summary Tables, Table VII, pp. xviii—xxxiii.

Such a situation points clearly to a growing problem of local government and administrative organisation in emerging conurbations in which the outgrowth of suburbs (or out-townships as they were often called) around the cities and the coalescence of formerly discrete industrial settlements both helped to create continuously urbanised areas (fig. 6). These were not necessarily fully built up into a single 'bricks and mortar' urban area, but were functionally related — especially in commercial and administrative matters — even though some included rural areas, both of farming and mining. Their existence pointed to the increasing problem of organisation of local government services and the need for adequate units of statistical analysis, a problem which has still to be solved.

Only in the case of the Metropolis had there been any real attempt to define and give some statistical basis to a conurban area (see above, p. 96). By 1871, the population of the County of London as defined for registration and census purposes was 3,251,804. But it was noted that '... this is now only a part of London; its population in intimate fusion and close relation, has overflowed these bounds; and within the radial lines of the Metropolitan Police District, drawn from 12 to 15 miles around Charing Cross, the population is 3,883,092'.[39] Therefore there was beyond the registration county an outer ring which was already the zone of fastest population growth.[40] Municipal organisation over this region was provided by a multiplicity of administrative units, though these were coordinated to some extent by the Metropolitan Board of Works set up in 1855.

The provincial conurbations were less fortunate in the coordination of their government, though the situation was sufficiently dynamic to permit the extension of borough boundaries and the creation of new local board areas to meet the needs of the day. The 1871 Census noted the enlargement of the boundaries of six industrial boroughs and the constitution of 11 new boroughs — all in the Metropolis or major industrial regions. Conversely, 13 boroughs were disfranchised, all in rural areas. Even so, it was noted that where towns had '... no recognised boundaries ... deemed suitable as a basis for a return of population, the Superintendent Registrar of the District has in each case distinguished the

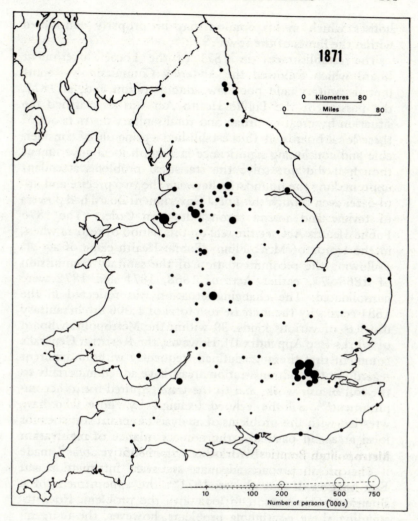

Figure 6 – URBAN POPULATION, 1871

The size of population of cities, municipal boroughs and other urban areas are shown on the scale used in figs. 2, 4, 8 and 10.

Based on *Census of England and Wales, 1871,* Preliminary Abstract, Table VIII, pp. 9–15.

houses which in his opinion may be properly considered within the limits of the town'.[41]

The establishment in 1871 of the Local Government Board which followed the Adderley Commission's Report united sanitary and poor law administration and, in 1872, the passing of the Public Health Act further clarified the situation by creating urban and rural sanitary districts out of these local boards. It thus established a principle of considerable and continuing significance in English local government though it did *not* solve the statistical problems attendant upon making the boundaries between the two precise and up-to-date, even though the Local Government Board had powers to review and amend through its own Orders. The 1875 Public Health Act set the seal on this period of reform when, in the words of M.W. Flinn, 'Public Health came of age'.[42] Following the recommendation of the sanitary commission of 1868–71, earlier Acts of 1868, 1871 and 1872 were consolidated. The changing situation was reflected in the 1881 census by the increase to a total of 1,006 urban sanitary districts of various kinds, 39 within the Metropolitan Board of Works (see Appendix II). However, the Registrar General's comment that these '... defined frequently without apparent regard to other administration areas, have added materially to the toil of our work, and to the time required for its accomplishment'[43] will be echoed feelingly by those who have wrestled with the problems of analysis of census statistics for local areas. In particular the non-accordance of registration districts and counties with other administrative areas[44] made it difficult to prepare adequate statistical information and Farr suggested as early as 1871[45] the appointment of a Boundary Commission to look into the problem. Notwithstanding these continuing problems, however, the reorganisation of local government areas in the centres of sanitary reform was leading to improvements of the ability of the census to distinguish urban from rural trends. As was noted in 1881, 'the recent division of the country into sanitary Areas some of which are styled Urban and the rest Rural Sanitary Districts, furnished the best available basis for such a calculation'.[46]

1891–1911

The continuing difficulty of precise definition of urban and rural populations was resolved to some extent by the Local Government Acts of 1888 and 1894. The basic and inter-related problems had long been recognised: the lack of an up-to-date administrative framework of government for both county and urban areas; and the uncoordinated series of *ad hoc* administrative units which had grown up since the mid-nineteenth century. The 1872 Local Government Act provided a framework of government for the towns which was adopted by the boroughs in the Municipal Corporations Act of 1882. But they did not integrate various functions within that framework. What was needed was a new and comprehensive system to put right the confusion caused by '... the legislation of this House which has created special authorities and special districts for special purposes, but, in doing so, has not proceeded on a uniform or symmetrical system'.[47] •

Rationalisation was achieved in two stages under the Local Government Acts of 1888 and 1894. The 1888 Act involved the creation of compendious authorities under which all functions of local government were combined in a single authority, but it also led to a separation of 'urban' and 'county' areas by the creation of county boroughs equivalent in status to the administrative counties which together formed a single tier of local government authorities. A good deal of discussion was involved as to the nature and definition of these new areas and, as a prelude to the legislation, the government passed a Local Government Boundaries Bill in 1887, appointing Commissioners to adjust county and local government boundaries, to avoid divided jurisdictions and to make appropriate proposals as to the boundaries of the new local government areas.[48] Thus the clearing up of many of the complexities of which administrators and census officials had complained was begun.

The Act itself was radical in that it recognised that the problems of the large towns were as great and comprehensive as those of the counties and could best be solved by separate borough authorities of county status. Much of the debate concerned the size of boroughs which should be separated and raised considerable matters of rating and finance. In the end it was decided that those towns of over 50,000 in 1881 should be accorded county borough status, together with all counties of cities irrespective of size, making 61 in all. The county areas were also reshaped and rationalised; 62 administrative counties were created out of the 52 ancient or geographical counties. London became an administrative county covering the 41 districts of the Metropolitan Board of Works, and incorporating the metropolitan parts of Middlesex, Surrey and Kent. Thus, in 1891, the administrative units used in the census were more clearly differentiated into urban and county areas, though the latter included, of course, many urban units still organised under boroughs and urban sanitary districts (fig. 7). In all some 1039 urban areas were distinguished: 63 county boroughs, 230 other municipal boroughs and 705 urban sanitary districts. While far from presenting a coordinated or even complete definition of urban England they nevertheless gave a reasonable indication of the urban populations which other estimates have confirmed (see table 3.1).

In 1893 it was the turn of the lower tier authorities — the municipal boroughs and urban sanitary districts — to undergo reform. The Local Government Act of 1894 consolidated powers into the hands of 302 town and 688 urban districts, though poor law and education still remained in separate boards.[49] In effect a considerable separation of urban areas and delegation of functions to the towns was achieved in 1888 and 1894 and the integration of most local government functions into unitary areas was achieved, a considerable gain in terms of simplification of administrative and statistical units, though at the cost of separation of urban from rural areas at a time when they were becoming more interrelated, especially in the areas around the great cities.

The new system allowed for flexibility in two ways: in allowing for boundary extensions and in permitting new Charters of Incorporation to be issued to boroughs and urban districts. While damaging to county administration, this process was necessary if statistical definition of urban areas were not to be rapidly outdated. The Registrar General noted that:

> unless the boundaries of a town are periodically adjusted, the relation between its area and its population must constantly alter as the latter increases. [50]

Indeed the rapid spread of large cities and the acceleration of the process of running together of separate municipalities in developing conurbations accentuated one of the weaknesses of the fragmentation of local government among many separate boroughs and county districts at a time when large urban regions were beginning to crystallise. Especially for the middle classes, growing separation between home and work-place came about with the development of suburban railways and electric tramways and the separation of home and work-place brought by sheer physical growth. The census itself noted:

> The growth of large urban communities can only be measured by considering jointly the population of the central area and all its suburbs, whether the latter do or do not happen to be under the same local government as the central area. [51]

The cases of Birmingham, Liverpool and Manchester were quoted to illustrate this point, but that of London was the most striking and is reflected in the decline in population in the Administrative County of London between 1901 and 1911, due largely to '... a group of districts in which the population had long been decreasing, owing to the substitution of business premises, warehouses, etc., for dwelling houses ...'[52] In contrast the rapid increase of population in an 'Outer Ring' extending deeply into mid-Surrey, north-west Kent, Middlesex, south Hertfordshire, and south-west Essex indicates the strength of suburban outgrowth which created a ring of satellite towns around London A.C. which included some of the fastest growing towns of the period.[53]

Thus the map of administrative and population units in 1911 (fig. 9) was still anachronistic in two ways: first, it still included a number of small historic towns of under 2,000 population and doubtful urban status; secondly — and more importantly — the major urban regions were sub-divided into a complex mosaic of urban administrative areas, lacking the necessary coordination to deal with urban problems over the

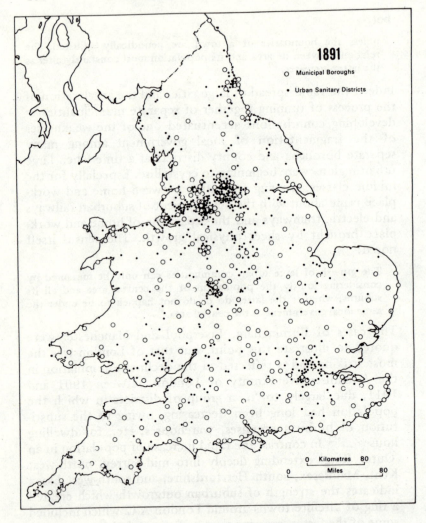

Figure 7 – URBAN AREAS, 1891

The categories of municipal (including county) borough and
urban sanitary districts are as given in *Census of England and
Wales, 1891*, Preliminary Abstract, Table IX, pp. 18–36.

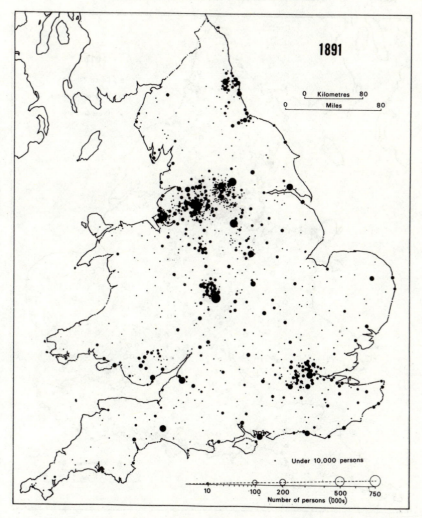

Figure 8 — URBAN POPULATION, 1891

The size of population of all country and municipal boroughs and urban sanitary districts are shown on the scale used in figs. 2, 4, 6 and 10.

Based on *Census of England and Wales, 1891*, Preliminary Abstract, Table IX, pp. 18—36.

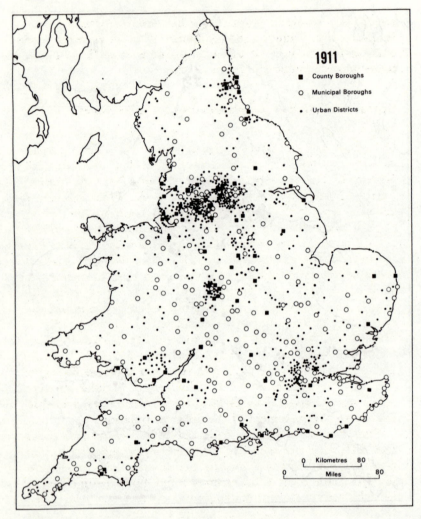

Figure 9 — URBAN AREAS, 1911

The categories of county borough, municipal borough and urban district are as established under the Local Government Acts of 1888 and 1894 are as given in the *Census of England and Wales, 1911*, Preliminary Abstract, Tables II and IV, pp. 2—25.

region as a whole, and with suburban areas constantly over-
reaching their administrative limits. For such areas the
comparative analysis of urban population is difficult or, in
many respects, impossible.

Census tabulation of population data for urban areas

Despite the problems of omission and changing legal definition, from 1851 the census reports give a reasonable picture
of urban population trends (table 3.1). The estimates for
'Principal Towns' together with London for the period
1801—41 are obviously far too low. R. Price Williams's
calculations of 1880[54] are probably closer to the mark,
though they may well overstate the early nineteenth century
situation since they are based on estimates for large towns
(of over 20,000) as they were in 1871. A.F. Weber[55] rejected
the purely legal definition of a town and tried to distinguish
simply between rural (hamlets and villages of under 2,000
people and towns of 2—10,000) and urban populations, the
latter including 'Cities' (10,000+) and 'great Cities'
(100,000+). In the case of England and Wales, Weber recognised that many urban centres had less than 10,000 people
and adopted a figure of 5,000. On the other hand, T.A.
Welton's[56] estimates of 'rural' and 'urban' population were
based upon a lower limit of 1000 for urban centres, probably
leading to overstatement of the urban population.

Such varying estimates from the same census data show
the difficulty of achieving accurate designation of urban
population for even a limited period of rapid population
growth (table 3.2). Valid estimates and comparison can only
be achieved by careful matching of population statistics and
topographic detail for *each* period in question as C.M. Law
has recently argued.[57] Law's recent recalculation of urban
population is based upon three-fold criteria: population size,
population density and degree of nucleation of settlement.
Though it is difficult to carry out such work with complete
accuracy, it is important to attempt to do so, especially in
large-scale studies.

Although the built-up areas of towns are rarely co-extensive
with administrative areas for which census data are tabulated,

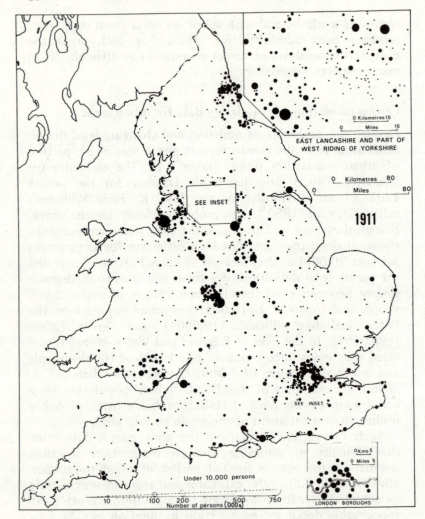

Figure 10 – URBAN POPULATION, 1911

The size of population of all county and municipal boroughs and urban districts are shown on the scale used in figs. 2, 4, 6 and 8.

Based on the *Census of England and Wales, 1911,* Preliminary Abstract, Tables II and IV, pp. 2–25.

these may often be adjusted from other evidence. Thus, the proportion of buildings within the continuously built-up area may be compared with outlying suburbs using detailed topographic maps and plans such as the Ordnance Survey 6-inch (1:10,560) and 25-inch (1:2,500) map series and the later '5-foot' (1:1,056) plans (published between 1843 and 1894) and '10-foot' plans (the 1:500 series of 1855–). There are usually, also, reasonably accurate maps and surveys available for the larger towns from the late eighteenth century.[58]

However, the continuously built-up area is not the only guide to urbanisation, for increasingly areas outside this were functionally an integral part of the city. The growing tendency of the middle classes to travel to work from adjacent areas, from the mid-nineteenth century, often makes it desirable to identify such suburbs. Local directories may assist this process, especially where the persons concerned are identified by both place of residence and place of work. On Merseyside, for example, as early as the 1840s, such people lived in Wirral and travelled to work by ferry.[59] In London this process was widespread, especially following the development of suburban railways.[60] Even smaller towns had journeys to work linking outlying industrial and residential units which can sometimes be traced by judicious use of directories, rate books and the census enumerators' books.[61]

Law's estimates provide consistent and comparable figures for the whole period 1801–1911 (table 3.1 and fig. 11) and underline the absolute and relative importance in urban population development of London and the large provincial cities, especially when one adds to them the substantial suburban development in the late nineteenth century in towns of under 20,000 around the large cities. The erratic pattern of change in the various size groups (fig. 12) underlines the need to look at *de facto* rather than *de jure* urban areas and draws attention to the importance of conurbations in the urban population growth of the later nineteenth century.

As the rate of increase of large urban areas declined, so residential and population development passed to separate suburban municipalities. Hence, the more densely occupied registration districts identified by Bowley[62] around the core

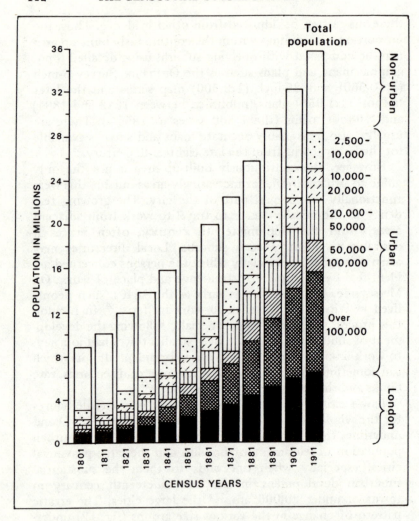

Figure 11 — URBAN POPULATION, 1801—1911

The population of London and several size groups of towns are shown as a proportion of the total population for each census year 1801—1911.

Based on C.M. Law 'The growth of urban population in England and Wales, 1801—1911' (fig. 2) *Trans. Inst. Brit. Geogr. 41* (1967), pp. 125—43.

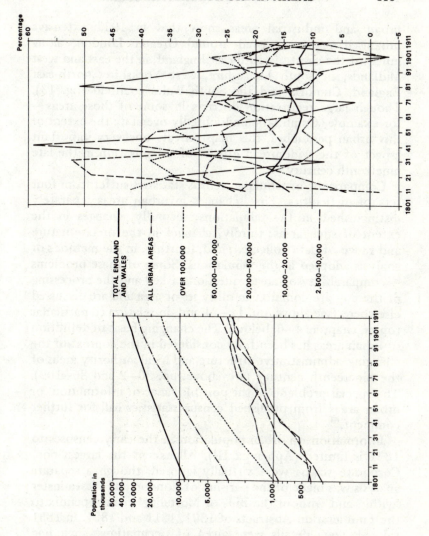

Figure 12 – URBAN POPULATION TRENDS BY SIZE
GROUPS, 1801–1911

The percentage decadal change in London and other size
groups of towns, 1801–1911, is plotted from C.M. Law
(op. cit.), Table XI, p. 141.

urban and industrial areas show that in 1911 extensive urbanised regions existed around Greater London, along much of the coast of south-east England, in the east and west Midlands, in south Lancashire, west Yorkshire, north-east England, Cumbria and the South Wales coalfield (fig. 13). Though large registration districts in some of those areas — for example, Cumbria — undoubtedly overstate the extent of this urban penumbra, this map reflects one very important aspect of the widespread effects of urbanisation in the late nineteenth century.

Comparisons of tabulated census statistics suffer from four sets of difficulties. First, changes in urban areas separately distinguished in the tabulations; secondly, changes in the extent of such areas; thirdly, changes in the precise nature and range of data collected; and, fourthly, in the methods of analysis adopted in the tabulations. Some of these problems — comparability of areas, questions asked and the processing of these — are common to all types of area and are discussed elsewhere (see above, pp. 11—21 and, in relation to particular topics, chapters 4—6, below). The changing basis of definition of urban areas has been fully considered in the context of the changing administrative structure and local authority areas of the nineteenth century (see above, pp. 30—2 and 86—109). The special problems of the possible range of information for urban areas from published census statistics call for further comment.[63]

Information on urban population in the early censuses to 1831 is limited (Appendix III). All except the largest non-Corporate towns were virtually ignored, though a separate analysis was made of the parishes of London and Westminster 'within and without the Bills of Mortality' in an appendix to the Enumeration Abstracts of 1801, 1811 and 1821. In 1831 valuable *new* details were given of occupations, including details of numbers engaged in three classes of agricultural activity, five classes of manufacturing, professional, commercial and labouring work, and male servants (over and under 20 years of age) and female servants were given for counties, boroughs and towns, though these were limited in number. The Parish Register Abstracts for 1831 (see above, pp. 87—91), as for the censuses of 1801—21, gave summaries of marriages,

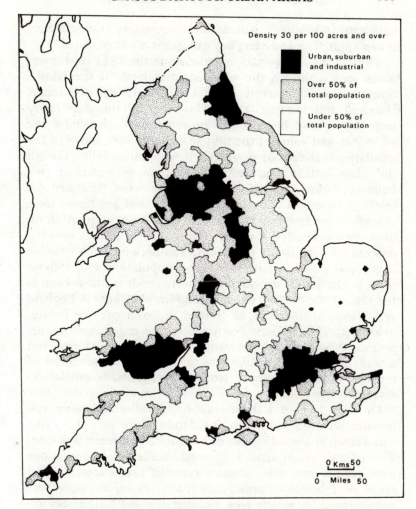

Density 30 per 100 acres and over

Urban, suburban and industrial

Over 50% of total population

Under 50% of total population

Figure 13 — URBAN, RURAL AND RESIDUAL AREAS, ENGLAND AND WALES, 1911

The proportion of population living at densities classified as 'urban, suburban and industrial' (i.e. at over 30 per 100 acres) is shown for registration districts in England and Wales.

The categories of over 50 per cent at over 30 per 100 acres and under 50 per cent may be classified as partly urbanised and rural, respectively.

Adapted from A.L. Bowley 'Rural populations in England and Wales. A study of the changes of density, occupations and ages', *Jnl. Roy. Stat. Soc.* 77 (1914), pp. 597—652 and based on *Census of England and Wales, 1911.*

baptisms and burials, but without separately distinguishing urban areas. The 1821 enquiry on ages was not repeated.

The range of information gathered in the 1841 census was much wider, though the administrative basis of the tabulations remained narrow and traditional, using county, Hundred and borough areas. However, by this date many large towns had become incorporated boroughs under the 1835 Act and some of the principal towns were added to the tabulations. Details of occupations were much fuller, though the classification had not yet become systematised (see Bellamy, below, p. 166—8), and these were tabulated for selected boroughs and large towns. Age and sex tables were compiled for five-year age groups and the new question on birthplace permitted the first glimpses of the rapidly growing process of urbanward migration. Tabulations for boroughs, large towns and counties grouped population under those born in the parish in which they were resident, those born in the rest of the county of enumeration, elsewhere in England and Wales, in Scotland, in Ireland and overseas (see Baines, below, p. 150). A new feature of some importance to the precise estimation of resident population of county and market towns in particular was the separate enumeration of inmates of institutions — workhouses, gaols, hospitals and asylums.

Only in 1851 did the census begin fuller and more systematic recording of urban population. Even so a sharp line was drawn in the 1851 census tabulations between 'Principal Towns' and urban areas in general. While total populations were readily available for most types of urban area, the full range of tabulations was restricted to cities, boroughs and large towns, for which ages, occupations and birthplaces are available. However some critical demographic information, notably the change in population due to births and deaths, was not given specifically for urban areas. Thus, only where towns and registration districts were reasonably co-extensive can the natural and migrational components of population change be fully analysed for urban areas. Additional, and very useful, summaries are available of population features in the principal towns (i.e. London and 61 major towns), indicating the attention now being given to urban areas in the census reports.

This essentially remained the basis of tabulation for urban areas until the 1871 census. Apart from basic population totals, given for 593 towns in 1861 and 976 in 1871, a full range of tabulations were available in 1861 for 79 'Principal Towns' (including London) and for 81 in 1871, the latter comprising 'a selection of the towns most remarkable for population and importance in their several counties'.[64] These tabulations related to age, occupations (males and females over 20 years of age) and birthplaces. Moreover in 1871 we see, for the first time, information on area, houses and inhabitants for the wards of the metropolitan parishes, though as yet there was no such information for provincial towns. As significantly, the 1871 census paid particular attention to the need for population statistics for urban areas and the difficulties of obtaining those. As the report noted: 'English institutions are flexible, but it is with difficulty that they keep pace with and meet all the exigencies of the increasing population'.[65]

In a classic report, Farr noted that 'In the absence of the old tried municipal form of local government, many towns have adopted improvement commissions and the special powers conferred by the Local Government Act. Every city, borough, district under either a local Board or an improvement Commission, and small towns have been carefully analysed in their constituent parts ...'[66] yet detailed tabulations for the various items gathered on the census schedule were still lacking (see Appendix III).

Indeed it was only with the adoption in the 1881 census of the newly formed urban and rural sanitary districts that some measure of standardisation of tabulation for urban areas was adopted. The basic data — area, houses, population and ages — were given for boroughs and urban sanitary districts. But the hard-to-code items (birthplaces and occupations) were tabulated only for counties and urban sanitary districts of over 50,000, soon to be the threshold population for the conferring of borough status under the Local Government Act of 1888. One gain in information in 1881 was that figures of area, houses and population were now available for wards of all urban areas.

This basis of tabulation remained essentially unchanged to 1911. Full tabulations were given for 61 boroughs and towns of over 50,000, but only basic demographic data for smaller towns. In 1891 the first census information on housing conditions — a simple statement of occupied rooms in tenements of less than 5 rooms, from which were derived numbers of persons per room as an index of overcrowding — was tabulated for London and the 32 largest boroughs.

The 1901 census was the fullest in coverage up to that time and the most clear-cut in terms of the distinction in tabulation between urban and rural districts. Indeed, it marked a transition between the mid-nineteenth century tendency to tabulate in terms of all-purpose units of county and registration district, restricting the range of information on towns either to the larger towns or to special tabulations. The Preliminary Report to the 1901 census paid particular attention to population trends in the various types of administrative area, including all types of urban area. The General Report contained valuable summaries of urban/rural contrasts, especially in a series of summary tables of the full range of census data: many of these — for area, houses and population, for ages and for occupations — aggregated information for urban districts, metropolitan and county boroughs. The County Reports for each administrative county (including London) contained much fuller information for local authorities than had hitherto been the case. Thus area, population and houses were given for *all* urban districts (including ward figures), as were data on tenements, ages and grouped occupations, though full occupational data, birthplaces and civil condition (as to marriage) were still classified only for municipal and county boroughs.

The 1911 census contains the most elaborate range of data and of tabulations for urban areas achieved to date. Workers were classified by industry and occupation. New information on marital condition and the fertility of marriage were of great value to population forecasting. But the fuller information on housing conditions was of more direct interest to urban areas, especially at a time when local authorities were beginning to concern themselves with slum clearance and municipal housing programmes — often for the first time —

under the consolidating Housing of the Working Classes Act of 1890.

The tabulation of the subject volumes was much more detailed than anything previously offered both in scope and topographical detail. The introduction to the *Report* on administrative areas drew particular attention to the 'number and complexity of areas'.[67] There were many summary tables for urban and rural areas, as well as the now customary emphasis for the 'Great Towns' of over 50,000 population which numbered 97. In the first main group of data, the population statistics — population, families (or separate occupiers) were given to urban district level, together with constituent Wards, and the numbers of inmates and officials in institutions were also given for urban districts and above. But the main gains in information were in the greater detail in which social statistics were tabulated. As in 1901 population was classified by age and civil condition down to urban and rural districts. Although other data — tenements, birthplace, occupation and industry, infirmities and fertility — were not detailed separately below the county borough level, except for towns of over 50,000, there were valuable aggregate tables. Moreover, in the case of birthplaces cross-tabulation by administrative county and large town made it possible to analyse both inward and outward lifetime movement (see Baines, below, pp. 151—4), while there is a first — and for the period to 1911 unique — tabulation of natives of counties living in London A.C. and three other counties and 10 selected towns by main age groups.[68]

In general, and particularly in terms of information on urban areas, the 1911 census was the high water mark of census-taking and tabulation, the latter no doubt assisted by punch-carding of data for the first time. Even so, only in 1921 when the registration district was abandoned as a major unit of tabulation, especially of vital data (births, deaths and marriages), did tabulation of the *whole* range of information in terms of local authority areas create comparability of all population data for urban areas. Thus, at no time in the nineteenth century is it possible to draw a portrait of the character of England's urban population as a whole or to isolate individual towns, other than the large urban centres of over 50,000 population, for detailed study. Moreover, through-out this period the administratively urban areas consistently omitted suburban populations in rural districts or county administrations (see above pp. 111—15).

During the second half of the nineteenth century, a period of rapidly increasing urban dominance, there were undoubtedly great improvements in the range and consistency of census coverage of large towns and in aggregate terms more data for urban populations as a whole. The general reports reveal this increasing concern with urban population and social conditions in their special tabulations and discussion of urban areas. Yet it is very difficult to compare urban population trends over the period 1841—1911, first, because of the changes in administrative structure and areas, secondly because of the changes in the content of the questions on the census schedule and the precise methods of tabulating this information. Appendix III attempts to summarise both aspects of this problem.

The internal structure of urban areas

Internal changes in the population and social structure of nineteenth century towns is a subject of increasing interest to urban historians.[69] The difficulties involved in micro-study of population within towns are three-fold. First, boundaries were not adjusted regularly enough to keep pace with urban growth (see above pp. 109—14). Secondly, published census reports contain very little areal breakdown of data, even within large towns, though some information on vital statistics is available for registration sub-districts from 1841,[70] while ward totals of area, houses and population were tabulated for boroughs from 1871. Thirdly, though the enumerators' books may be used for minutely detailed studies of population and urban structure, they are available to the public only after a 100-year confidentiality period and — as yet — cover only the censuses 1841—1871:[71] moreover, the immense labour of handling such detailed information at the individual or household level for even a medium-sized town has so far restricted their use to studies of individual towns, though it would be possible to derive some information for enumeration districts which would be of great assistance in the study of trends over time and in comparative studies between towns (see below pp. 132–4 for a fuller discussion).

WARD DATA

Contrasts in population growth between the various areas of large towns, in particular, reflect economic and social change within the city. Most central areas reached their maximum population capacity in early Victorian times though the fastest growth was taking place in suburbs from the early nineteenth century. Where boroughs and other urban areas comprise several parishes or townships it is possible to distinguish the general pattern and chronology of population development, especially in the large cities, from details given for the constituent parishes which, in the case of medieval cities such as Norwich, gave a considerable areal break-down of the information. In many of the large towns similar details were given in the 1801 Abstracts for 'districts': in the case of Manchester, for example, there were 28 such districts and in Liverpool there were 5 'districts'. In addition the tables in the 1801–21 Abstracts and the *Report* to the 1831 census analyse the population trends in the Greater London area, within and outside the area covered by the Bills of Mortality.[72] Some of this detail is lost in the 1851 summaries of population totals 1801–51: but in Liverpool, where by 1851 the population of central areas had passed its peak, the process may be traced from population figures for the sub-districts within the Liverpool Registration District (co-extensive with the old borough) and for adjacent townships.[73]

In the 1871 tables areas, population and houses were given for the wards of metropolitan parishes but not for other cities. In 1871 similar information was tabulated for boroughs and in 1901 this was extended to all urban areas. Unfortunately, no other information was tabulated for wards and thus any analysis at this level based on published information is restricted in range and chronological depth.

ENUMERATION DISTRICTS

For worthwhile analyses of changes in population distribution and structure *within* the nineteenth century town, we must turn to the unpublished material in the enumerators' books.

Despite the lack of a systematic format in the collection of census data in the period 1801—1831, it is possible to reconstruct enumeration districts from the enumerators' lists where these have survived (see above pp. 13—14). Though survival is sporadic, county and urban archives often have such lists. For example, lists for 1821 and 1831 contain a short description of the enumeration district or, where this is missing, the detailed schedules of households together with contemporary directories and town plans, permit analysis of early nineteenth century urban population in detail which has not hitherto been realised.[74]

The procedures by which the taking of censuses by the Registrar General were governed were laid down in 1841. These are outlined above (pp. 14—17) and discussed in more detail by Dr Armstrong (Chapter 2).[75] However the directions 'concerning the manner in which Entries may be made in the Enumeration Schedule' are worthy of closer examination in the context of problems of population analysis within urban areas. The 1841 instructions required a statement at the head of each page of the city or borough, or parish or township in which the enumeration district is located: the enumerator was specifically instructed:

> In the Column marked Place, write the name of the house (if it has a name), or of the street or other part of the town ... opposite to the mark denoting each house, or the first house in the street, etc., and write *'do'* opposite to every other in the same street, etc.[76] (see Appendix I, chapter 2, above).

In 1851 these instructions were more precise, asking for the location of the enumeration district in terms of 'Parish or Township, Ecclesiastical District, City or Borough, Town or Village'. The widening range of published tabulations on urban areas were clearly founded on more precise information at enumeration district level, though enumerators did not always find it easy to carry out their instructions, especially around the periphery of towns. Within the towns they were asked to name the 'Street, Square, etc.' and to give the number or name of the house, while the procedure for noting uninhabited houses or house building was clarified. By 1861 greater precision was achieved for urban areas by the require- ment that in cities and municipal boroughs the ward in which the enumeration district was located should be stated.

Where the instructions concerning the numbering of houses and naming of streets and of the allocation of enumeration districts to administrative units are followed there should be little difficulty in precisely assigning households and districts to administrative areas: for example, the 1851, 1861 and 1871 instructions stated that at the end of the schedule for 'any one Parish or Township, Borough, Ward, Town, Hamlet, etc., or Ecclesiastical District' the enumerator should write across the page 'End of the Parish . . . etc'. Despite the care with which these orders were drawn up, it was not always easy to follow them. Indeed the 1881 census noted that 'the point in which the enumeration books . . . were found to be most deficient and to show the most serious amount of inaccuracy, was the matter of boundaries' in which 'numerous subdivisions of the county overlap and intersect with such complexity, that the enumerators and the local registrars in a vast number of cases failed altogether to unravel their intri- cacy'.[77]

Taken in conjunction with the procedure by which enumeration districts were to be 'formed with careful refer- ence to those various divisions of the county'[78] which the Act stated should be separately enumerated (namely, in 1851, 'Parishes, Townships, Ecclesiastical Districts, Parliamentary Boroughs and Incorporated Cities and Towns'), it is thus possible to use the enumeration districts as 'building bricks' from which to construct topographic and structural analysis of areas *within* the city. Registrars were charged with dividing sub-districts into enumeration areas which were revised by the Superintendent Registrar who, in turn, submitted the areas for approval by the Registrar General.[79] The enumera- tion districts are described in the enumerators' summary (see Appendix I, Chapter 2), but if maps were ever compiled of these areas they have not survived. Indeed, the first maps of enumeration district boundaries available from the Registrar General are for the 1961 census.

While local knowledge was used to draw up enumeration

districts and care taken to fit these into the administrative framework, a number of difficulties arise in their design and use. In the first place, by their very nature, enumeration districts were *ad hoc* units which changed from census to census: as administrative areas changed (even down to ward level), enumeration districts had to adjust to new boundaries; the changing distribution of population in towns led to enlargement of districts in areas of declining population and to division of districts in areas of rapid increase. The recommendations for the 1841 census were that no district should have fewer than 25 or more than 200 inhabited houses.[80] But in practice districts varied considerably in size and population, even in urban areas: for example, in 1871 the average enumeration district had 131 houses and 696 people, but three London enumeration districts contained 3599, 3860 and 4800 people, respectively.[81] Physical changes in the towns led to demolition of older residential areas, for roads and railways,[82] offices and works, or for slum clearance schemes. Such continuous modification of the residential area was paralleled by vigorous expansion throughout the nineteenth century which added new residential areas within and around the towns. Since enumeration districts were — and still are — topographically defined, such changes led to continuous adjustment of boundaries and there is little consistency in enumeration districts over any period of time, or even from one census to the next. Hence it is very difficult to make comparisons within towns on the basis of enumeration district totals. In figure 14, for example, we may see the changes in the enumeration districts for Birkenhead, a 'new town' of the 1820s and '30s which was growing rapidly in the period 1841—71.[83]

A second major set of problems arises from the principle of topographical definition in that suitably sized and shaped enumeration units were often too heterogeneous in character to provide coherent units for demographic and social study. For example, certain of the Birkenhead enumeration districts — especially those around Birkenhead Park — contain basically working class areas near the town centre but extend into new suburban villa development (fig. 14). Frequently streets were used as boundaries, separating areas of similar character

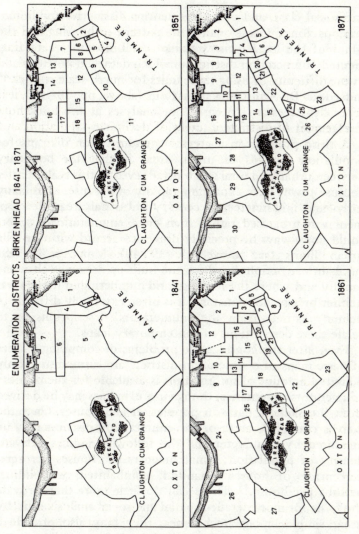

Figure 14 — ENUMERATION DISTRICTS OF
BIRKENHEAD, 1841–71

Based on the descriptions contained in the census enumerators'
books, 1841–1871.

I am indebted to Mr W.D. Jacobsen for permission to use this
map.

and social class, and often fragmenting distinctive and homogeneous zones. Occasionally, the pattern of housing and the
whim of the local registrars alike combined to create fragmented enumeration districts in which detached portions add
to the difficulty of using these units for micro-scale studies.[84]
Indeed, as Dr Armstrong points out (above, pp. 39–41), it is
generally necessary to carry out analyses at the household
level, especially in smaller towns.

A third problem in aggregating enumeration districts for
population analysis of urban areas is that the boundary
between urban and rural was blurred, even at this scale. Either
because towns were expanding rapidly or because, as in many
early- and mid-nineteenth century industrial areas, development was urbanised rather than civic, enumeration districts
could not always be precisely drawn to accord with the true
urban limits (see above pp. 39–40). Moreover, in the
rural–urban periphery where the built-up area was changing
rapidly and where the naming and numbering of houses was
neither precise nor constant, it is often extremely difficult to
delimit districts from the enumerators' descriptions or to
relate these descriptions to contemporary maps.

Even after the considerable problems of compiling a series
of basic maps of enumeration districts are surmounted, only
a limited amount of information is available for them in the
enumerators' summaries, though useful indices may be derived
from the skeletal data on population and houses. Once the
map is compiled, areas of the enumeration districts may be
measured by planimeter and the following indices derived:
density of population; female:male ratios; houses per acre;
percentage of houses inhabited, uninhabited or building;
persons per house.[85] These can do little more than provide
the basis for more detailed spatial and social analysis. But, by
using simple linkage techniques, they may also provide a
satisfactory operational framework both for sampling at the
household level (see Armstrong, above, pp. 45–7 for a fuller
discussion) and for the analysis of particular aspects of urban
population study. As an example of the latter, P.J. Taylor in
an analysis of middle class population mobility in mid-
nineteeth century Liverpool derived some eight areas ('opera-

tional taxonomic units') from 302 enumeration districts by
linking enumeration districts with similar 'social distance'
scales (derived from F:M ratios, population density, and
intensity of occupation as measured by persons per house).[86]

Preliminary work also suggests that certain of the indices
derived from enumeration district summaries may be of
value as diagnostic variables of social class, as well as providing
much more detailed information on population density and
distribution, and housing development within the city. For
example, residential domestic servants (mainly female) 'inflate'
the F:M sex ratios in middle-class areas and it *may* be possible
to use these to outline, in broad terms, middle class areas.
Similarly, though occupancy rates (showing persons per house)
are not in themselves a very accurate index of social class
(because of variations in house size) they seem to be indicative
of broad class differences at the enumeration district level.
Further refinements may be possible by using the enumeration
district scores derived from more than one variable to give a
fuller idea of spatial variations of population in the city.

Any full-scale analysis of urban population at the micro-
scale must go beyond the few indices available in the
summaries. Though the precise stages of the 'classification of
facts' mentioned in the census reports are not clear,[87] the
enumerators' books must have been used as the basis of the
'hand tabulation' of returns which were then built up into
the published tables of the census reports. However, all data
for this intermediate stage of totalling have been destroyed.
The Office of Population Census and Surveys states:

> departmental records of tables of totals extracted from the enu-
> meration books in anticipation of the data printed in the census
> volumes . . . were destroyed as soon as practicable after a report was
> published because there was no justification for retaining them as
> the figures, although not available in toto, could again be derived
> from the Enumerators' Record Books.[88]

Indeed, for many purposes enumeration districts have
provided a satisfactory areal framework for studies which
have retabulated the full range of topics on which information
was gathered though, to date, these tend to be available for
limited areas only.

STREET, HOUSE AND HOUSEHOLD

The general problems of handling data from the enumerators' books are fully discussed in chapter 2 by Dr Armstrong (see above, pp 39—45). However, those problems of using household data for analysis of urban populations will be briefly indicated.

The establishing of identity between household, dwelling and street is of basic importance in both spatial and chronological studies of towns, especially in detailed comparisons between one census and another. There are sometimes difficulties in distinguishing separate households, despite procedures laid down for enumerators by the Registrar General (see above, pp. 48—54). Changes in the boundaries of enumeration districts cause difficulties in comparative studies (see above, pp. 124—5). But more fundamental are the problems of matching individual, or personal, data and group characteristics of households or families — the basic concerns of population censuses — with realistic topographic and social areas.

Topographic identification requires both precision in the enumerators' books and accurate and up-to-date town plans or directories from which households may be located. Even where the enumerator gave a full and accurate description of the location of his district (by registration district, superintendent registrar's district, borough, ward, townships, parish etc.), it is sometimes difficult to allocate houses to enumeration districts. Boundaries between districts often ran along streets and it is often difficult to assign houses to one side or another. Similarly, where a long street or road is divided between enumeration districts the exact location of the houses must be known, while in areas of housing development and on the edges of towns both descriptions of the districts and the precise placing of houses within them is often very difficult.

Absolute certainty in identification depends on correctness and consistency of numbering or naming in the census books and the ability to identify houses on contemporary plans. Two major difficulties exist. First, street numbering systems did not become formalised in most towns until the 1850s, at earliest.[89] Even as late as 1871 it was noted in the census:

The census is taken with comparative ease in a town where all the streets and the courts are named, where all houses are consecutively numbered, and where all the boundaries are distinctly marked. Such business-like arrangements are always made where the municipal government is intelligent and energetic; but the duty is unfortunately neglected in many places . . . [90]

Even where 'such business-like arrangements' were made, changes in systems of numbering or, in unnumbered areas, of naming houses by their occupants, often create a second difficulty, that of comparison between one census and another, which may seriously inhibit identification or comparative studies. For example, the identification of the Manchester house of the novelist, Elizabeth Gaskell, from 1842—50 created problems because of subsequent renumbering of the address in Upper Rumford Street.[91] Even where systems of coding are used for topographic identification, if renumbering is undetected it is difficult to devise consistent areal units for comparative areal studies.

For the mid-nineteenth century this process is hampered by the lack of a consistent series of town plans showing the contemporary numbering of properties. The first large-scale Ordnance Survey town plans (the five-foot series of 1843—), did not give house numbers, nor did the more ephemeral second series (the 1:528 or '10—foot' of 1850 —) or the more general third (1:500) series published from 1855 to 1894. Indeed, not until the '50—inch' plans (1:1250) were introduced in 1911 ' . . . to facilitate amongst other things the needs of land registration and land valuation'[92] did house numberings appear on Ordnance Survey plans.

An example from Liverpool may help to illustrate the problem of house identification, though this is not claimed as typical of every town in the country: indeed, as Dr Harley has shown, the Ordnance Survey plans for London have a rather different history from that of provincial towns.[93] An official numbering system in the Borough of Liverpool was first established in 1848 by the Health Committee and in 1856 the houses ' . . . were renumbered on a uniform system . . . [involving] the painting or affixing of 40,538 new numbers'.[94] But this did not solve all problems as the following account by Iain Taylor indicates.[95]

The enumerators' books of 1851 examined for Liverpool used a numbered street address system, an exception [being] 'court' property where individual court houses are not numbered.

Care has to be taken in checking house numbers as the system apparently remained somewhat fluid, especially in middle class areas where properties were built at different time intervals. The street directories may prove valuable evidence here as might also the records of the Corporation department responsible for street names and house numbers. It is known that various revisions took place from time to time, though on a piece-meal basis, probably as infilling took place along a street.

A particular difficulty in Liverpool was the large number of court dwellings, estimated as providing homes for 20 per cent of the population in 1841. Courts, which were named in the Ordnance Survey '5–foot' plans (of 1848), were numbered by the Health Committee in 1848 to 'enable easy identification of property by inspectors': The Corporation's numbering system was used by the census enumerators from 1851, but this and the plans fit together remarkably well and . . . a close comparison between the census and plans will allow allocation of house numbers [to census households] (fig. 15).

Where Ordnance Survey town plans fail or, as for censuses up to 1841, are not available, other town plans are often available in municipal libraries or archives, though published lists of such plans are limited.[96] Such plans are numerous for the nineteenth century, especially from the 1830s, and include the town plans which accompanied the enquiries into municipal government of the 1830s and later parliamentary enquiries into urban conditions. Perhaps the most valuable are the independent surveys by borough engineers resulting from increasing concern from the 1840s with sanitary and housing conditions within towns. For specific areas of towns, however, detailed property and housing plans may be used to trace the development of housing which, even in limited areas, may be spread out over a considerable time period.[97] Among the numerous statutory plans, those concerned with transport development are of particular value. The railway plans, especially the statutorily required plans which, from 1853, accompanied applications for demolition of property are very useful for the inner city areas which were much affected by railway development in the mid-nineteeth century.[98]

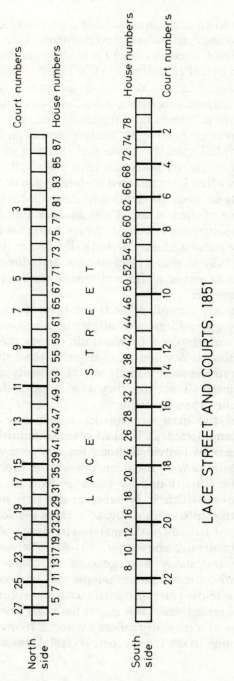

Figure 15 – HOUSES AND COURTS, LACE STREET, LIVERPOOL, 1851

Even where good town plans are available they rarely give a continuous chronology of urban development. Thus in identifying houses listed in census books it is often necessary to supplement maps by other sources such as rate books and directories. Where available, the rate books provide a continuous record of occupied properties. They have been used to good effect, both in providing additional variables for analysis of social areas of nineteenth century towns and in helping to trace morphological evolution and changing social characteristics.[99] However, rate books are extremely bulky to handle and have too often been allowed to deteriorate in the cellars of town halls or been thoughtlessly destroyed. As a supplementary source of data in social area analysis, rateable assessments suffer because they are not always based on the same criteria and are reassessed only periodically. Hence they do not provide a fully accurate, up-to-date and directly comparable set of data either within any one urban area or from one region to another.

Directories are mainly compiled for trades or professions and do not generally give addresses of all the population.[100] However, complete topographical or postal directories, are of very considerable value as a guide to changes in the urban plan. Moreover, directories were usually issued annually and updated at regular intervals so that they give an up-to-date picture of the changing urban situation.[101]

The processing of the mass of evidence which may be derived from the enumerators' books, often comprising hundreds of thousands of individual items for a large town, requires careful organisation of the data, though the precise methods used will be conditioned by the objectives of the study and the scale at which it is being made. It is now generally accepted that in studies of urban areas some form of sampling is required to reduce the material to manageable proportions (see Armstrong, above, pp. 45—8). Where the town is small and reasonably homogeneous in character a straightforward systematic or random sample may be taken, either selecting every tenth entry (or whatever proportion is required) or by numbering households sequentially and selecting the sample by use of a table of random numbers. In many cases, however, it is important to represent several distinctive areas of a town in the sample and this may require some form of areal sampling. Such samples may be derived by selecting areas for analysis on the basis of prior knowledge, using other information as the basis of choice.[102] Perhaps more correctly, the areas to be studied may be grouped or stratified, or using indices for enumeration districts or other large-scale units (see above pp. 126–7), the household sample then being drawn from the smaller number of areas derived from this preliminary grouping. For certain purposes – especially areal studies – individual households may not adequately reflect the character of small but highly distinctive districts. In such cases some form of clustering of the sample to cover a larger area – for example a street or a group of streets – may be necessary.

The problems of handling the sampled data from the enumerators' books are discussed above by Dr Armstrong (pp. 58–62). For most purposes, coding of data and storage on punched cards will accommodate all the required information for a household. However, computer-linked reference systems could be valuable especially where households can be given grid references by which they may be located on the town plan.[103] Problems are raised by the need to devise appropriate grid referencing systems both for individual towns and more generally. Indeed, work is being currently undertaken by Dr M. Anderson of Edinburgh University to extract an approximately one per cent sample of enumeration districts for the whole of Great Britain which will be of fundamental value to comparative studies in providing yardsticks against which more detailed studies may be measured.[104]

Conclusion

Detailed studies of the structure and evolution of towns and urban society in nineteenth century England are still in their infancy. Basic themes with some supporting case studies have been discussed by Asa Briggs in his most stimulating book on *Victorian Cities*. There are many good individual studies, especially of medium-sized nineteenth century industrial towns, in which social and economic forces which shaped the form and character of the town have a prominent place.[105]

These studies have paved the way for some preliminary drawing together of the field of the 'new' urban history, a field in which detailed social and spatial analysis of population have a fundamental place and in which the techniques of many social scientists are being linked in a truly interdisciplinary fashion.[106]

We are already beginning to move towards general hypotheses or models concerning the evolution of nineteenth century urban society[107] and in relation to particular aspects of population growth and patterning within the nineteenth century city. But before satisfactory general models can be produced a great deal more work is needed. These studies may range in scale from macro-studies of general population trends in urban areas, in which the basic data are to be sought in the enormous quarry of information contained within the published censuses and the returns and annual reports of the Registrar General,[108] to micro-studies of individual towns or even of districts within towns in which much of the basic evidence lies in local records but with a core of tremendously valuable data in the unpublished records of the census enumerators' books.[109] Much of the latter work, though demanding in time and the care with which data must be handled, can be carried out by part-time local investigators as well as large research teams, as Armstrong observes (see above pp. 58—62).

To yield maximum returns for the considerable effort involved, it is important that the census data be handled with scrupulous care and that methodology be standardised as far as is possible. This essay has sought to contribute to this general area of study by reviewing the availability, potential and some of the problems of handling the material for the study of nineteenth century towns contained in both published and unpublished census returns for England and Wales.

NOTES

1. 'On the increase of population in England and Wales', *Jnl. Statist. Soc.* 43 (1880), pp. 462—508.
2. 'The growth of the urban population in England and Wales, 1801—1911', *Trans. Inst. Brit. Geogr.* 41 (1967), pp. 125—43.

3. R. Vaughan, *The Age of Great Cities, or Modern Society Viewed in its Relation to Intelligence, Morals and Religion* (1843).

4. A.F. Weber, *The Growth of Cities in the Nineteenth Century: a Study in Statistics* (1899, reprinted 1965).

5. See A.L. Bowley, 'Rural population in England and Wales. A study of the changes of density, occupation and ages' *J.R. Statist. Soc.* 77 (1914), pp. 597—65 for a discussion of these areas. For a more recent view of urbanisation on a county basis see D. Friedlander, 'The spread of urbanisation in England and Wales, 1851—1951' *Population Studies 24* (1970), pp. 423—43.

6. Office of Population Censuses and Surveys, *Information Paper No. 1* (Census Division, General Register Office, 1970).

7. R. Lawton, 'Population changes in England and Wales in the later nineteenth century' *Trans. Inst. Brit. Geogr. 44* (1968), pp. 55—74.

8. For example, in 1846 France defined as urban those communes with a population cluster of 2,000; in Canada the definition starts at 1,000 but in India a minimum of 5,000 is required. The United Nations' definition emphasises criteria of size (over 2,000) and degree of clustering.

9. Municipal Corporations Act (5 and 6 Gul. IV, c. 76).

10. See J. Tait, *The Medieval English Borough* (1936) and C. Stephenson, *Borough and Town: A Study of Urban Origins in England* (1933) for a discussion of medieval origins, and for a brief outline in the administrative context J.J. Clarke, *A History of Local Government of the United Kingdom* (1955).

11. See above, pp. 11—14 for a fuller discussion.

12. Sample copies for a few Bedfordshire parishes of the overseers' and Clergy's summaries for the Censuses of 1801—31 have been preserved in GRO records and may be consulted in the Public Record Office.

13. Census, 1831, pp. 410—7.

14. According to V.D. Lipman, *Local Government Areas, 1834—1945* (1949), pp. 4—5 there were, in 1834, 99 boroughs or Liberties which 'levied a rate in the nature of a county rate'. Not all had their own quarter session but represented broadly a group with historic status and privileges which included four elements: 16 cities (or city and county); 70 boroughs; 8 towns (including 'Town and County') and 5 Liberties, etc. In addition 10 'Cinque Ports' could be distinguished.

15. See Census, 1851. *Report* pp. cvii—cviii, Table 18 for further examples.

16. See R.H. Kinvig and M. J. Wise (eds.), *Birmingham and its Regional Setting: a Scientific Survey* (Brit. Assn. for the Advancement of Science, 1950), pp. 213—21 and 232—41.

17. The metropolitan area was not satisfactorily defined until the Metropolis Local Management Act of 1855 (see below, p. 96). The 1831 Census distinguished between 6 units: London within

the walls; London without the walls; the Borough of Southwark; the City of Westminster; parishes within the Bills of Mortality; other Metropolitan Parishes. Census, 1831; *Report*, pp. 8–12.

18. For example, Birmingham obtained a Local Improvement Act in 1769 Manchester in 1765–6.

19. See V.D. Lipman, *op. cit.*, pp. 27–33 on which much of the following discussion is based.

20. Initially by a bill for Registration of Births, Deaths and Marriages in England (6 Gul. IV, c. 85 and 86, 1836). This was never entered upon the Statute Book, being deferred by 7 Gul. IV, c.1, 1837 and was implemented by the Act of 1 Vic., c. 22, 1837 which brought into being the Office of the Registrar General.

21. Returns of Marriage under 6 and 7 Gul. IV.

22. Census, 1851, Appendix to *Report*, Table 42, p. cxxvi.

23. Census, 1851, *Summary Tables*, Table VII, pp. cciv.

24. The Reform Act of 1832 had removed parliamentary representation from some boroughs and extended the parliamentary limits of others, thus destroying the previous identity between the two definitions *(Guide*, p. 102). One must be careful to distinguish between the two areas for the populations within the parliamentary borough boundaries were often much greater than within the municipality.

25. For example, New Radnor District of Boroughs was made up of the small market towns of New Radnor (2,345), Presteigne (1,617), Knighton (1,388) and Rhayader (1,007), together with Knuclas (251) and Cefnllys (45).

26. Towns of all sizes often made considerable population gains under the 1835 boundary extensions; for example, in 1851 the population of Liverpool within the extended limits was 375,955 and within the old 258,236, of Bristol 137,328 as against 65,716, of Hull 84,690 compared with about 16,000, of Stockport, 53,835 compared with 30,589 and of Carlisle 26,300 compared with 8,307.

27. Census. 1851, *Report*, p. lxxx.

28. See J. J. Clarke, *A History of Local Government of the United Kingdom* (1955), pp. 242–5 on which the following is based.

29. T.W. Freeman, *Geography and Regional Administration* (Hutchinson, 1968), p. 155.

30. Lipman, *op. cit.*, p. 59.

31. Especially under the Public Health Act of 1848 and the Sanitary Act of 1866: for a convenient summary see M. W. Flinn, *Public Health Reform in Britain* (1968).

32. For example under the Lodging-houses Acts of 1851 and the Artisans' and Labourers' Dwellings Act of 1869 and the Artisans' and Labourers' Dwellings Act of 1875.

33. The Local Government Board Act of 1871 permitted the development of a series of local government Board areas under specific Board Orders.

34. *The Report of the Royal Commission on Sanitary Inspection* (the Adderley Commission), Parlty. Papers, 1868/1869/XXXII and 1871/XXXV.
35. Introducing his Rating and Local Government Bill to the House of Commons, 1871. See also his *Report on Local Taxation,* Parlty. Papers 1870/LV.
36. Quoted by Lipman, *op. cit.* p. 81.
37. See M.W. Flinn, *op. cit.* p. 48-*seq.* for a discussion of the Public Health movement.
38. Census, 1871, *Summary Tables*, Table VII, p. xviii.
39. Census, 1871, *Report*, p. vi.
40. Between 1861 and 1871 the registration county's population increased by 14.9 per cent, but in the 'outer ring' the increase was 41.9 per cent.
41. Census, 1881, *Report*, p. iv.
42. M.W. Flinn, *op. cit.*, p. 47.
43. Census, 1871.
44. In 1871, 181 registration districts overlapped the boundaries of geographical counties.
45. Census, 1871, *Report*.
46. Census, 1881, *Report*, p. 9.
47. Lipman, *op. cit.* quoting H.H. Fowler, 1893, in *Parliamentary Debates*, 4th series, Vol. 10, col. 683.
48. See Lipman, *op. cit.* pp. 136—42, for a discussion of the work and proposals of the Commissioners.
49. Lipman, *op. cit.*, p. 157.
50. Census, 1911, *Preliminary Report*, p. xii.
51. *Ibid.*, p. xii.
52. *Ibid.*, pp. xiv. The formation in 1899 of 28 metropolitan boroughs absorbed many *ad hoc* administrative bodies and tidied up administration without really solving anomalous boundaries or consistently resolving the problem of defining the urban limits of the Metropolis.
53. See J.T. Coppock and H.C. Prince (eds.) *Greater London* and, for illuminating case studies, W. Ashworth, 'Suburban Metropolitan Essex since 1850', *Victoria County History of Essex* , *5*, pp. 1—92 and H.J. Dyos (ed.), *The Study of Urban History* (1968) especially pp. 253—71 (D.A. Reeder, 'A Theatre of Suburbs; Some Patterns of Development in West London, 1801—1911').
54. R. Price Williams, 'On the increase of population in England and Wales' *Jnl. Stat. Soc. 43* (1880), pp. 462—508.
55. This was a comparative international study: A.F. Weber, *The Growth of Cities in the Nineteenth Century. A study in statistics* (1899).
56. T.A. Welton, 'On the distribution of the population of England and Wales and its progress in the period of ninety years from 1801—1891', *Jnl. Roy. Stat. Soc. 63* (1900), pp. 527—89, and *England's Recent Progress* (1911).

57. C.M. Law, 'The growth of urban population in England and Wales' *Trans. Inst. Brit. Geogr. 41* (1967), pp. 125—43.

58. See J.B. Harley, 'A guide to Ordnance Survey maps as historical sources IV: The Town Plans and small-scale maps of England and Wales' *The Amateur Historian 5* (No. 8) (1963), pp. 251—9. See also pp. 129—32.

59. I am indebted to Mr D. Jacobsen for this information. For an account of such a community see E. Hubbard, Commuter Country, 1851'. *The Cheshire Round 1* (No. 6) (1966), pp. 185—87 and 194.

60. J.R. Kellett, *The Impact of Railways on Victorian Cities* (1969). For specific case studies see D.A. Reeder, *op. cit.* footnote 53, and J.E. Vance, 'Housing the Worker', *Econ. Geog. 43* (1967), pp. 100 ff.

61. For a case study see A.M. Warnes, 'Early separation of homes from workplaces and the urban structure of Chorley', *Trans. Hist. Soc. Lancs. and Cheshire* 122, (1970) pp. 105—35, and also his 'Residential patterns in an emerging industrial town', pp. 169—89 of B.D. Clark and M.B. Gleave (ed.), *Social Patterns in Cities* (1973), *Inst. Brit. Geogr.* Special Publication No. 5.

62. A.L. Bowley 'Rural population in England and Wales. A study of the changes of density, occupations and ages' *Jnl. Roy. Stat. Soc. 77* (1914), pp. 597—652.

63. In the following section the account and tables of the *Guide* have been used, together with the tabulations and *Reports* of the individual census publications. Appendix III attempts to summarize the classes of data tabulated for urban areas.

64. Census, 1871, *Report*, Vol. III, summary tables.

65. Census, 1871, Vol. 1, *Preliminary Report*, p. vi.

66. Census, 1871, Vol. IV, *Report*, pp. xxxi—xxxiv.

67. Census, 1911, *Report on Administrative Areas* (1912).

68. Population was grouped by male and female (under 20, 20—24, 25—34, 35—44, 45—54, 55—64, 65—74 and 75 and over) for London, eight county boroughs (Birmingham, Bradford, Burton on Trent, Coventry, Hastings, Liverpool, Manchester and Middlesborough), Swindon Municipal Borough and Rhondda Urban District.

69. For a general approach via case studies see Asa Briggs, *Victorian Cities* (1960); for a review and massive bibliography of the present state of the art see H.J. Dyos (ed.), *The Study of Urban History* (1968).

70. These may be linked with sub-district information in the Registrar General's Annual Reports.

71. See, for a general description of the background to these, M. Beresford, 'The unprinted census returns of 1841, 1851, 1861 for England and Wales', *The Amateur Historian 5* (1963), pp. 260—9.

72. Census, 1831, Statement of Progress under the Population Act of 1830, pp. 8—12.

73. R. Lawton, 'The population of Liverpool in the mid-nineteenth century', *Trans. Hist. Soc. Lancs. and Cheshire 107* (1956), pp. 89—120.

74. My colleague Paul Laxton has found a number of such schedules from archives in Norwich, Reading and Lancashire, including a number for Bolton, Lancs.

75. See also M.W. Beresford, *op. cit.*

76. Census, 1841, *Report.*

77. Census, 1881, *Report*, p. 3.

78. Census, 1851, *Report*, p. xii.

79. Census, 1851, *Report*, p. cxxxv ('Instructions to Registrars of Births and Deaths').

80. See Beresford, *op. cit.*, p. 262.

81. Census, 1871, *Report*, p. ii.

82. For examples see J.R. Kellett, *The Impact of Railways on Victorian Cities* (1969).

83. I am indebted to Mr D. Jacobsen for permission to use this map.

84. See P.J. Taylor, 'Interaction and distance: an investigation into distance decay functions and a study of migration at a microscale' (unpublished Ph. D. thesis, University of Liverpool, 1969) for a discussion of this problem in the Toxteth Park area of Liverpool.

85. I am indebted to Mr I.C. Taylor and Mr D. Jacobsen for information on and discussion of these problems.

86. P.J. Taylor, 'The locational variable in taxonomy', *Geographic Analysis 1* (1969), pp. 181—95.

87. See, for example, Census 1851, *Report*, p. xix.

88. I am grateful to Mrs. M. Havord of the Office of Population Censuses and Surveys for this information (Letter ref. E.510/8/1, 19th August 1971).

89. In a letter to *The Times* (November 13th, 1973), Mr T.W. Benford notes that '... the Towns Improvement Clauses Act, 1847 provides in Section 64 that the Commissions under that Act ... shall from time to time cause the houses and buildings in all or any of the streets to be marked with numbers as they think fit'. This requirement was also incorporated into the Public Health Act of 1875. M. Drake (*op. cit.*, p. 23), however, refers to '... quite chaotic numbering systems' of nineteenth century towns and notes that 'To help enumerators still further, the Census Commissioners tried to get local authorities to adopt a more rational numbering of houses' (*ibid*).

90. Census, 1871, *Report*, p. ii.

91. B. Kay, 'The riddle of Rumford Street', *The Amateur Historian 7* (1967), pp. 263—4.

92. J.B. Harley, 'A guide to Ordnance Survey Maps as Historical Sources IV: The Town Plans and small-scale Maps of England and Wales', *The Amateur Historian 5* (1963), pp. 251—9.

93. *Op. cit.*, p. 254.

94. T. Baines, *Liverpool in 1859*, p. 101 (London and Liverpool,

1859). The river and a west-east line from the city centre were used as base-lines: streets were numbered evenly on the right-hand and oddly on the left-hand sides beginning at the river end (and increasing eastwards) or (in north-south aligned streets) at the central west-east line (and increasing northwards or south-wards).

95. I.C. Taylor, private communication. I am greatly indebted to Mr Taylor for this information and for many discussions concerning the processing and analysis of data from the enumerators' books for Liverpool.

96. See J.B. Harley, 'Maps for the Local Historian: a Guide to British Sources I: Maps and Plans of towns', *The Amateur Historian 7* (1967), pp. 196—208 for a valuable general account of town plans and, especially pp. 203—8 for nineteenth century and specialized town plans.

97. For a general discussion see R. Lawton, 'An age of great cities', *Town Planning Review 43* (1972), pp. 199—224, especially pp. 213—6.

98. See J.R. Kellett, *The Impact of the Railways on Victorian Cities* (London and Toronto, 1969) for a general discussion of this question.

99. For example, B.T. Robson, *Urban Analysis: a study of city structure with special reference to Sunderland* (Cambridge, 1969).

100. See J.E. Norton, *Guide to the National and Provincial Directories of England and Wales before 1856* (1950) for a general guide to early directories. Care must be taken to check the frequency and accuracy with which directories were updated.

101. W.K.D. Davies, J.A. Giggs and D.T. Herbert, 'Directories, rate books and the commercial structure of towns', *Geography 53* (1968), pp. 41—52.

102. For example as by R. Lawton, 'The population of Liverpool in the mid-nineteenth century', *Trans. Hist. Soc. of Lancs. and Cheshire 107* (1956)', pp. 89—120.

103. Techniques in this area are developing rapidly. For a general review see I. Taylor and C.G. Pooley, 'Problems of topographical indexing and spatial analysis of small-area data', in *Methodological Problems in the Statistical Analysis of Small Area Data: Working Paper No. 2*, Social Geography of nineteenth century Merseyside project (Dept. of Geography, University of Liverpool) (1973).

104. Social Science Research Council *Newsletter*, 17 (December 1972), p. 25.

105. For example W.H. Chaloner, *The Social and Economic Development of Crewe, 1780—1923* (1950), T.C. Barker and J.R. Harris, *A Merseyside Town in the Industrial Revolution* (St. Helens 1959).

106. For a review see H.J. Dyos (ed.), *The Study of Urban History* (1968) and P.M. Hauser and L.F. Schnore (eds.) *The Study of Urbanization* (1965). 'For a stimulating methodological study of the towns of England and Wales in the nineteenth century which

is, according to the author 'more theoretical than empirical' but which provides a perspective of population growth, see B.T. Robson, *Urban growth: an approach* (London 1973).

107. See, for example, P.G. Goheen, *Victorian Toronto, 1850–1950*, (1970) especially chapters 1 and 2, and D. Ward, *Cities and Immigrants. A geography of change in nineteenth century America* (1971).

108. As for example in A.F. Weber, *op. cit.*, C.M. Law *op. cit.* and R. Lawton *op. cit.*, 1968.

109. See, for example, H.J. Dyos, *Victorian Suburb: a study of the Growth of Camberwell* (1961) for an exemplary study. More recently there have been a large number of studies from both geographers and historians. A convenient selection of recent work is found in papers on nineteenth century towns in 'Change in the Town', *Transactions, Institute of British Geographers*, New Series, 2 (No. 3) (1977). For methods of analysis of enumerators' returns for a large city see R. Lawton and C.G. Pooley, *The Social Geography of Merseyside in the Nineteenth Century: Final Report to the SSRC* (Liverpool, 1976).

APPENDIX II

Urban areas in England and Wales, 1801–1911[1]

Census	Borough and City		Other urban areas		All urban areas
1801	136 (all cities and towns)				136
			Towns	*Other urban*	
1831	94		35	—	129
1841[2]	171		45	753	969
1851[3]	286		248	—	534
	Other	*London and Metropolitan*			
1861[4]	302	(39)	291	—	593
			Other Local Boards		
1871[5]	308	(39)	576	92	976
			Urban Sanitary Districts		
1881[6]	228	39	739		1006
	C.B. *M.B.*				
1891[7]	63 230	41	705		1039
			Urban districts		
1901[8]	67 248	29	806		1150
1911	75 249	29	812		1165

Notes

1. The precise designation is given for each census.
2. 'Other urban' include those places described under tables of the population of 'Principal Towns' as Liberty, Parish, Township, or even paradoxically, Hamlet: urban townships adjacent to towns which are listed individually are not separately distinguished in this

table; the metropolitan area is counted as 3 units only — London, Within and Without the Walls (together with 24 adjacent 'urban' townships), Westminster (plus 7 townships) and Southwark (plus 8 townships).

3. Boroughs are the municipal and/or parliamentary boroughs, including the 45 individual components of 13 'contributory parliamentary boroughs'; the metropolis is included as three units — London, Tower Hamlets and Westminster.

4. Boroughs are as in 1851. The 39 London areas are Districts of the Metropolitan Board of Works established in 1855 (see also p. 96). These are not included in the total of all urban areas.

5. Boroughs and Metropolitan Districts are excluded from the total as in 1861. Local Boards (which here includes the Metropolitan Board of Works) are a variety of 'Improvement', 'Lighting' and 'Paving' areas, many of which were precursors of later urban districts.

6. The metropolitan areas and urban districts are sanitary districts set up under the Public Health Act of 1872 (see above p. 102).

7. County boroughs (CB) are those established under the Local Government Act of 1888 (see above p. 103).

8. Municipal boroughs (MB) and urban districts were established under the Local Government Act of 1894 (see above p. 104). The units given in 1901 and 1911 for London and the Metropolitan area are the 28 Metropolitan boroughs established by the Act of 1899, together with the City of London.

Sources:

1801 *Census, Abstract of Answers and Returns.*
1831 *Census, Report;* pp. 410—6 (Table of population of Hundreds and towns).
1841 *Census, Report; Enumeration Abstract.*
1851 *Census, Report; Summary Tables,* Table VII, pp. cciv—ccvii.
1861 *Census, Report; Summary Tables,* Table IX, pp. xxi—xxv.
1871 *Census, Report; Summary Tables,* Table VII, pp. xvii—xxxiii.
1881 *Census, Report; Preliminary Abstract,* Tables VIA (pp. 13) and VII (pp. 13—28).
1891 *Census, Report; Preliminary Abstract,* Tables V (p. 16) and IX pp. 18—36).
1901 *Census, Preliminary Report;* Tables VII (pp. 18—19) and XI (pp. 21—41).
1911 *Census, Report; Preliminary Abstract,* Tables II (pp. 2—4) and IV (pp. 5—25).

APPENDIX III

Census information on urban areas in England and Wales, 1801–1911

Census	Area (Acres)	Nos & Sex	Population Ages	Civil condition	Infirmity	Birthplace	Occupation	Families	Housing Houses	Condition	Institutions
1801 1811 1821	London, Boroughs and Principal Towns	L,B, T	(1821 B only) 0–5, 5–10, 10–15, 15–20, 20–30 and then 10 yr. groups	— — —	— — —	— — —	Families in agriculture; manufacture, trade and handicraft; other (by parish)	Families occupying L,B,T.	Inhabited and uninhabited L,B,T.	— — —	— — —
1831	B,C,T,L	B,C, T, Met. B.	(Males over 20 by occupation) B	—	—	—	3 classes of agric; 5 classes of manufacturing, professional and commercial; labourers; male and female servants B	Families occupying L,B,T	Inhabited houses; houses building & uninhabited B	—	—
1841	B,C,T,L	B,C,T,L 'other urban' townships	B,C,T,L 'other urban' townships (5 year groups)	—	—	B,T (own county, rest of E. & W., Scotland, Ireland, Overseas)	Selected occupations B & T	—	Selected B & T;L	—	(Work-houses, hospitals & Asylums) B & T
1851	B,C,T,L	B,C T,L	(5-year groups) T	T	(blind, deaf & dumb) T	B,C,T (county in E & W; Scotland, Ireland, overseas)	T	—	B,C,T,L	—	B & T

1861	1871	1881	1891	1901	1911*
B,L, L.B., Met. ward	B,L, L.B., Metropolitan wards	MB, UD; Met. B, Met. ward	CB, MB, UD; Met. B, wards of boroughs	CB, MB, UD; Met. B, all urban wards	CB, MB, UD, Met. B, all urban wards
B,C,T,L	B,C,T,L	MB, UD; Met. B	CB, MB; UD; Met. B	CB, MB, UD; Met. B, all urban wards	CB, MB, UD, Met. B, Met. B
—	—	MB, UD; Met. B, wards of boroughs	CB, MB, UD; Met. B, wards of boroughs	CB, MB, UD; Met. B, wards of all urban areas	CB, MB, UD; Met. B, wards of boroughs
—	—	UD over 50,000	UD over 50,000	UD over 50,000	MB, UD; Met B, wards of boroughs
—	—	UD over 50,000	UD over 50,000	UD over 50,000	(Tenements of under 5 rooms) UDs; (summary of over-crowding) T
—	CB and Met. B	CB and Met. B	Of foreigners only for CB & Met. B	CB, Met. B; and grouped occupations for T over 50,000	CB, MB, UD, Met. B
T	CBs and towns over 50,000	CBs and towns over 50,000	CBs and towns over 50,000 special tabulations by age group for London AC & 13 other towns	CBs and towns over 50,000	(Families per tenement; persons per room) CBs, towns over 50,000
T	CB & towns over 50,000	CB; and Met. B	CB; and Met. B	CB, MB, UD, Met. B, urban wards	(Families or separate occupiers) CB, MB, UD, Met. B, urban wards
T	CB, MB, UD, Met. B, all urban wards	CB, MB, UD, Met. B, Met. B	CB; MB; UD	(Type of building) CB, MB, UD, Met. B	Admin. area in which located to UD level

Key columns (type codes): B,C,T,L | T | T | T | T | B,C,T,L | — | B,C,T,L | T

* New tabulations for urban areas in 1911 included the following: *Industry:* CBs and towns over 50,000; *Welsh Language:* UDs in Wales and Monmouth; *Fertility:* (children born to each marriage and living): CBs

Key to abbreviations

B = incorporated borough; C = city; CB = county borough; MB = municipal borough; Met. B. = metropolitan borough (or district); L = London; L.B. = London borough; AC = Administrative county; UD = urban (sanitary) district; T = principal or large town; — = not separately available for urban areas.

CHAPTER 4

Birthplace Statistics and the Analysis of Internal Migration [1]

D.E. BAINES

Information for the direct and indirect measurement of migration can be obtained from a number of sources and several methods of estimation can be used to partially make up deficiencies in the original data. The main sources and estimation methods are detailed below. The data available for nineteenth century England and appropriate methods of analysis will be discussed in more detail later in this chapter.

General methods of measurement of migration

CONTINUOUS POPULATION REGISTER

The legal liability to notify all changes of address, though common on the Continent, has never been thought desirable in Britain in peacetime. In wartime it was necessary because of rationing and the direction of labour so that a National Register was begun in 1939 and retained until 1952. A study based on the National Register carried out under the auspices of the General Register Office was able to estimate average annual migration by taking a one per thousand sample of addresses and subsequently checking each individual's location.[2] But no equivalent data exist before 1939 or after 1952.

OTHER CONTINUOUSLY GATHERED DATA

In the absence of national registration, registers kept for some other purpose have been used to measure migration. National insurance records are among the best. One researcher used the exchange of cards at National Insurance offices (when a man changed to a job in another area) to measure migration to London in the 1930s.[3] But this method only covers employees and unemployment insurance only started (for a few) in 1913. No continuously kept register had an equivalent coverage for the years before 1913, but in *local* studies some information on migration can usually be found in trade union, friendly society or even chapel registers.

DISCONTINUOUSLY GATHERED DATA

Since 1837,[4] all births, deaths and marriages have been compulsorily registered. Hence, the location of every person (except immigrants and emigrants) should have been recorded at least twice. In addition, if they married and had children their location at those points in their lives will also be recorded, while each certificate[5] should also record the subject's address and occupation at that time. Initially not all births, marriages, and deaths were registered but in 1874 the imposition of penalties for failure to register improved coverage considerably. Even so more than 90 per cent of births were always registered.[6] Occupations, however, may have been considerably upgraded, particularly on the marriage certificates. Some systematic use has been made of this material,[7] but the considerable cost of individual search at Somerset House and the enormous demands in time have limited such studies to very local areas or selected groups of persons. Consequently, despite the ability to pinpoint individuals from the certificates, Registrar General's material has normally been used in the *aggregate* — that is in published form — and in conjunction with the census (this is discussed below, p. 149).

THE CENSUS

The census is and will remain the most important source for nineteenth and early twentieth century migration studies. Unlike the registration data discussed above, the nineteenth century censuses of England and Wales were taken at regular intervals of ten years. They therefore provide a series of 'photographs' of the condition and location of the entire population rather than occasional glimpses of individuals at intervals determined by events in their life cycles (like the birth of their children) largely unconnected with migration.

Moreover, each enumeration was virtually complete. The main disadvantages of the census arise from its confidentiality. The published returns do not detail the characteristics of individuals (age, sex, occupation, etc.) in anything like the detail possible (see chapter 2, pp. 39–45 and below, p. 154). For example, in the later censuses tables are frequently given enumerating the county of birth of the inhabitants of a particular area and also tables enumerating their ages and occupations: but no tables are ever given correlating all three. While these tables might show that one quarter of the population was born outside the town and one tenth of the population of that town were domestic servants, they do *not* show how many born outside the town were domestic servants. The investigator must remember that the criteria used for selecting published tabulations were those which were considered important and useful *at the time.* Deficiencies of tabulation can be overcome by going back to the original returns,[8] more specifically the enumerators' books into which the original schedules were transcribed. But these returns are protected by a one-hundred year confidentiality rule which means that for practical purposes[9] the data cannot at present be used for periods after 1871 except in its published census form.

In fact tracing migration from the original census returns is very difficult, as well as laborious (see above, p. 37). Different spelling of surnames, mis-statements of age and the chaotic nature of nineteenth century addresses means that in most urban areas rarely more than one quarter of those enumerated in, say 1851 can be found in the 1861 census: since it is unreasonable to expect that three quarters of them had died or migrated in only ten years, it follows that a large proportion of the apparent out-migrants were still in the town in 1861. To trace the missing individuals from other sources (e.g. directories and registration statistics) is even more difficult. Despite these problems, detailed local migration studies are of immense value as a complement to the aggregate data retrievable from the published returns. In consequence, as a general rule, the more comprehensive the geographical and chronological coverage of a study, the less detailed it can be.

The simplest form of migration estimate which can be made from the published census is derived from comparing the enumerated population of an area at one census, say 1871, with the enumerated population at the previous census (1861) plus the births, minus the deaths in the intervening period. If this projected population is more than the enumerated population at the second census there must have been net out-migration by the amount of the difference and if the projection is less there must have been net in-migration by the amount of the difference.[10] This calculation can be done for either males or females.

For example:—

Enumerated population of county X, 1861	50,000
Enumerated population of county X, 1871	60,000
Births, 1861—1870	17,000
Deaths, 1861—1870	10,000
The 'projected' population in 1871	= 50,000 + 17,000 − 10,000
	= 57,000
Enumerated population, 1871	= 60,000
Net migration, 1861—70	= 3,000 (inward)

Total populations can be obtained from the census tables for areas as large as counties or regional groups of counties, or as small as registration districts.[11] Births and deaths for equivalent areas are given in the *Annual Reports* of the Registrar General. A useful summary of births and deaths at a county level is given in the *Decennial Supplements,* but to break them down by sex in the early decades of registration means summing annual or even quarterly births and deaths from the annual returns themselves.

Net migration estimates can be made with great accuracy subject to the proviso that the two populations compared and the numbers of births and deaths refer to the same *area*. Failing this the data must be adjusted to take boundary changes into account. This critical problem is discussed below (p. 156). It is important, however, to understand what an estimate of net migration means. In the example above, the net in-migration of 3,000 persons could conceal an outflow of 10,000 in the ten years balanced by an inflow of 13,000: moreover, those leaving and returning within the inter-censal period would still not be counted. These estimates are best described as 'net population change by migration'.

The other main source for the study of nineteenth century migration is the enumerations of the 'Birthplaces of the People' in the census tables. This is the most useful information that the present day investigator could reasonably expect the census to provide. Ideally, place of residence at some specified earlier date would be more useful but, unless the time lag is very short, even in modern censuses such information is very difficult to obtain with any accuracy.[12] 'Residence' is very difficult to define and memories are notoriously short. Such an enquiry in the nineteenth century could not have provided very accurate information. Several intuitive measures of migration can, however, be derived from the birthplace tables such as the ratio between, say, Norfolk-born in London and London-born in Norfolk.[13] A better approach is to attempt to estimate the deaths of migrants (Norfolk-born in London) from the appropriate Registrar General's returns.[14] This entails estimating the probable age distribution of the Norfolk-born in London. Net movement of Norfolk-born into London can then be estimated for each ten-year period in the same way as above. Similarly net movement of Norfolk-born out of Norfolk can be estimated by the same method. This type of calculation can be made for any pair of the fifty-three counties of England and Wales. In this way the most important shortcomings of the place of birth data — that no evidence is given of *when* migrants left their birthplace or some intermediate place of residence — can be partially remedied. It must be emphasised, however, that *direct* evidence of migrant death rates, for example, is virtually non-existent.

Every census between 1841 and 1911, inclusive, contained information on the birthplaces of the population.[15] In 1841, the census gave the numbers, first, of those enumerated in their parish of birth and, secondly, of others: but for counties the census distinguished between the proportion of the population born in that county, those born in another English or Welsh county, those born in Scotland and those born in Ireland. From 1851 the 'Birthplaces of the People' were tabulated by 53 English and Welsh counties, Scotland,

Ireland, 'Islands in the British Seas', 'at sea' and abroad (a typical lay-out is shown in Table 4.1). These enumerations were divided by sex from 1861 and between 1851 and 1871 inclusive into 'under 20' and '20 or over' age groups. Migrant age structure is not only important in its own right, as one of the most common migration differentials, but also, because it enables the mortality of migrant groups to be estimated, it is an important tool of analysis.[16] Unfortunately, before 1911 no comparable data on migrant age structure were tabulated, and then only for four counties (three in Wales) and selected towns.

The tables were designed to show where the inhabitants of each area had been born, with place of birth read down and place of enumeration across the page. In 1881, 1891 and 1901 additional tabulations were included to show where those born in each county had been enumerated — the 'mirror image' of the usual tabulation (see Table 4.2). The smallest area for which birthplaces were enumerated were the registration districts, but tabulations for these areas were produced only in 1851 and 1861. Tabulations for urban areas were uneven: birthplaces for inhabitants of 'principal towns' were given in 1851, 1861 and 1871; birthplaces were tabulated for urban districts with 50,000 population or more in 1881, 1891 and 1901; and for all urban areas (municipal boroughs and urban districts) with 50,000 or more together with all county boroughs in 1911. Except in 1911, however, the *place of birth* was never given for an area smaller than a county. But while the county of birth remained the basic unit from 1851 to 1901, the county of enumeration changed: and *both* changed in 1911. On the census schedule the head of the household was required to enter for each member of his household the 'county and town or parish' of birth, if in England or Wales, and, if outside England and Wales whether born in Scotland, Ireland, Islands in the British Seas, overseas or foreign. Before the administrative reforms of the late nineteenth century the county — as it was generally understood — was the so-called 'civil' or 'ancient' county (see above, ch. 3). Before 1911 the county of birth was always recorded in terms of the civil county. But in 1851 and 1861 birthplaces were enumerated for registration districts and their summation

TABLE 4.1

A typical 'Birthplaces of the People' enumeration, 1881

where born	where enumerated					
	Eastern Counties		Essex		West Ham	
	Males	Females	Males	Females	Males	Females
Total of inhabitants	678,052	700,024	288,180	288,254	65,410	63,543
Monmouthshire & Wales	1,219	1,303	873	890	337	352
Monmouthshire	216	230	168	179	71	91
Glamorganshire	275	267	190	189	76	81
Carmarthenshire	59	59	48	40	17	15

Source: Census, 1881 (B.P.P. 1883 vol. LXXX, pp. 156–7 (pp. 206–7 if renumbered when bound))

TABLE 4.2
Enumeration of inhabitants of counties, 1881 (as for 1891 and 1901)

where enumerated	Monmouthshire and Wales		Monmouthshire		Glamorganshire		Carmarthenshire	
where born	Males	Females	Males	Females	Males	Females	Males	Females
Eastern Counties	1,219	1,303	216	230	275	267	59	59
Essex	873	890	168	179	190	189	48	40

Source: Census, 1881 (B.P.P. 1883 vol. LXXX p. 518
(p. 568 if renumbered when bound))

was in terms of *registration* counties. In 1861 registration districts were still distinguished but the county totals were *civil* counties. The 1911 census was the first to take account of the administrative changes under the Local Government Acts of 1888 and 1894 (see above, chapter 3) and birthplaces were enumerated in terms of county boroughs and administrative counties. This enumeration was far more comprehensive than any previous. Instead of the usual matrix limited to counties, the places of birth and enumerations included also all county boroughs and all municipal boroughs and urban districts of 50,000 or more population. For example, Swansea-born were enumerated in East Ham and Aberdare-born in West Ham: similarly the Glamorgan tables enumerated East Ham-born in Swansea and West Ham-born in Aberdare (see Table 4.3). The tables were in alphabetical order of counties instead of the customary order by geographical 'divisions' and the county totals were for the administrative county *less* its county boroughs. Unfortunately the detail of the 1911 census was unique. Except for a simple listing of one-time migrants its enormous coverage was largely wasted since this detail of tabulation was never repeated. The only inter-censal calculations that can be made from the 1911 birth-place data are net change by migration — for which the birthplaces are irrelevant — and net movement of natives of counties — for which only the county totals are necessary. The county, therefore, remains the critical unit.

Between 1861 and 1901 the same units (civil counties) were used both for birthplace and residence. Neither registration, civil nor administrative counties coincided with each other nor were their boundaries consistent from census to census. Numerous adjustments must be made to equate the various units. The history of these administrative changes, the importance of consistency and the way adjustments can be made will be discussed in more detail below.

There seems little reason to doubt the basic accuracy of the place of birth statistics (see above, chapter 2, p. 57). The enumerators' clerks were responsible for translating the entry in the enumerator's book (or on the form as appropriate) into the appropriate *county*. Actual errors were probably rare and modern demographers rate birthplace and migration data

TABLE 4.3

A typical 'Birthplaces of the People' enumeration, 1911
(the maximum possible census coverage)

| where born | where enumerated | | | | | | | |
| | Essex Administrative County | | West Ham CB | | East Ham CB | | Ilford UD | |
	Males	Females	Males	Females	Males	Females	Males	Females
Glamorgan	230	252	59	56	20	33	21	27
Cardiff, City of CB	236	261	83	88	57	47	36	39
Merthyr Tydfil CB	21	34	15	14	1	6	1	5
Swansea CB	128	150	47	46	28	19	9	23
Aberdare UD	11	24	4	4	2	1	2	4
Rhondda UD	7	14	4	2	1	3	1	1

CB – county borough, MB – municipal borough, UD – urban district.
Note that the urban districts (italicised) are included in the county total. The county boroughs and municipal boroughs are not. The male inhabitants of West Ham born in the county of Glamorgan are therefore 59 + 83 + 15 + 47 = 204.

Leyton UD, Southend-on-Sea MB and Walthamstow UD were also enumerated with Essex.

amongst the most accurate in censuses.[17] In the nineteenth century, however, there was possibly a bias in favour of the locality of enumeration (i.e. *against* migration). The 'not stated' column given in the published census tables in some years (1881—1911) was a minute proportion of the total birthplaces. Otherwise, those enumerated by birthplace always equalled the total enumerated population. Presumably, in the absence of other information, blank returns were counted at some stage as if the birthplace was the county of residence. The only major exception to this practice was in the case of those Welsh who wrote 'Wales' instead of the county of birth and who were enumerated separately. They pose a special problem since at most censuses such persons numbered about 10 per cent of those who gave a Welsh *county* of birth. These 'Wales' returns must be distributed in proportion to those Welsh- (and presumably Monmouth-) born who *did* give their county of birth in that census, on the reasonable assumption that all Welsh were equally unlikely to know their county of birth.

Since the county was the smallest geographical area for which consistent data were given, any migration estimates must therefore conform at least in part with the county unit. It is, of course, possible to calculate net intercensal migration (i.e. net population change by migration) down to the level of registration sub-district, but it is not possible to trace, say, Liverpool-born (as opposed to Lancashire-born) in other counties nor to calculate the migration of Liverpool-born persons to such counties. Similarly, English counties of birth were not tabulated to the censuses of Scotland and Ireland nor were the counties of birth given for Irish- and Scottish-born enumerated in England and Wales. This restricts detailed studies attempting to show the geographical origins and direction of migration to inter-county movement inside England and Wales.

The importance of boundary adjustments to this type of study can be easily demonstrated. Consider the example given above (p. 149) calculating net population change by migration. All estimates of this type are residual, therefore errors in the final estimate are directly dependent on errors in the original data. Since the number of migrants is usually much less than the total population, originally small percentage errors are magnified. For example, if in the previous calculation the 1871 enumerated population of 60,000 included 1,500 persons added from an adjoining county by a boundary change, then the county population within the boundaries of 1861 would be 58,500: net in-migration would then be only 1,500, rather than 3,000. On the other hand, the adjoining county would have 1,500 more people within the boundaries of 1861 and its in-migration would be 1,500 more, and out-migration 1,500 less (or some intermediate figure). Errors of this kind can easily change the *direction* of the migrant flow calculated. It is vital, therefore, that the total populations, number of births and number of deaths all refer to exactly the same area, irrespective of the area for which the inform-ation was given on the date in question. If the county is to be the unit — as it must be for the purpose of most studies — it is necessary to assume that one particular type of county within one particular set of boundaries existed for the whole period studied. All census and Registrar General's data must be altered to conform with the boundaries chosen. Unadjusted data have been used in several studies. Acceptable results are possible for non-adjacent counties but adjacent county estimates are much more seriously distorted. In fact, the most comprehensive study to date only calculated migration between non-adjacent counties.[18]

A geographical (standard) area can be useful to the historian if it is completely arbitrary (i.e. superimposed on an existing population distribution): but it is much more useful if it has some economic or social meaning for the period in question. Unfortunately, nineteenth century counties are neither completely arbitrary units nor indisputably meaningful historical areas: for example, their boundaries often cut through urban areas (see chapter 3). The county unit with the greatest economic and historical meaning in the nineteenth century, and that most used and thought of in everyday life, was the civil (or 'ancient') county: this unit was also the most common area used in the census tables. Civil counties, based on old, pre-Norman units and twelfth century creations, were originally much fragmented, but with the operation of the Counties (Detached Parts) Act of 1844 they had become, with a few major exceptions,[19] geographically discrete units. They were not exclusive administrative units, however, because they nearly all included urban areas with varying degrees of political and administrative independence (see above, chapter 3, pp. 86–109).

Under the Local Government Act of 1888 the administrative units became the county borough and the administrative county. The boundaries of the new administrative counties (even including their county boroughs) did not coincide with those of the civil (ancient) counties whose names they carried. Fortunately, birthplaces were not given in terms of administrative counties until 1911. More seriously the Registrar General's (vital) data were recorded in terms of registration districts – derived from the surviving Poor Law Unions of 1782 and 1834 – and hence registration counties. The Poor Law Unions and the later registration districts were areas served by local market centres and when aggregated into registration counties they did not always coincide with civil counties. For example, part of the registration district of Stourbridge (Worcestershire), containing 29,354 inhabitants in 1851, was in the civil county of Staffordshire: these people were enumerated as born in Staffordshire but living in the registration county of Worcestershire. They therefore appear as 'migrants' though they may have never moved.[20] Although it was obviously more convenient to use the same unit for all purposes, attempts to standardise the areas of counties in the nineteenth century met with little success, largely because changes might affect financial responsibility. No ratepayer was prepared to subsidise an adjoining area, hence administrative counties could not be made co-extensive with either registration or civil counties.

Mitchell[21] tabulates nineteenth century population totals for civil counties assuming they had the boundaries of 1891. It is suggested that this hypothetical standard be used for all migration calculations that use county units. For smaller areas we suggest using the local government boundaries of 1891.

'London' only became an administrative county in 1888 (see above, chapter 3, pp. 103–4). Prior to this the best statistical definition of London is the area defined by the

Metropolis Management Act of 1855 which contained the
'Intra-Metropolitan' parts of the counties of Middlesex,
Surrey and Kent (which corrected to the boundaries of 1891
became the County of London as used in the census of that
year). The 'extra-Metropolitan' parts of these three counties
became the counties of Middlesex, Surrey and Kent for the
purposes of population calculations. The migrant population
has to be estimated where the 'London' column is insufficiently broken down,[22] and for 1851 and 1911 considerable
estimation is necessary to obtain 'London' data.

The crucial assumption necessary to adjust county (or
other) boundaries to a hypothetical standard is that the
smaller part 'transferred' reproduces the features of the county
of which it is a part: i.e.

$$\frac{\text{Population (old area) 1871}}{\text{Population (new area) 1871}} = \frac{\text{Female population (old area) 1871}}{\text{Female population (new area) 1871}}$$

For example: the population in county A in 1861 is 100,000
with 45,000 under 20 years old and 55,000 20 and over.
County B has 50,000 people with 20,000 under 20 years of
age and 30,000 of 20 years and over. Between 1861 and 1871
county A gains 3,000 people from B through a boundary
change. The 1861 population of A within the new borders
aged under 20 will be

$$45,000 + \left(3,000 \times \frac{45,000}{100,000}\right) = 46,350$$

and the population 20 and over will be

$$55,000 + \left(3,000 \times \frac{55,000}{100,000}\right) = 56,650$$

The 1861 population of B within the new borders aged under
20 will be

$$20,000 - \left(3,000 \times \frac{20,000}{50,000}\right) = 18,800$$

and the population 20 and over will be

$$30,000 - \left(3,000 \times \frac{30,000}{50,000}\right) = 28,200$$

It will be noted that though county A 'gained' 1,350 persons under 20, county B only 'lost' 1,200. There is no illogicality in this, since the objective is to find the hypothetical characteristics of the population at all censuses but within the boundaries of 1891. Strictly, it might be better to use the characteristics of the losing county for both changes (or perhaps some average) but the above method has the great practical disadvantage that innumerable calculations would then be necessary whereas to convert a county of 1891 boundaries on the original criteria needs effectively only one operation per decade. In any case, it seems reasonable to assume that the smaller parts mirror the characteristics of the whole area.

In practice, it is not necessary to convert registration counties to our 1891 standard civil counties. Birth and death rates can be used because when they are applied to the converted mid-decade population the adjusted number of births and deaths will be given. The process is mathematically identical to adjusting the numbers of births and deaths for boundary changes because the rates given in the Registrar General's returns are no more than the actual number of births and deaths divided into the average population. Such rates today are normally adjusted to take into account the rate applied to the larger population at the end of the decade. They cannot therefore be simply grossed up in this way. That registration decades do not correspond to census decades can be safely ignored.[23]   Finally, birth rates must be inflated to include unregistered births. Glass[24] calculated that four per cent of births were unregistered in the 1850s and two per cent in the 1860s; female births were less likely to be registered than male.

Once the raw data have been reduced to hypothetical standard areas they can be manipulated to provide a range of results, some of which have been mentioned before and which are reiterated by way of a conclusion.

The most valuable feature of census-based migration estimates is their comprehensiveness, particularly since so much information is lost by the process of calculation (and in the publication of the census). Such estimates can, of course, be supplemented by local studies based on the enumerators' books (see above, chapter 2), local newspapers or vital registration. Government reports can also yield valuable results: for example, Redford's study of migration in the early nineteenth century used a special Poor Law Report.[25]

Simple calculations of net migration (by sex) are highly accurate but only show the *effect* of migration on population change. Large migrant inflows can be masked by only a slightly larger outflow. 'Nearer gross' migration[26] can be obtained (by sex) by calculating the net outflow of natives (for example, Devon-born in Devon). If the reduction is made in the Devon-born enumerated in other counties by an estimated migrant death rate, the differences in Devon-born between one census and another must be due to the net movement of Devon-born into and out of other English and Welsh counties or abroad — assuming also that the boundary problems have been taken into account. Estimation of a migrant death rate (both for all counties and for an individual county) is the critical problem in all such studies. Assuming that age-specific migrant death rates approximate to those of natives, the death rate of a migrant group in another county depends on its age structure. But a migrant group is composed of two elements; *current* migrants who have arrived during the past decade and *previous* migrants who are the survivors of the current migrants of a previous decade. The presumed ages of current migrants can be estimated, but the ages of the previous migrants present in the current decade is dependent on the decades in which they arrived and the number arriving in each of those decades. If current migrants are assumed to have a constant age distribution, the longer ago previous migrants arrived, the older the survivors must now be.

Net decadal migration change can also be calculated for each age group by applying survivorship factors[27] and comparing the result with the enumeration at the next census. A forward survival method (the chance of surviving to the end of the decade) misses migrant deaths in the intervening period and therefore overstates in-migration. A reverse method (the chance of having survived since the beginning of the decade) overstates immigrant deaths and therefore understates in-migration.

In conclusion, we must detail what census-based migration

estimates *cannot* show. The census was a *de facto* enumeration, so seasonal migrants are generally missed. County units are frequently arbitrary and divide rather than enclose meaningful economic or social units (see chapter 3, above, pp. 109—21). Migration within a county normally exceeded migration across its boundaries: in addition, a migrant is only counted once if he makes a series of moves in a decade and not at all if he returned to his original birthplace, so that birthplace tables always understate population mobility. But, accepting these problems, any study which stresses the ebb and flow of migration is worthwhile. Moreover, overall estimates are an essential pre-requisite to more detailed local studies for which other sources of information must be used.

NOTES

1. This chapter is a revised version of part of my 'The use of published census data in migration studies' in E.A. Wrigley (ed.), *Nineteenth Century Society* (1972).
2. M.P. Newton and J.R. Jeffery, *Internal Migration*, General Register Office, Studies in Medical and Population Subjects, No. 5 (HMSO 1951). See also, J.A. Rowntree, *Internal Migration*, General Register Office, Studies in Medical and Population Subjects, No. 11 (HMSO 1957).
3. B. Thomas, 'The movement of labour into South-East England 1920—1932', *Economica* (New Series), 2 (1934), pp. 220—41, and 'The influx of labour into London and the South-East 1920—1936', *Economica* (New Series), 5 (1937), pp. 323—36.
4. 1838 was the first complete year of civil registration in England and Wales. Vital registration only began in Scotland in 1855. See above, chapter 1, for a discussion of earlier forms of registration.
5. Parish Registers still continued to be kept and good use has been made of them. See for example P.J. Perry, 'Working class isolation and mobility in rural Dorset 1837—1936: a study of marriage distances', *Transactions, Institute of British Geographers*, 46 (1969), pp. 115—35.
6. See D.V. Glass, 'A note on the under-registration of births in the nineteenth century', *Population Studies 5* (1951—52), pp. 70—88.
7. See R. Duncan, 'Case studies in emigration: Cornwall, Gloucestershire and New South Wales, 1877—1886', *Economic History Review*, 16 (1963), pp. 272—89. For a recent study using such data see R.J. Dennis, 'Distance and social interaction in a Victorian city', *Journal of Historical Geography* 3 (1977), pp. 237—50.
8. A good example of such a study is C.G. Pooley, 'The residential segregation of migrant communities in mid-Victorian Liverpool'. *Transactions, Institute of British Geographers*, New Series 2

(1977), pp. 364—82. See above, chapter 2 and, for urban data, chapter 3.

9. Attempts have been made to examine the enumerators' books with the names blocked out, but it is then virtually impossible to match individuals from one census to another. Moreover, individual names can be the only way of resolving ambiguities in the composition of households and relationships inside the family.

10. This may be expressed simply as $\pm T = \pm N \pm M$ where $T =$ total population change, $N =$ natural change (the balance of births and deaths) and $M =$ the balance of migration (or net migration). The majority of migration estimates have used this method. See, for example the Preliminary Report of the Census of 1961, and A.K. Cairncross 'Internal migration in Victorian England', *Manchester School 17* (1949), pp. 67—87, reprinted in his *Home and Foreign Investment, 1870—1913* (1953), pp. 65—83.

11. See R. Lawton, 'Population changes in England and Wales in the later nineteenth century: an analysis of trends by registration districts', *Transactions, Institute of British Geographers, 44* (1968), pp. 55—74.

12. See for example the discussion of the questions in the 1961 and 1966 censuses in B. Benjamin, *The Population Census* (Heinemann for SSRC, 1970), pp. 79—81.

13. See C.T. Smith, 'The Movement of population of England and Wales in 1851 and 1861', *Geographical Journal 117* (1951), pp. 200—10, and R.H. Osborne, 'Internal Migration in England and Wales 1951', *Advancement of Science 12* (148) (1956), pp. 424—34.

14. See below for further comments on this method of analysis which is discussed in detail in D.E. Baines, *op. cit.*

15. See chapter 3 for details for urban areas.

16. A.B. Hill, *Internal Migration and its effects upon the death rates with special reference to the county of Essex* (Medical Research Council 1925), D.S. Thomas, *Research Memorandum on Migration Differentials,* New York, Social Science Research Council, Bulletin No. 43 (1938). A.L. Bowley, 'Rural Population in England and Wales. A study of the changes in density, occupations and ages', *Journal of the Royal Statistical Society 78* (1914), pp. 597—645 and the Census of 1911, *General Report,* p. 61 ff. are the most useful of a considerable literature.

17. See, for example, the 1966 follow-up to the 1961 Census of England and Wales.

18. D. Friedlander and D.J. Roshier, 'A study of internal migration in England and Wales, Part 1', *Population Studies 19* (1966), pp. 239—79.

19. Worcestershire and Flint had detached parts in neighbouring counties until 1972, and a great confusion of local government areas on the Warwickshire, Worcestershire and Gloucestershire borders was only rectified in 1931. For details of boundary

changes and the legislation affecting them see V.D. Lipman, *Local Government Areas 1834–1945* (1949).

20. This is discussed in H.C. Darby, 'The Movement of Population to and from Cambridgeshire between 1851 and 1861', *Geographical Journal 101* (1943), pp. 118–25.

21. B.R. Mitchell and P. Deane, *Abstract of British Historical Statistics* (1962), pp. 20–23.

22. In 1861, 1871 and 1881: in 1861 the intra-metropolitan parts of Surrey, Kent and Middlesex can only be calculated by summing parishes and subtracting them from the county totals. Greenwich was in both intra-Metropolitan Surrey and intra-Metropolitan Kent. Its population has to be divided on the basis of the known 1871 distribution.

23. In fact, it is best to assume that the *census* was always taken on the 1st January: the migration decades then become 1861–70, 1871–80 etc. This is effectively the same as assuming the registration year began in April and in any residual calculations the error would be identical.

24. D.V. Glass, *op. cit.*

25. The Poor Law authorities had to assess the reasons for any emigration in the six months prior to the 1841 census. The results of this enquiry were published in the census tables. See A. Redford, *Labour Migration in England 1800–1850* (Manchester, 1926). Cf. the use of the marginal notes in some published census tables used by C.T. Smith, *op. cit.*

26. See also D.E. Baines *op. cit.*, which also contains a full appraisal of the other methods mentioned here, D. Friedlander and D.J. Roshier, *op. cit.*, H.A. Shannon, 'Migration and the growth of London 1841–1891', *Economic History Review 5* (1935), pp. 78–86, and B. Thomas, 'Migration into the Glamorganshire Coalfield 1861–1911', *Economica 30* (1930), pp. 275–94.

27. See E.S. Lee, A.R. Miller, C.F. Brainerd and R.A. Easterlin, *Population Redistribution and Economic Growth, United States 1870–1950,* Vol. 1 American Philosophical Society (Philadelphia) (1957).

CHAPTER 5

Occupation Statistics in the Nineteenth Century Censuses

JOYCE M. BELLAMY

The census occupation statistics provide the most complete information available on the employment of the population in the nineteenth century and extensive use has already been made of the printed tables for studies of national[1] and local[2] employment trends. Modifications in methods of collection and presentation, have, however, somewhat restricted comparative analyses over long periods. The official *Guide* to the census reports[3] contains much detail on the occupation enquiries but says little about their effect on the comparability of the statistical material and omits altogether some points of interest to research workers. In this chapter the census occupation data published in the decennial census reports for England and Wales from 1801 to 1911 will be evaluated in the light of the principal classification changes; and their limitations, as well as their value, for research purposes will be discussed.

Some information on occupations was collected in 1801 but the results were unsatisfactory. In the census enquiries for 1811 and 1821 the basis was changed to family units by two main classes — 'Agriculture and Trade', 'Manufacture and Handicraft' — but in 1831 additional details were collected. These distinguished agricultural from other labourers and male persons working in the manufacture of machinery or other manufacture from those employed in retail trade and handicrafts. Capitalists were grouped with bankers, professional and other 'educated men'. Only those males aged 20 or above were included in these categories but some information was given relating to male servants under 20 and female servants whose ages were unspecified. Since these statistics were given for parishes and townships they have a value, though limited, for local research but a more detailed occupational breakdown was supplied for the larger towns and this throws some light on the employment of local residents.

It was not, however, until 1841 that an occupational enumeration of the total population, as individuals, was attempted. Even so, doubt has been cast on the validity of comparing the 1841 figures with subsequent returns: Charles Booth, in his early analysis of the occupation statistics, stated,[4] 'owing to the different methods of tabulation as to ages and the imperfections of the returns, the figures for 1841 do not ... offer a very safe basis of comparison' and, though included in annexed tables, they were not used in his paper to the Royal Statistical Society. W.G. Hoffman in his analysis of industrial output and employment in England and Wales criticised the 1841 occupation data on the grounds that the figures did not adequately reflect the proportion of the population in industrial employment when compared with later census reports.[5] This point is pursued further by D.J. Coppock who suggests that 'the occupations of many women and children must have failed to be enumerated' in 1841.[6] He quotes a figure of 37 per cent as the proportion of occupied to total population in 1841, compared with 46 per cent ten years later. Discrepancies of a similar order of magnitude have been derived from an analysis of the occupation data for Hull published in the 1841 and 1851 census volumes. These showed that total occupied to total enumerated population for part of the Hull borough area[7] in 1841 was 35.4 per cent; comparable data for the same areas were not available from the 1851 census but the ratio of total occupied to total enumerated population in the Hull borough for that year was 43.6 per cent.[8] However, data from an independent study undertaken in 1839 by the Manchester Statistical Society and relating only to the town part of Hull showed that 40.3 per cent of the total population was occupied at that time.[9] Mitchell and Deane refer to the fact that many people described as unoccupied in the 1841 census would have been allocated to an occupation in later returns.[10] They also emphasise that unoccupied men apparently declined by half a million between 1841 and 1851 whereas women occupied in the latter year had risen by over a million.

Although changes of such magnitude would appear to be due to inaccuracies in either the enumeration or inter-pretation of the returns, the *Introductory Remarks* (1844) to the 1841 census did refer on several occasions to persons being temporarily out of employment owing to trade depression — although such details were rarely recorded on the schedules. It is also relevant to note Tooke's comment that 'as the summer [of 1841] advanced it became evident that the continued high price of corn and cattle, together with the general scarcity of employment for the labouring population precluded any material improvement for the present'[11] especially as the census was taken in early June — the latest date of any nineteenth century census — and might, therefore, have reflected to some extent the lack of employment opportunities. A decade later, by contrast, a factory in-spector's report for April 1851 indicated that there was 'not much evidence of unemployment' even though there was some short-time working in Yorkshire, and in October 1851 a report on trade in Lancashire stated that 81 new factories had been built or started working in the previous twelve months.[12]

Since quantification of the effects of economic conditions on the accuracy of the census reports is impossible, caution must clearly be exercised when using the 1841 occupation statistics for comparative purposes. They should not, however, be dismissed as of little worth for economic and social research. Those seeking information on local industry will find much in the 1841 census occupation statistics of interest and value for their studies. W.F. Spackman reproduced census data extensively in his early occupational analysis[13] and for more localised studies the details are of special interest. So meticulously were the designations of occupations utilised by those compiling the tables that it is possible to group them under the headings used in later returns with the proviso that direct comparisons may not give an accurate picture of rates of growth for individual categories (see above, chapter 2 for a discussion in the context of local data). Mitchell and Deane draw attention to those occupations where special caution is needed:[14] nurses (returned as domestic servants in Scotland), domestic servants (whose numbers included coachmen, gardeners and grooms), commercial occupations (where the general category of clerk was used somewhat indiscriminately) and the 'general labourer' for whom, especially in mid-century returns, there was generally no indication of the type of labouring work undertaken.

By 1851 the accumulated experience of the earlier enquiries resulted in a more comprehensive survey of the occupations of the people and gave rise to the first scientific attempt to analyse the information: collected into classes and sub-classes which were renamed orders and sub-orders in later census reports. For the first time also, masters in trade and manufacture were requested to indicate this fact and to give details of the number of men they employed. Whilst the results of the latter inquiry were not considered sufficiently accurate for detailed statistical analysis, they were published for county groups (except for London and Yorkshire which were separately designated.). The original details given in the enumerators' schedules are now available for inspection at the Public Record Office.[15] These are especially useful for local studies as they are frequently the only source of information on the size of the labour force of individual mid-century enterprises although not all employers made returns. Whilst the broad pattern of classification laid down in 1851 survived during the remainder of the century (and later) some important changes and modifications were subsequently introduced which have restricted direct comparisons for the years from 1851 to 1911. It is essential that those wishing to undertake research involving the use of occupation statistics should examine the census reports closely and the suggestion in the *Guide* that the later census reports should be studied before extraction of the data from earlier ones is very pertinent.[16]

The most important of the modifications to the census classification occurred in 1881 when clerks employed in any branch of industry or commerce were no longer assigned to that particular branch but grouped into a general heading.[17] At the same time retired persons, previously classed to their former occupation, were assigned in 1881 to the unoccupied category. The effect of this latter change was not, however, considered to be large: the *General Report* for 1881 indicated, in fact, that for an entire county the inclusion of the retired increased the total occupied by an average of two per cent.[18] In 1891 Army and Navy pensioners were included in the unoccupied, but retired clergymen and medical practitioners were still being included with the active members of their profession (until 1911).

The employment of relatives also caused some confusion and the *Guide* fails to explain these discrepancies. Until 1881 the number of wives, widows, sons, daughters and other relatives were shown separately in the occupation tables; for the years 1851–71 a wife who assisted in her husband's business was designated separately as innkeeper's wife, butcher's wife, shoemaker's wife, etc. It was realised in 1881[19] that, by this method, the same woman might be reckoned twice, once as a wife and again if she had a specified occupation of her own, and from that year wives, *per se,* were no longer included among the occupied population.

The *Guide* did not refer, either, to several other changes in the classification of the female population. Numbers in domestic service in 1891 cannot, for example, be compared with those for earlier or later years as female relatives of the head of the family were included, in that year, with the totals for domestic servants; in 1901[20] it was decided to revert to the 1881 method and include them among the unoccupied. Female relatives of farmers, returned as assisting in farm work in 1901,[21] were not shown at all in 1891. In the schedule for 1911 women who were regularly engaged in assisting relatives in trade or business were asked to state the fact; this naturally increased the numbers of women returned and affected comparisons between those orders in which dealers were included.[22]

Furthermore the *Guide* contains no reference to the changes in the classification of the student population. In the census returns for the years 1841 to 1881 students were included in the totals for their respective professions. In 1891 a total figure for all students was given and from 1901 they were included among the unoccupied. It should also be pointed out that the number of fishermen recorded in the

1881 census is not comparable with totals given for other years in the century. The *Guide* indicates[23] that 'from 1851 to 1921 the enumeration of those aboard ships was restricted to vessels in port on Census night and vessels which arrived during the following day'. It does not, however, mention that in 1881 all fishermen coming into port during the succeeding fourteen days were taken into account.[24]

In the matter of age groupings covered by the occupation tables details are given in the *Guide*[25] but no specific reference is made in the text to the effect on the comparability of the data of the exclusion of persons under 20 years of age from the 1871 tables for the principal towns.[26] In 1851, 1861 and 1881 the occupation statistics for these areas were tabulated for all males and females; the exclusion of the younger age group for 1871 thus seriously impairs the comparability of absolute figures between these dates. For 1891, 1901 and 1911 the occupation data related to persons aged 10 years and over.[27]

In 1861, for the first time, the census for Scotland was taken by the Registrar General for Scotland and a separate report, comprising two volumes, was published. It was realised that the English 'Classification of Occupations' had defects and the Scottish census authorities suggested that, before the next census, delegates from the census offices of England, Scotland and Ireland should discuss a mutually acceptable and practical occupation classification to which each country could adhere.[28] This suggestion was not adopted and although the Scottish tables in 1871 could be compared with the English and Irish classifications they also contained additional information which included the allocation of the number of dependents to the classes to which they belonged.

In the early census returns large numbers of persons were classed as general labourers since no other indication was given on their schedules of the actual work on which they were engaged. As Booth has pointed out,[29] 'skilled and common labour are inextricably confused' in the census returns, a fact which applies especially to Building, Manufactures and Transport as 'Dealing affords little employment for common labour, and Agriculture, Fishing and Mining return their own'. Improvements in educational standards during the second half of the century, in conjunction with more comprehensive census schedules, reduced the numbers in undefined occupations. The *Guide* confirms the improvement in the completion of the schedules[30] but does not draw attention to the effect of these improved returns. As stated in the 1901 census,[31] the apparent increase in some specific occupation group may be obtained at the expense of the undefined occupations. Changes in the nomenclature of certain occupations become necessary as industrial mechanisation increased and the *General Report* for 1891 included a table noting the differences between the classification used in 1881 and in 1891.[32] The extent to which the changes from the undefined groups to more specific categories — such as the transfer of general labourers to the Building Class as builders' labourers, bricklayers' or masons' labourers and the like — affected the individual categories is not known, but the *Guide* emphasises that 'substantial changes in the grouping of and consequently the occupations assigned to, Orders formerly included in the Industrial Class made comparison between Orders in this Class in 1891 and 1901 very difficult.'[33] Nevertheless the census authorities published a comparative analysis for the years 1881–1901.[34]

The statement in the *Guide* that 'the occupational classification has changed so considerably as to make it difficult to relate earlier and later figures' is undoubtedly true in specific categories but it is somewhat countered by the subsequent remark that 'the form of classification was basically the same [in 1851] as that in use at the present day'.[35] The census authorities themselves had attempted comparisons over several decades[36] and it has already been shown that much work has been done in this field from the 1880s to the present day;[37] Mitchell and Deane have also provided some useful comparative tables on the British labour force.[38] Whilst it is essential to study the changes in classification in detail, and imperative to indicate that comparisons between the years 1851–1871 and 1881–1911 may be seriously affected by the 1881 amendments, it is still possible to trace the principal trends in the occupational structure of a local area during the nineteenth and early twentieth centuries by reclassification of the occupations listed in the census volumes from 1841.[39]

But where boundary changes have occurred it is necessary to use proportions instead of absolute numbers.[40]

To facilitate comparison with 1901, the census authorities decided against any important classification changes in 1911, although groups within Orders were revised and fuller details of occupational designation provided. In addition, those working at home were classified by status: employer, employee or self-employed.

Despite the criticisms which can be made of the inconsistencies in the census data, they are unquestionably the only source providing such detailed accounts of the activities of nineteenth century working population. Apart from the changes mentioned, their limitations for more sophisticated studies such as those seeking information on skilled workers are apparent; not until 1911 was sufficient detail provided for research on this aspect of the labour force.[41] Nor can one state with accuracy the relative share of the occupied population engaged in the distributive trades. The separation of 'dealers' from 'makers', first made in the Scottish census of 1891, was not available in the census for England and Wales until 1901. Neither is it possible to determine the incidence of unemployment from nineteenth century census returns, for it was admitted in 1881 that persons 'out of employ' were 'abstracted by their occupations as being possibly only temporarily debarred from them',[42] a policy which was continued until 1931. As pointed out during a discussion on the paper by D.C. Jones, 'there was little mobility of labour, particularly in the lower ranks and a man would, for instance, still go on calling himself a miner, although he might get but a few days' work in the year'.[43]

There is no doubt, as the census authorities readily admit, that their task was hampered by inadequate replies and by persons with more than one occupation, although this latter contingency was usually met by including only the first occupation listed. In such cases, the published census data would, therefore, ignore the existence of dual occupations: coalmining might, for example, be undertaken in the winter with a transfer to farm work in the summer. Furthermore, dual occupations of farmer and textile worker were quite widespread in the Craven district of the Pennines in the early

nineteenth century.[44] Local studies based on enumerators'
books could, therefore, provide a more accurate picture of
the occupational structure of a district where dual occupations
are noted than the use of published census data, but it must
be emphasised that seasonal labour could completely escape
the notice of the census authorities. These workers would
normally arrive after the censal date since their services were
usually required for haymaking and harvesting.[45]

No account was taken in the nineteenth century of differences between place of work and place of residence, but this
was less of a problem than in the present century. The basis
of the mid-century analysis of the occupied population was
primarily industrial, and persons were included within the
broad groups irrespective of whether the nature of their own
employment was in producing or distributing a particular
commodity. Modifications to the original scheme were introduced in 1881 when, for example, some of the commercial
clerks were listed under one heading, whereas in earlier years
they had been included in the industry to which they were
attached.[46] When all this is said, however, the wealth of source
material provided by the census returns is invaluable for such
studies as the changing pattern of female employment, the
decline in workers in agriculture and the expansion of other
sectors of the economy — especially in transport and com-
munications. By using the original detailed occupational
headings from the 1841 and subsequent census returns and
adjusting, where appropriate, for classification changes, it is
still possible to analyse the material by the twenty-three
Orders introduced in 1891.[47] These can be grouped to provide
an overall picture of changes in the primary (extractive),
secondary (industrial) or tertiary (service) sectors of the
economy. But care must always be taken in interpreting the
trends in the light of the classification amendments made
from time to time and also in relation to technological
developments. Whilst the occupation statistics are an essential
tool in historical studies of employment trends they should
preferably be used in conjunction with other economic source
material such as factory inspectors' returns, trade statistics
and — from the early twentieth century — Census of Production data. Information on capital invested, numbers employed

and output may sometimes be located in local contemporary archives such as bank and other business records,[48] Chamber of Commerce reports and newspapers, all of which are especially useful sources to supplement the official census occupation data. For contemporary economic trends, the *Annual Register* provides much relevant background information and the recent Government publication on labour statistics[49] could usefully be added to the other source material when the census occupation data are being analysed. It must be emphasised, however, that the published data can only be used for the geographical areas to which the statistics relate, namely local government administrative areas, and in some cases Registrar General's districts. It may, therefore, be impossible to study the occupation structures of villages and small towns from the printed tables and use must then be made of the original census schedules.

NOTES

1. C. Booth, 'Occupations of the People of the United Kingdom, 1801–1881', *Journal of the Statistical Society*, XLIX (1886) pp. 314–335; T.A. Welton, 'On Forty Years' Industrial Changes in England and Wales', *Manchester Statistical Society* (1897-8) pp. 153–266 and 'Occupations in England and Wales, 1881 and 1901', *Journal of the Royal Statistical Society*, 73 (1910) pp. 164–6; C. Day, 'The Distribution of Industrial Occupations in England, 1841–1861', *Trans. Connecticut Academy of Arts and Sciences*, 28 (March 1927) pp. 79–235; W.A. Armstrong, 'The Use of Information about Occupation' in E.A. Wrigley (ed.) *Nineteenth-Century Society: essays in the use of quantitative methods for the study of social data* (Cambridge, 1972) pp. 191–310.
2. J. Bellamy, 'Occupations in Kingston upon Hull 1841–1948', *Yorkshire Bulletin of Economic and Social Research*, 4, no. 1 (Jan 1952) pp. 33–50; P.G. Hall, *The Industries of London since 1861* (1962); D.J. Rowe, 'Occupations in Northumberland and Durham, 1851–1911', *Northern History*, VIII (1973) pp. 119–31.
3. Interdepartmental Committee on Social and Economic Research, *Guides to Official Sources No. 2 Census Reports of Great Britain 1801–1931* (1951) [later as *Census Guide*].* See p. 178.
4. *Loc. cit.*, p. 319; see also below, Chapter 6.
5. W.G. Hoffman, *British Industry 1700–1950* (1955) p. 38.
6. D.J. Coppock, 'The Climacteric of the 1890's: a critical note', *Manchester School*, 24 (1956) pp. 5–6. I am indebted to Miss

Janet Blackman, Hull University for drawing my attention to this discussion.

7. Hull (town part) and Sculcoates Parish only. This area's total population was about 86 per cent of the Hull borough total in 1841.

8. These statistics were derived from material collected for my thesis: 'Some Aspects of the Economy of Hull in the Nineteenth Century with Special Reference to Business History', Ph. D. Thesis University of Hull, 1965.

9. Statistical Society of Manchester, 'Report on the Condition of the Working Classes in the Town of Kingston upon Hull', *Journal of the Statistical Society*, 5 (1842) pp. 212–21. The town part of Hull had a total population of 41,150 in 1841, equivalent to 61 per cent of the Hull borough total. The figure of 40.3 quoted above was calculated from data published in this article.

10. B.R. Mitchell and P. Deane, *Abstract of British Historical Statistics* (1962) p. 59.

11. T. Tooke, *History of Prices ... for 1839 to 1847 inclusive* (1848) p. 46.

12. T. Tooke and W. Newmarch, *A History of Prices*, 5 (1857) pp. 259–60.

13. W.F. Spackman, *An Analysis of the Occupations of the People ... of the United Kingdom of Great Britain and its Dependencies* (1847).

14. *Op. cit.*, p. 59.

15. The enumerators' schedules for the years 1841, 1851, 1861 and 1871 are now located away from the P.R.O. itself and are at the Land Registry, Lincoln's Inn Fields. Only those for 1851, 1861 and 1871 contain employment data. For a full discussion see above, chapter 2.

16. *Census Guide, op. cit.*, p. 6.

17. This included all clerks except those in the Civil Service, Army, Navy, Law, Bank, Insurance and Railway Service: *ibid*. pp. 31–2.

18. Census of England and Wales (1881) IV, *General Report*, p. 28.

19. *Ibid.*, pp. 32–3.

20. Census of England and Wales (1901) *General Report*, pp. 76–7.

21. *Ibid.*, p. 101.

22. Census of England and Wales (1911) part 1, p. xxxvi.

23. *Census Guide, op. cit.*, pp. 94–5.

24. Census of England and Wales (1891) IV *General Report* p. 45. The statistics for fishermen in 1881 may, however, be compared with those given in the 1931 census which were compiled on a comparable basis: *Census Guide., op. cit.*, p. 95.

25. *Census Guide., op. cit.*, 43–51.

26. Census of England and Wales (1871) III. The occupations of males and females of all ages are given for London but for the other principal towns (Tables 18 and 19 in the County Sections) only those of twenty years and over.

27. *Census Guide, op. cit.*, p. 42.
28. Census of Scotland (1871) II, p. xxxvi.
29. *Loc. cit.*, p. 336.
30. *Census Guide, op. cit.*, p. 36.
31. Census of England and Wales (1901) *General Report*, p. 90.
32. Census of England and Wales (1891) *General Report*, Appendix B.
33. *Census Guide, op. cit.*, p. 34.
34. Census of England and Wales (1901) *General Report*, Appendix A.
35. *Census Guide, op. cit.*, pp. 6 and 30.
36. In addition to the table in the 1901 *General Report*, see Census of England and Wales (1871) IV, *General Report*, Appendix A, Table 107 for the years 1861 and 1871 and Census of England and Wales (1911) *Occupations and Industries*, Tables 26 and 27, Summary Tables 64 and 65 for the years 1881—1911.
37. See footnotes 1 and 2 above and also D.C. Jones, 'Some Notes on the Census of Occupations for England and Wales', *Journal of the Royal Statistical Society* LXXVIII (1915) pp. 55—81 for useful comments on the comparability of the census returns.
38. *Op. cit.*, p. 60.
39. See Appendix IV to this chapter for details of method used.
40. J. Bellamy, *loc. cit.*, p. 45.
41. G. Routh, *Occupation and Pay in Great Britain 1906—1960* (1965). I am indebted to Dr E.W. Evans, Hull University, for drawing my attention to this analysis.
42. Census of England and Wales (1881), *General Report*, p. 28.
43. D.C. Jones, *loc. cit.*, p. 79.
44. See R. Lawton, 'The Economic Geography of Craven in the Early Nineteenth Century', *Transactions, Institute of British Geographers*, 20 (1954), pp. 93—111. I am indebted to Professor Lawton, Liverpool University for this reference and for other very helpful advice.
45. R. Lawton, 'Rural Depopulation in Nineteenth-Century England' in *Liverpool Essays in Geography*, edited by R.W. Steel and R. Lawton (1967), p. 249.
46. For a further discussion of this point see H.R. Wilkinson, 'The Mapping of Census Returns of Occupations and Industries', *Geography*, vol. 37 (1952) pp. 37—46 and F.J. Monkhouse and H.R. Wilkinson, *Maps and Diagrams* (3rd ed., 1971), pp. 318—19.
47. See Appendix IV at the end of this chapter for the method of analysis and adjustments made to the occupation data for the census statistics from 1841 to 1911. For later amendments and for the details of the individual occupation groupings by the Orders see J. Bellamy, *loc. cit.*, pp. 45—50.
48. For advice on these consult the Business Archives Council, London, the National Register of Archives, London and see T.C. Barker, R.H. Campbell, P. Mathias and B.S. Yamey, *Business History* (Historical Association, revised edn. 1971).
49. HMSO, *British Labour Statistics: Historical Abstract 1886—1968* (1971).

APPENDIX IV

Method of analysis and adjustments to the Hull occupation data from the Census Reports of 1841 to 1911

All the occupations for the Hull population in the census volumes for 1841 to 1891 were reclassified into the twenty-three Orders introduced in 1891. Throughout the analysis the occupational headings were allocated to the most appropriate Order. As far as possible the definition of industry given in the 1931 census was followed, namely: 'The industry in which any individual is engaged is determined (whatever may be his occupation) by reference to the business in, or the purpose of which, his occupation is followed'. This was essential as in some cases the description of the actual work performed was given in the returns — e.g. carpenter, engine driver, etc. — whilst in others general categories only were given e.g. cotton manufacture. The following amendments were made to the original data:

(1)   Certain occupational headings, included in the census volumes for 1851–71 but not thereafter, were transferred to the Unoccupied Order (XXIII). These were:

   (a)   Wives (with no special occupation), widows, sons etc. The only exceptions were the male relatives of farmers and graziers who were included in the total for agriculture.

   (b)   Wives assisting their husbands, e.g. innkeeper's wife, shoemaker's wife etc. Although no reference is made to these in subsequent census reports, it is possible that some were included under the heading in which they assisted.

   (c)   Land proprietors, shipowners and house property owners.

   (d)   The student population in 1891 was transferred to Order XXIII but in 1841–1881, since students had been included in the totals for their respective professions, it was impossible to adjust the figures for these years.

(2)   No attempt was made to adjust the data to account for the changes in classification introduced in 1881 affecting some clerks, messengers, porters etc., nor for the exclusion of the retired from the 1881 and subsequent returns.

(3)   In 1911 retired clergymen and doctors were included among the unoccupied. No allowance could be made for this change of classification for they had previously been included with the professions.

(4)   No account could be taken of the new instructions in 1911 which affected women regularly engaged in assisting relatives but it is possible that this may have affected those Orders in which dealers were included.

These Orders were then numbered on the basis of the 1931 Industry Tables and were as follows: I, Agriculture; II, Fishing; III, Mines and Quarries; IV, Bricks, Pottery, Cement, Glass; V, Chemicals, Oils, Paints etc.; VI, Metals and Engineering; VII, Precious Metals; VIII, Textiles; IX, Skins and Leather, etc.; X, Dress; XI, Food, Drink and Tobacco; XII, Woodworking (including Furniture and Fittings) etc.: XIII, Paper, Books, Printing etc.; XIV, Building; XV, Gas, Water and Electricity; XVI, Transport; XVII, Commerce; XVIII, National and Local Government; XIX, Defence; XX, Professions; XXI, Domestic and Other Service; XXII, Other Occupations and Industries; XXIII, Without Specified Occupation or Unoccupied.

*   *   *   *   *

Acknowledgements

I am greatly indebted to the Editors of the *Yorkshire Bulletin of Economic and Social Research* for permission to use material from my article in volume 4 (1952) of that Journal, to Professor D.V. Glass, Editor of *Population Studies*, who has also permitted me to incorporate details from my article 'A Note on Occupation Statistics in British Censuses' published in *Population Studies*, 6 (1953), pp. 306—8, and to Dr. G.J. Crossick, Department of Economic and Social History, Hull University, for his most helpful comments and advice.

* A revised edition of the *Census Guide* was published after this chapter was written: see *Guide to Census Reports Great Britain 1801—1966*, HMSO (1977), pp. 47—79 for the section on occupation and industry statistics, 1801—1931.

CHAPTER 6

The Social Structure of Nineteenth Century England as seen through the Census

J.A. BANKS

At the present time the Registrar General uses two forms of classification which may be regarded as attempts to go beyond the initial ordering of census data to a rather more fundamental conception of the social structure of the community. The older of these forms — social class — is based upon the unit *groups* of the occupational census and consists of the arrangement of these into five broad categories. As the 'General Explanatory Notes' to the Occupational Tables of the 1961 Census of England and Wales put it, each of these social class categories is intended to be 'homogeneous in relation to the basic criterion of the general standing within the community of the occupations concerned',[1] though in these 'Notes' no account was actually given of how such a criterion was defined and employed. The new classification — socio-economic groups — contains 17 categories, based upon the occupations and employment status of *persons,* and in this case reference in the 'Notes' was made to the much more specific definitions of employment status and economic position given in *Classification of Occupations, 1960* (HMSO, London, 1960), as well as to the fact that such definitions are not definitions of socio-economic grouping as such. 'Ideally', the authors emphasised, 'each socio-economic group should contain people whose social, cultural and recreational standards and behaviour are similar. As it is not practicable to ask direct questions about these subjects in a population census, the allocation of occupied persons to socio-economic groups is determined by considering their employment status and occupation'.[2] Since questions about the general standing

179

of an occupation within the community are not asked at a census, it may also be emphasised that what is true of the socio-economic groups is true of the social classes. The use of either form of classification implies an inference from whatever is recorded on a census schedule about an individual's occupation and the nature of his employment to a conception, regarded as more socially fundamental, of a structured order of divisions within communities which is not directly investigated by those who make a census.

The concept of social structure, from this point of view, entails the notion that in spite of their obvious differences several occupations are more like one another in some, unspecified, way than they are like the other occupations which the Registrar General puts together in one of the other social classes or socio-economic groups. These likenesses and differences, moreover, are not simply attributable to intrinsic characteristics of the occupations which occur in a society but to some other feature of social life which is thought to be *related* to occupation, but which is not usually made very clear. Thus, when T.H.C. Stevenson first introduced this manner of grouping occupations in 1911 he asserted that his classes were 'designed to represent as far as possible different social grades'. Yet, his justification for his method of arrangement was purely pragmatic, namely, that in spite of the imprecision in some cases, the analysis of *infant mortality* in these terms made scientific sense in that it enabled a hypothesis about such mortality to be tested by reference to statistics. He wrote:

> It will be seen from what has been said, as to the method of arrangement of these occupational classes, that insofar as infant mortality depends upon social position it may be expected to be lowest in Class 1 and to increase regularly down to Class 5 ... There are naturally some irregularities where individual causes of death are shown for separate portions of the first year of life, but where all causes are dealt with there is no exception at any age to the steady increase of mortality from Class 1 to Class 5, and almost the same may be said for the first year of life as a whole of the groups of causes and individual causes of death except where the latter are numerically insignificant.[3]

Infant mortality was thought to be a consequence of 'social

position' and the social position of an infant to be most easily ascertained from knowledge of its father's occupation; and this initial use of occupation as an index of social class, socio-economic group or social grading has been continued in the twentieth century. The concept of 'social structure' indicated by the classification of occupations into a small number of groups or classes, is not to be interpreted, therefore, as identical to the occupational structure of a community as this is produced by the organisation of its economic activities (see above, Chapter 5) nor, indeed, is it to be taken as equivalent to other structural features of a society, such as its pattern of income distribution, which might be said to flow from the occupational structure. The criterion of 'general standing within the community' referred to in the 'Notes' to the 1961 Census of Occupations, for example, was further commented upon in precisely these terms: 'This criterion is naturally correlated with (and the application of the criterion conditioned by) other factors such as education and economic environment, but it has no direct relationship to the average level of remuneration of particular occupations'.[4] Taken in conjunction with the application of occupational categories to the analysis of infant mortality statistics, such notions seem to suggest that the census makers have in mind a concept rather like that referred to by sociologists when they talk about *differential* life chances and *differential* life experiences. The social structure of a community comprises an ordered set of opportunities which are offered to its members in such a fashion that whether or not an individual can take advantage of them depends to a very large degree on those prior opportunities which he, or his parents before him, have already experienced or been denied.

In looking at the nineteenth century censuses these preliminary observations should be borne in mind; for, though the Registrar General did not use the term 'social structure' at any time between 1801 and 1901, the different *systems* of classifying occupations during the century suggest that the compilers had some kind of structural simplification in mind, which is worthy of attention today as possibly implying different opportunities in the 'social structure' sense. The division of the population into three classes in the 1801 census, for example — or four, when it is recalled that the numbers of men in the Army and Navy were not included — indicates that the framers of the schedule, which was attached to the Population Act of 1800, had some idea that information divided in this way gave a socially significant picture of the country. In the event not all parishes made returns for the occupations of their inhabitants; but from those that did the following 'structure' is ascertainable, (see Table 6.1).

TABLE 6.1
England and Wales, 1801; persons in occupational classes

	numbers	percentage
Agriculture	1,713,289	20.3
Trade, Manufacturers, Handicraft	1,843,353	21.9
Other	4,873,103	57.8
Total	8,429,745	100.0

(Derived from *Abstracts of the Answers and Returns to the 1801 Census of Great Britain, Enumeration*, (1801) Part I, p. 497)

The tabular returns in the Report provide details for various subdivisions within Great Britain which show the extent to which industry had already begun to make its impact on the social structure. The relative insignificance of agriculture in Lancashire (8.1 per cent), for example, is apparent in comparison with 20.3 per cent for England and Wales as a whole, and even more so when compared with a county such as Devonshire (28.1 per cent) which was little affected by industrialisation, as the contrasts by reference to the proportions for Trade, Manufactures and Handicraft show even more clearly. Urban-rural contrasts can also be seen in the figures for two major urban areas in these counties, Liverpool and Exeter (Table 6.2).

The suggestion that in such comparisons the emphasis might be laid on the contrast between agriculture on the one hand, and trade, manufactures and handicraft on the other, derives from the fact that the residual category is not altogether meaningful. The comparisons can only be said to make sense, indeed, on the assumption that in every case the errors of enumeration have been evenly distributed between the first two categories or, rather, that the third does not contain

TABLE 6.2
Occupational classes in Devonshire and Lancashire, 1801

| | Devonshire | | Exeter | |
	No.	%	No.	%
Agriculture	96,208	28.1	183	1.1
Trade, Manufactures, Handicraft	60,844	17.7	4,429	26.3
Other	185,835	54.2	12,205	72.7
Total	342,887	100.0	16,817	100.0

| | Lancashire | | Liverpool | |
	No.	%	No.	%
Agriculture	52,018	8.1	174	0.2
Trade, Manufactures, Handicraft	269,259	42.1	11,269	14.5
Other	318,712	49.8	66,210	85.3
Total	639,989	100.0	77,653	100.0

(Derived from *Abstracts 1801 (op. cit.)*, pp. 79, 173 and 451.)

a disproportionate number of persons who should have been
returned in either one of these, despite the fact that it obviously includes too great a proportion from them both. It
was for this last reason, of course, that John Rickman regarded
the question about the occupations of *persons* as an entire
failure 'from the impossibility of deciding whether females
of the family, children, and servants were to be classed as of
no occupation, or of the occupation of the adult males of the
family'.[5] In the census of 1811 he accordingly asked the
Overseers to provide occupational returns on families, and he
repeated this procedure in 1821 in spite of the fact that other
problems of enumeration had been noticed. For example,
'in the answers respecting the Families employed in Agriculture', he wrote, 'a remarkable proof occurred of the difficulty
of putting any Question which shall be universally understood.
In some places the *Occupiers* of Land, but not *Labourers* in
Agriculture, are supposed to belong to that Class; in other
places exactly the contrary'. He was not, apparently, unduly
worried by this problem. 'Such mistakes', he continued,
'were usually apparent, and of course corrected in forming
the Abstract.'[6]

The results of the censuses of 1811 and 1821 demonstrate the degree to which the inclusion under the residual, 'Other', of many individuals who should have been in the first two categories, undoubtedly inflated the proportion for 1801 (Table 6.3).

TABLE 6.3
Families by occupational class in England and Wales, 1811 and 1821

| | numbers | | percentage | |
	1811	1821	1811	1821
Agriculture	770,199	847,957	36.0	34.0
Trade, Manufactures, Handicraft	959,632	1,159,984	44.8	46.5
Other	412,316	485,491	19.2	19.5
Total	2,142,147	2,493,432	100.0	100.0

(Derived from the 'General Summary', *Abstracts of the Answers and Returns to the 1811 Census of Great Britain* (1812), p. 509, and 'General Summary', *Abstracts of the Answers and Returns to the 1821 Census of Great Britain* (1822), p. 542).

On the other hand, if the residual category of 1801 is reduced to roughly the proportions of 1811 and 1821 (19.0 per cent) and the remaining percentage (57.8 minus 19 per cent) redistributed proportionately between the other two classes, Agriculture becomes responsible for roughly 39 per cent of the 1801 figures, and Trade, Manufactures and Handicraft for roughly 42 per cent. The twenty-year comparisons of these two classes, giving a surplus of industry over agriculture of 3 per cent in 1801, 8.8 per cent in 1811 and 12.5 per cent in 1821, do not seem unreasonable indicators of the industrial growth of the time. Despite Rickman's misgivings about the accuracy of the statistics, more can be made of structural comparisons from these early censuses than has customarily been the case. Although they are 'somewhat frustrating sources', they are nevertheless 'important',[7] and provided it is understood that the analysis of social structure in the nineteenth century must perforce always be rather crude, comparisons based on rough estimates of this kind may be used, not only at the national but at county, borough and parish levels.

Rickman, to be sure, also declared himself dissatisfied with the family method of assessing occupation on the ground that it was difficult to define a family. Accordingly, in 1831 he supplemented the question on the occupational category of families with a question about the occupations of males, aged 20 years and upwards, on the assumption that men who have 'arrived at Twenty Years of Age' have usually settled 'in their occupations for life'.[8] He also introduced a further number of subdivisions, possibly as a means of simplifying the preparation of Abstracts, but also undoubtedly because he had a concept of the social structure in mind. Thus, agriculture was now divided into (1) occupiers employing labourers, (2) occupiers *not* employing labourers, and (3) agricultural labourers. Such a 'Division of Classes', he wrote, was 'more generally illustrative of the grade and condition of those under whose care the soil is cultivated',[9] although he went on to add the cautious rider, 'in what degree, this minute analysis of Social life may be useful in Statistical investigation, experience only can decide'.[10] The 'grade and condition' of those employed in Trade, Manufacture and Handicraft was not made so obviously apparent in the subdivisions of this census, but this category as a whole would seem to have been replaced by (4) capitalists, bankers, professional and educated, (5) employed in manufacture or in making manufacturing machinery, and (6) employed in retail trade or in handicrafts as masters or workmen. 'Other' seems similarly to have been replaced by (7) labourers not employed in agriculture, (8) male servants, and (9) other males. At least, if these two categories are assumed to be subdivided in this way, the occupational class structure shown in Table 6.4 may be estimated, for comparison with those in Tables 6.1 and 6.3.

On this occasion the 'industrial' dominance over agriculture for the employment of men of 'upwards of twenty years' was 12.9 per cent as compared with 12.5 per cent for families in 1821, suggesting that the estimated 'Other' category which may be said to have increased by 4.2 per cent between 1821 and 1831 (Tables 6.3 and 6.4) contains some men who should have been included under 'Trade, Manufactures and Handicraft'. Nevertheless, the general trend in the statistics follows the line which might have been expected.

TABLE 6.4
Estimated occupational classes of males aged 20 and upwards,
England and Wales, 1831

	numbers	percentage
Agriculture	1,075,912	31.7
Trade, Manufactures, Handicraft	1,512,914	44.6
Other	805,864	23.7
Total	3,394,690	100.0

(Derived from 'Preface' to the *Abstracts of the Answers and Returns to the 1831 Census of Great Britain*, (1833), Vol. 1, p. xiii.)

In considering whether more use should be made of these early census reports for numerical estimates of social structure, it is pertinent to consider whether the class divisions employed for agriculture in 1831 are capable of extension to other occupational categories, despite the failure of the census compilers to do this. It is possible to take exception to the agricultural analysis as it stands. Dyos and Baker, for example, have objected that the *'agricultural self-employed* and *agricultural labourers* were not always so sharply different in social status as might appear, though landowners operating on a very small scale were still superior socially to the men they employed'.[11] Was, however, the leaseholder employing one labourer so very different from the freeholding *paterfamilias* who relied solely on his own labour and that of his family? Any occupational classification used for social structure analysis is certain to raise questions of this kind; for the designated middle class of three classes is certain to contain some persons who overlap in status the occupations on either side, and *vice versa*. Short of abandoning structural analysis altogether, occupational classifications may be used on the assumption that discrepancies in one direction have been balanced by discrepancies in the other. On this basis the occupational structure in agriculture in 1831 may be seen in 'class' terms in Table 6.5.

As it happens, these proportions are almost identical with those in agriculture in 1851[12] when the comparable position in 'Trades' was roughly 10 per cent employers, 5 per cent self-employed, and 85 per cent employees.[13] If it is assumed

TABLE 6.5
Sub-divisions in occupational status of males, aged 20 and over,
in agriculture, England and Wales, 1831

	numbers	percentage
I Occupiers employing labourers	161,188	15.0
II Occupiers not employing labourers	114,849	10.7
III Agricultural labourers	799,875	74.3
Total agricultural	1,075,912	100.0

that in both Agriculture and in Trade, Manufactures and
Handicraft little structural change had occurred in respect of
occupational status over the twenty years, these percentages
may be used to make estimates for the earlier period. Thus
the 185,187 male Capitalists, etc. of 1831 may be assumed to
include no manual labourers and therefore be divided into
two-thirds employers, one-third self-employed: the 1,327,727
men employed in Retail Trade, Handicrafts, Manufacture and
Making Machinery may similarly be divided in the proportions
10:5:85; and the 805,864 labourers not employed in Agriculture may be wholly deemed to have been 'labourers'.
Allocating estimated employers to Class I, estimated self-
employed to Class II and employees to Class III, the following
structural analysis is obtained for Trade, Manufactures,
Handicrafts and Other, and for the combination of these
groups with those in Table 6.5 above (see Table 6.6).

Thus, the census of 1831 may be said to be the first to
provide the kind of detail which makes possible structural

TABLE 6.6
Estimated Social Class composition, males, aged 20 and over,
England and Wales, 1831

Social Class	Occupations other than in Agriculture		All occupations	
	numbers	percentage	numbers	percentage
I	256,231	11.1	417,419	12.3
II	128,115	5.6	242,964	7.2
III	1,934,432	83.4	2,734,307	80.6
Total	2,318,778	100.0	3,394,690	100.0

TABLE 6.7
Estimated social class composition, males, aged 20 and over,
in Devonshire and Lancashire, 1831

(a) Devonshire

Social Class	Agriculture		All other occupations		All occupations	
	Nos.	%	Nos.	%	Nos.	%
I	9,328	19.4	7,638	11.2	16,956	14.6
II	3,356	7.0	3,819	5.6	7,175	6.2
III	35,311	73.6	56,736	83.2	92,047	79.2
Total	47,995	100.0	68,193	100.0	116,188	100.0

(b) Lancashire

Social Class	Agriculture		All other occupations		All occupations	
	Nos.	%	Nos.	%	Nos.	%
I	6,658	17.8	30,103	10.9	36,761	11.7
II	9,714	26.0	15,051	5.5	24,765	7.9
III	20,949	56.1	230,622	83.6	251,571	80.3
Total	37,321	100.0	275,776	100.0	313,097	100.0

(c) Exeter

Social Class	Agriculture		All other occupations		All occupations	
	Nos.	%	Nos.	%	Nos.	%
I	15	7.7	782	12.3	797	12.1
II	25	12.8	392	6.1	417	6.3
III	156	79.6	5,203	81.6	5,359	81.5
Total	196	100.0	6,377	100.0	6,573	100.0

(d) Liverpool

Social Class	Agriculture		All other occupations		All occupations	
	Nos.	%	Nos.	%	Nos.	%
I	39	11.6	5,624	12.7	5,663	12.7
II	165	49.1	2,812	6.3	2,977	6.7
III	132	39.3	35,954	81.0	36,086	80.7
Total	336	100.0	44,390	100.0	44,726	100.0

analysis along lines which eventually led to the Registrar General's socio-economic groupings, though strict comparisons with twentieth century data are not valid; and a more extended treatment of this early census information, using varying estimates of the ratios of employers, self-employed persons and manual employees, is needed. Some indication of the stability and uniformity of the general social structure, despite marked regional and local variations in agriculture, is seen in the examples on p. 188 (Table 6.7).

Unfortunately, the 1841 census returns did not distinguish between the three classes in agriculture. Instead the compilers used a mixed three-fold classification of (1) farmers and graziers; (2) agricultural labourers; (3) gardeners, nurserymen and florists. However, this census represents the first tentative steps away from a structural analysis based on social standing towards the system of Orders and Sub-Orders, devised by reference to the materials worked upon by the individuals in diverse occupations, which was introduced in 1851 and which dominated census occupational enumerations for the rest of the century.

By comparison with 1830, the three main occupational groupings are shown in Table 6.8.

Thus, rough estimates of the occupational class structure of the country, over forty years, can be made from these statistics (Table 6.9).

The returns from the 1841 census do not preclude the possibility of making a rough estimate of the class structure at that time. For example, since the social divisions in agri-

TABLE 6.8
Estimated occupational class of males, aged 20 and over,
in England and Wales, 1841

	numbers	percentage
Agriculture	1,041,980	25.7
Trade, Manufactures, Handicraft	2,000,560	49.3
Other	1,017,386	25.1
Total	4,059,926	100.0

(Derived from the *Census of Great Britain, 1841, Abstract of the Answers and Returns, Occupations* (1844), pp. 52–3.)

TABLE 6.9
Estimated change in occupational class structure,
England and Wales, 1801 — 1841.

	percentages				
	1801	1811	1821	1831	1841
Agriculture	39.0	36.0	34.0	31.7	25.7
Trade, Manufacture, Handicraft	42.0	44.8	46.5	44.6	49.3
Other	19.0	19.2	19.5	23.7	25.1
	100.0	100.0	100.0	100.0	100.0

culture seem to have been unchanged in 1851 as in 1831, the
crude proportions 15:10:75 (derived from Table 6.5 and
footnote 12) may not unreasonably be used for 1841, along
with the other conventions already employed for the analysis
of the 1831 statistics (Table 6.6). The estimates shown in
Table 6.10 have been derived (compare Table 6.6).

In 1851 George Graham, William Farr and Horace Mann
introduced a system for the classification of occupations
which took as its point of departure not the social standing
of an occupation in the community, but its impact on the
personalities of those who followed it. Stating that in the
past the work a man did could be inferred from his characteristic dress, they went on to claim that occupations could
be distinguished by (1) the skill, talent or intelligence exercised in them, (2) the tools, instruments, machines and
'structures' employed in the work, (3) the materials which
were worked upon, (4) the processes of making or manufacturing used, and (5) the products which are the outcome.

TABLE 6.10
Estimated Social Class composition, males aged 20 and over
England and Wales, 1841

Social Class	Occupations other than in Agriculture		All occupations	
	numbers	percentage	numbers	percentage
I	341,968	11.3	498,265	12.3
II	170,978	5.7	275,176	6.8
III	2,505,000	83.0	3,286,465	80.9
Total	3,017,946	100.0	4,059,926	100.0

All these elements and their conflicting claims have been considered in the classification but, in conformity with the first notions of mankind of which we have record, the greatest weight has been given to the *materials* in which people work, as they generally imply important modifications not only in the tools, in the machines, in the processes, and in the products, but in the characters of the men. By his trade, and by the matter which surrounds him, how different is the blacksmith from the tailor; the shoemaker from the hairdresser; the butcher from the baker; the horsedealer from the grocer; the sweep from the navvy; the fisherman, the waggoner, the pedler, and the cotton-spinner, from each other![14]

Viewed thus, each of the seventeen 'classes' — and even each 'sub-class' — may be thought of as socially distinctive, and in this sense the 1851 and subsequent systems of classification comprise a social structure of some importance. However, this type of structure necessarily lacks the element of superiority-inferiority which is implicit in the social standing or class structure analysis as this is usually understood. Thus, the 23 'Orders' used in the 1911 census range across the spectrum of classes employed by Stevenson (Table 6.11).

Hence, any attempt to use the Graham, Farr, and Mann system must take account of the fact that the impact of the materials worked on a man's personality is different from the impact of his social standing in the community.

The use of occupation data for the analysis of social structure, therefore, requires a series of *ad hoc* adjustments to be made to the returns printed in the census reports from 1851 to 1901. Such adjustments are of two types: (1) to make the occupational classifications as comparable as possible from census to census; (2) to make as reasonable a subdivision of the returns under separate occupations as possible wherever there is evidence that people of different social standing have been put together under the same occupational name. Two attempts have already been made to derive estimates which are crudely comparable at the occupational level. First, in 1886 Charles Booth published an account of the occupations of the people which included a statistical appendix on the figures from 1841 to 1881, divided into eleven separate 'industrial' groups, each further subdivided into 'occupations' numbering 51 in all.[16] Secondly, in the 1911 Census Report on Occupations and Industries the Registrar General published

TABLE 6.11
Class distribution of occupational Orders 1911

Order No.	Title	Class 1	2	3	4	5	6	7	8[15]
I	General and Local Government	1	1	—	3	—	—	—	—
II	Defence of the Country	2	—	—	2	—	—	—	—
III	Professional Occupations	14	14	—	—	—	—	—	—
IV	Domestic Offices or Services	—	1	4	7	—	—	—	—
V	Commercial Occupations	11	1	—	—	—	—	—	—
VI	Conveyance of Men, Goods, and Messages	1	4	8	5	9	—	—	—
VII	Agriculture	—	1	1	5	—	—	—	1
VIII	Fishing	—	—	—	1	—	—	—	—
IX	Mines and Quarries	4	1	—	2	5	—	8	—
X	Metals, Machines, Implements and Conveyances	—	2	30	25	8	—	—	—
XI	Precious Metals, Jewels, Watches, Instruments etc.	—	2	7	—	—	—	—	—
XII	Building and Construction	2	1	13	1	7	—	—	—
XIII	Wood Furniture etc.	—	4	5	8	—	—	—	—
XIV	Bricks, Cement, Pottery	—	—	1	2	2	—	—	—
XV	Chemicals, Oil, etc.	1	—	3	6	4	—	—	—
XVI	Skins, Leather, Hair etc.	—	1	2	4	1	—	—	—
XVII	Paper, Prints, Books	—	3	7	3	—	—	—	—
XVIII	Textile Fabrics	—	2	—	—	—	10	—	—
XIX	Dress	—	10	6	5	—	—	—	—
XX	Food, Drink, Lodging	1	16	5	10	1	—	—	—
XXI	Gas, Water, etc.	—	—	—	4	1	—	—	—
XXII	Other General and Undefined Workers and Dealers	—	9	3	9	6	—	—	—
XXIII	Unoccupied etc.	2	1	—	—	—	—	—	—
Total		39	74	95	102	44	10	8	1

(Derived from the *74th Annual Report of the Registrar General, op.cit. Table 28A, et seq.*)

a table containing a much more detailed set of comparisons from 1881 to 1911.[17] Both sets of figures are subdivided by age and sex. They have been used by way of example to show the decline of agriculture over seventy years (Table 6.12)

The details of the class distribution of occupational Orders

TABLE 6.12
Estimated proportion of the male population of England and Wales
employed in agriculture, 1841 — 1911

Census date	Booth, age 20+	Registrar General, age 15+
1841	28.3	—
1851	27.0	—
1861	24.1	—
1871	19.5	—
1881	15.8	14.9
1891	—	12.1
1901	—	10.5
1911	—	9.2

in 1911 (Table 6.11) has made it plain that any such crude classification is almost certain to include a number of the Social Classes in any occupational cluster. Booth's 51 varieties are no exception, and as can be seen in Appendix V only a minority of his 'occupations' may reasonably be said to have been composed of the members of a single Social Class, whether the 1911 or the 1951 system for assigning such class membership is used. Consequently, there must always be some unknown dimension of error in any attempt to apply Social Class divisions to Booth's occupational headings, and the attempt makes sense only on the gross assumption that the errors in one direction are cancelled out by compensatory errors in the opposite direction (see also above, chapter 2). Thus the following treatment of Booth's figures (Table 6.13) is based upon rudimentary and obviously false premises. Where an occupation is deemed to have included the members of more than one Social Class, Booth's figures have been divided by the number of Social Classes assigned to that occupation and each fraction *counted* separately under each Class heading. Since it is most unlikely that 50 per cent of miners, say, were in Class III and 50 per cent in Class IV at any census, it is assumed that the error involved is redressed by some adjustment of the Class totals over the whole range of occupations. Clearly almost any other convention could have been employed but this convention has the advantage of simplicity and has been used here for illustrative purposes only.

TABLE 6.13

Estimated Social Class composition of males, aged 20 and over, England and Wales, 1841 – 1881 (thousands)

	1841		1851		1861		1871		1881	
	No.	%	No.	%	No.	%	No.	%	No.	%
I	355.1	9.4	395.3	8.5	472.6	9.1	566.1	9.9	696.5	10.9
II	464.6	12.3	646.2	14.0	715.2	13.8	772.1	13.5	816.7	12.8
III	758.7	20.0	930.5	20.1	1083.7	21.0	1189.6	20.7	1371.3	21.5
IV	1675.3	44.1	1999.8	43.2	2161.8	41.8	2208.3	38.4	2315.4	36.3
V	538.9	14.2	654.8	14.2	739.0	14.3	1004.7	17.5	1727.7	18.4
Total	3792.6	100.0	4626.6	100.0	5172.3	100.0	5740.8	100.0	6372.6	100.0

(To reduce the number of Social Classes from eight in 1911, as in Table 6.11, to five in this table, the 1951 system of classification was used for occupations grouped in Classes 6, 7 and 8.)

In the analysis of comparative data from the 1911 census a less crude set of assumptions have been employed, since the figures obtained in the 1911 census itself are all immediately open to classification by reference to Stevenson's categories or — with rather more difficulty — to the 1951 version of Social Class. Hence any amalgamation of classes which has occurred under single occupational headings in the figures from early censuses may be 'unscrambled' in terms of proportions calculated from the 1911 figures and often from the 1901 figures as well. Thus Tanners (Class IV) included Dealers in 1881 and 1891, but the latter were put under 'Dealers in Skins, Leather, Hair and Feathers' (Class II) in 1901 and 1911. The procedure adopted to separate out the Dealers from the Tanners in 1881 and 1891 consists in calculating the proportion of Dealers in all the sub-groups of Leather, etc., occupations at the two later dates and to work back by geometrical progression to estimates of the proportion of Dealers on the other occasions. All the relevant occupations have then been reduced by the relevant proportions and the sum of the reductions recorded as the estimated number of Dealers in 1881 and 1891. The final figures are presented, by occupation, in Appendix VI.

In other cases, for example that of distinguishing between Naval Officers and Men, the procedure was less tedious because the geometrical progression, once estimated, could be applied directly to the data for 1881 and 1891. In yet others, where only in the 1911 figures were occupations of different Social Classes separately distinguished, the simple 1911 proportions have been applied to all three previous censuses. Where, on the other hand, the separations had been made from the time of the 1891 census and a geometrical progression could be fitted to the proportions, a mean of them was employed for estimating the 1881 figures.

The comparison between these two systems has been made here for two reasons. First, since 1911 the allocation of occupations to the five Social Classes has been modified from census to census in order to accord with what the 1961 census called 'changes in economic conditions and with the intention of preserving the gradient rather than literal continuity'.[18] A comparison of the same *data* classified according to different systems, used forty years apart, indicates the range of differences which may occur in any attempt to analyse the social structure in this way, when one method is compared with another. In this instance, as Table 6.14 shows, the selection of the 1951 system of classification in preference to that of 1911, while it leaves Classes II and IV virtually unchanged, augments Class III by nearly 50 per cent, largely at the expense of Classes I and V. Indeed, Class III predominates in this system, whereas under that of 1911, Classes III and IV predominate, with the latter slightly in the ascendent. Secondly, recent attempts to estimate the social structure of selected districts in the nineteenth century from the census returns of the time have employed the 1951 system of classification[19] or some modification of it.[20] Both, for example, include Clerks in Class III, as opposed to the 1911 practice of including them in Class I.

Of course, as David Glass pointed out in 1940, 'a very large arbitrary element is involved in grouping occupations — on *a priori* grounds — into social classes' and, as he also emphasised, especially where estimates of social mobility are the object of the exercise, 'more realistic results might be obtained if, instead of constructing arbitrary groups based on occupations, sociologists attempted to discover, by means of empirical investigation, what are the factors which produce, or are at least associated with, roughly homogeneous culture groups'.[21] The outcome of this observation was a series of studies on social mobility in Britain and an attempt to create a scale of ranking derived from enquiries amongst a sample of the population.[22] These showed that although there was a high degree of consensus on the social grading of occupations in the 1940s there was, at the same time, always a range of ranking employed. Thus, while 54 per cent of the respondents put Routine Clerks in Class III, 6 per cent put them in Class II, 37 per cent in Class IV and 3 per cent in Class V.[23] Class III, indeed, tended to be the 'residual' class for those occupations which the rankers were not sure about.[24] This element of ignorance applies to all surveys of this kind. Thus, Reiss and his colleagues in America found local and regional variations at work similar to that carried out in Britain, they concluded:

while the general public may be expected to know something about such occupations as barber, bartender, shoe-shiner, janitor, and policeman, one wonders how large the proportions of 'don't knows' or random responses would be to a request to rate glazier, job-setter, molder or photo-engraver, not to mention a request to rate differentially the operatives in such manufacturing industries as meat products, dairy products, bakery products, and beverage industries. Actually, we know too little about the psychological salience of occupations for this kind of speculation to be worth much.[25]

TABLE 6.14
Social Class composition of males over 15,
England and Wales, 1881 – 1911 (Estimates)

(a) using the 1911 system of classification

	percentages			
Social Class	*1881*	*1891*	*1901*	*1911*
I	11.6	12.1	12.5	12.3
II	14.5	14.9	15.1	16.8
III	27.7	27.2	28.3	27.9
IV	29.2	28.6	27.7	28.5
V	17.0	17.2	16.4	14.5
	100.0	100.0	100.0	100.0

(b) using the 1951 system of classification

	percentages			
Social Class	*1881*	*1891*	*1901*	*1911*
I	2.1	2.3	2.5	2.7
II	14.6	14.4	14.5	15.3
III	39.8	40.6	42.5	43.1
IV	30.5	29.6	29.2	29.2
V	13.1	13.1	11.4	9.7
	100.0	100.0	100.0	100.0

(Derived from the calculations given in Appendix VI).

This was true in 1961 of the people at that time. It is equally true of data collected nearly a century ago. Obviously, there is always an arbitrary element in any ranking system. What is important is not the fact of arbitrariness, but whether the basis of the ranking has been made plain by the ranker.

The justification for the arbitrary judgements made in this chapter lies in this fact. If there is a criticism to be levied at the various methods employed, however, it is that the number of different systems used might have been increased so that the estimates could have recorded that the 'true' figure lay between the range and nearest to one or other of the calculated numbers in a class. Nevertheless, enough has been done to show that the social structure can be analysed from the printed census data and that it is not necessary to conclude, as David Marsh has done, that comparison between censuses cannot be made 'because of changes in classification of occupation'.[26] While it is undoubtedly useful to provide data on the separate occupations, as he has done, and even more accurate to go back to the occupations listed in the original returns, as French and English historical demographers regularly do,[27] it is notorious that such work is laborious, to the degree that it will be a very long time before the whole of the nineteenth century returns will have been worked over in this way. In the meantime there is no need merely to wait for the work to be done. Assumptions such as those employed here may validly be applied to the published volumes to give a general impression of the social structure at a given census date for the country as a whole, and even, where local and regional details about occupations are available, for towns, counties and regions. Provided that the procedures are always made clear, gross changes in such structures over time may also be estimated. There is a wealth of data in the census volumes still to be analysed in this way.

NOTES

1. General Register Office, *Census 1961*, England and Wales, *Occupational Tables* (HMSO, 1966), p. xiii
2. *Ibid*, p. xi
3. T.H.C. Stevenson, 'Review of the Vital Statistics of the Year, 1911', *Seventy-Fourth Annual Report of the Registrar General of Births, Deaths and Marriages in England and Wales, 1911* (HMSO, 1913), p. xli.
4. *Occupational Tables*, 1966, *op. cit.* p. xiii
5. John Rickman, 'Statement of Progress in the Enquiry regarding the occupations of Families and Persons, and the Duration of

Life', *Comparative Account of the Population of Great Britain in the Years 1801, 1811, 1821 and 1831* (1831), p. 3.

6. 'Preliminary Observations', *Abstracts of the Answers and Returns to the 1811 Census of Great Britain* (1812), p. x. Italics in the original.

7. W.A. Armstrong, 'Social Structure from the Early Census Returns', in E.A. Wrigley (ed.), *An Introduction to English Historical Demography* (1966), p. 209.

8. Rickman, 'Statement of Progress', *op. cit.* p. 3.

9. 'Preface' to the *Abstract of the Answers and Returns, Enumeration, Census of Great Britain, 1831*, (1833), Vol. 1, p. ix.

10. *Ibid*, p. xi.

11. H.J. Dyos and A.B.M. Baker, 'The Possibilities of Computerising Census Data', H.J. Dyos, ed. *The Study of Urban History* (1968), p. 105.

12. *Census of Great Britain, 1851, Population Tables, II*, Vol. 1 (1854), Table 32, p. lxxix. 133,620 farmers (15.0 per cent) employed 665,651 labourers (74.7 per cent). 91,698 farmers (10.3 per cent) employed no labourers.

13. *Ibid*, Table 31, p. lxxviii: 87,270 masters (10.2 per cent) employed 727,468 men (84.9 per cent): 41,732 masters (4.9 per cent) employed none.

14. *Census of Great Britain, 1851*, II, 1, *op. cit*, p. lxxxiii.

15. Stevenson introduced 'three other "classes" or, rather, important groups of the working-class population which it seemed desirable to distinguish separately, and they are therefore not treated either as skilled or unskilled. Class 6 consists of textiles workers, Class 7 of miners, and Class 8 of agricultural labourers'. T.H.C. Stevenson, *op. cit*, p. xli.

16. Charles Booth, 'Occupations of the People of the United Kingdom, 1801–91', *Journal of the Statistical Society*, 49 (1886), Appendix A (i) pp. 351–371.

17. *Census of England and Wales, 1911* Vol. 10, *Occupations and Industries*, Part I, Table 26, pp. 540–551.

18. *Census of England and Wales, 1961, Occupation Tables*, (1966) p. xiii, footnote.

19. W.A. Armstrong, 'The Classification of Occupations', Appendix D of Wrigley, ed. *op. cit.* pp. 272–3. See also W.A. Armstrong, 'The use of information about Occupation' in E.A. Wrigley ed. *Nineteenth-century Society* (1972) Ch. 6, which was published after this chapter was written and provides an industrial classification for 1841–1891.

20. Dyos and Baker, *op. cit.* note 29, p. 101.

21. D.V. Glass, *Population Policies and Movements in Europe*, (1940) note mm, pp. 431–2.

22. C.A. Moser and J.R. Hall, 'The Social Grading of Occupations' in D. V. Glass, ed. *Social Mobility in Britain* (1954).

23. *Ibid*, Table 4, p. 39. In point of fact the rankers were asked to use

the letters A to E, but the Classes I–V can hardly be distinguished from such 'grades'.

24.   *Ibid*, p. 38. For a later discussion of this attempt to grade occupations socially see J.H. Goldthorpe and K. Hope, 'Occupational Grading and Occupational Prestige' in Keith Hope, ed. *The Analysis of Social Mobility, Methods and Approaches*, (1972) and K.I. Macdonald, 'The Hall-Jones Scale: a Note on the Interpretation of the main British Prestige Coding' in J.M. Ridge, ed. *Mobility in Britain Reconsidered*, (1974).

25.   A.J. Reiss, Jr. et. al., *Occupations and Social Status* (1961), p. 130.

26.   D.C. Marsh, *The Changing Social Structure of England and Wales, 1871–1951* (1958), p. 194. In the 2nd edition (1965) Marsh is more open to making comparisons between 1931, 1951 and 1961, p. 198.

27.   Wrigley, ed. *op. cit.* passim. See also T.H. Hollingsworth *Historical Demography* (1969), Ch. 2.

APPENDIX V

Social class classifications of 1911 and 1951, as applied approximately to Charles Booth's categories, 1886.

Booth's industrial classification of occupations	Social class categories employed 1911	1951
A. Agriculture		
Farmers and their Relatives	II	II
Agricultural Labourers and Shepherds	IV	IV
Nurserymen, Gardeners, etc.	IV	IV.
Drainage and Machinery Attendants	IV	IV
Breeding and Dealing	IV	IV
B. Fishing		
Fishermen	IV	IV
C. Mining		
Miners	III IV	III IV
Quarrying and Brickmaking	IV V	III IV
Salt and Water Works	IV V	IV V
D. Building		
Management	I	II
Operative Builders	III IV V	III IV V
Roadmaking	I V	II IV V
E. Manufacture		
Machinery and Tools	III IV V	III IV V
Shipbuilding	III IV V	III IV
Metal Workers	III IV V	III IV
Earthenware, etc.	IV	III IV
Fuel, Gas and Chemicals	IV V	IV V
Furs, Leather, Glue etc.	III IV V	III V
Wood, Furniture and Carriages	III IV	III IV
Paper, Floorcloth and Waterproof	III IV	III IV
Textiles and Dyeing	III IV	III IV
Dress	III IV	III IV
Food, Drink and Smoking	III IV V	III IV
Watches, Instruments and Toys	II III	II III
Printing and Bookbinding	III	III
Unspecified	III IV V	III IV V

Booth's industrial classification of occupations	Social class categories employed 1911					1951				
	I	II	III	IV	V	I	II	III	IV	V
F. Transport										
Navigation and Docks		II	III	IV	V		II	III		V
Railways	I		III	IV	V		II	III	IV	V
Roads		II	III	IV	V		II	III		V
G. Dealing										
Raw Materials	I		III				II	III		
Clothing Materials and Dress		II					II			
Food, Drink and Smoking	I	II					II	III		
Lodging and Coffee Houses		II	III	IV			II	III	IV	
Furniture, Utensils and Stationery		II					II			
General Dealers and unspecified		II		IV				III	IV	
H. Industrial Service										
Commercial	I						II	III		
General Labour					V					V
Public Service and Professional										
Administration	I	II		IV		I	II	III	IV	
Army and Navy	I			IV		I		III		
Police and Prisons				IV				III		
Law	I					I		III		
Medicine	I	II				I	II	III		
Art and Amusement	I	II				I	II	III		
Literature and Science	I	II				I	II	III		
Education	I	II				I	II			
Religion	I	II				I		III		
Domestic Service										
In-door			III	IV				III	IV	
Out-door			III	IV				III	IV	
Extra			III	IV				III	IV	
Property Owning and Indefinite										
Property Owning	I					I				
Indefinite	Omitted					Omitted				

APPENDIX VI

Social class classification of occupations, 1881–1911, based on estimates derived from the Census of England and Wales, 1911, Vol. X, Occupations and Industries, Part I, (London, 1913), Table 26, pp. 540–51.

In the following tables the figures have been either taken directly from the Census Table 26, as is the case with 1911 figures, or calculated on the basis of 1911 proportions or 1901–11 geometrical increases from the figures for the preceding decades. Occupations have been attributed to classes on the nearest approximation of title to that classified in the 74th Annual Report for the Registrar General, 1911 and in the census of 1951. The titles are, in fact, best understood by reference to Vol. X, pp. 540–551. This is apparent of titles below beginning 'Other . . .' or 'Others in . . .' but it is also true of other occupations which have in fact been abbreviated from the original for convenience.

Class IA

Occupation	1881	1891	1901	1911
Accountants	7,456	7,923	9,026	9,479
Architects	6,875	7,779	10,775	11,122
Army Officers	10,252	12,969	13,115	16,206
Authors, etc.	5,778	7,473	9,807	12,005
Bankers, Bank Clerks	15,932	20,765	30,036	39,881
Barristers and Solicitors	17,386	19,978	20,998	21,380
Clergymen, Church of England	21,663	24,232	25,235	24,859
Clergymen, Other	11,823	12,568	14,660	15,583
Dentists	3,538	4,562	5,149	7,337
Engineers	8,667	9,042	10,268	7,207
Finance Agents, Clerks	601	989	978	3,165
Insurance Officials, Clerks	4,124	10,139	20,812	41,586
Medical Practitioners	15,091	18,936	22,486	24,553
Naval Officers	2,389	2,942	4,797	6,997
Scientists, etc.	1,170	1,849	3,171	6,171
Surveyors	4,849	5,059	5,745	4,028
Total Class IA	137,594	167,205	207,058	251,559

All attributed to Class I, 1911; and to Class I, 1951.

Class IB

Occupation	1881	1891	1901	1911
Civil Service Officers and Clerks	19,556	29,233	42,403	61,152
Coal Mine Owners, Managers	2,064	3,445	4,313	6,293
Metal Mine Owners, Managers	192	321	402	585
Quarry Owners, Managers	964	985	1,411	1,220
Total Class IB	22,776	33,984	48,529	69,250

All attributed to Class I, 1911; 50 per cent to Class I and 50 per cent to Class II, 1951.

Class IC

Occupation	1881	1891	1901	1911
Brokers, Agents, Factors	30,601	36,173	41,086	41,404

All attributed to Class I, 1911; 33.3 per cent to Class I, 33.3 per cent to Class II and 33.3 per cent to Class III, 1951.

Class ID

Occupation	1881	1891	1901	1911
Auctioneers, House Agents etc.	9,995	11,714	13,932	17,613
Builders	23,821	25,959	40,114	39,723
Dealers in Stone etc.	2,451	2,032	2,375	1,807
Merchants (Commodity undefined)	10,287	8,372	5,132	5,402
Painters, Artists, etc.	5,428	5,521	6,151	7,410
Railway Officials, Clerks	34,249	42,264	66,538	84,086
Road Contractors, Surveyors	1,324	1,646	2,173	1,168
Salesmen, Buyers	3,145	3,803	1,908	1,204
Teachers, etc.	44,181	49,072	57,829	68,651
Total Class ID	134,881	150,383	196,152	227,064

All attributed to Class I, 1911; and to Class II, 1951

Class IE

Occupation	1881	1891	1901	1911
Chemists, Druggists	19,014	21,387	24,911	26,507
Commercial Clerks	173,161	221,044	298,001	353,622
Commercial Travellers	35,447	43,867	63,940	85,824
Insurance Agents	10,606	20,584	33,971	53,428
Law Clerks	23,549	26,244	32,705	33,345
Wine and Spirit Merchants	7,431	7,216	8,378	6,794
Total Class IE	269,208	340,342	461,906	559,520

All attributed to Class I, 1911; and to Class III, 1951

Class IF

Occupation	1881	1891	1901	1911
Private Means	82,840	97,379	93,381	52,432
Students	242,744	282,595	290,395	283,048
Total Class IF	325,584	379,974	383,776	335,480

All attributed to Class I, 1911; not classified, 1951

Class I — 1911 system of classification

Sub Groups	1881	1891	1901	1911
IA	137,594	167,205	207,058	251,559
IB	22,776	33,984	48,529	69,250
IC	30,601	36,173	41,086	41,404
ID	134,881	150,383	196,152	227,064
IE	269,208	340,342	461,906	559,520
IF	325,584	379,974	383,776	335,480
Total	920,644	1,108,061	1,338,507	1,484,277

Class I — 1951 system of classification

Sub Groups	1881	1891	1901	1911
IA	137,594	167,205	207,058	251,559
IB	11,388	16,992	24,264	34,625
IC	10,200	12,058	13,695	13,801
IIE (See below)	574	1,027	1,820	2,768
Total	159,756	197,282	246,837	302,753

Class IIA

Occupation	1881	1891	1901	1911
Bakers, Bread Dealers	15,562	21,850	30,155	43,259
Boot etc. Dealers	5,035	8,606	13,813	21,724
Butchers	74,765	88,628	102,190	120,651
Cattle Dealers	5,706	5,291	5,328	4,864
Church etc. Officials	4,469	5,894	5,653	7,791
Clothiers, Outfitters	6,936	10,686	17,323	26,562
Coal, Coke Merchants	19,397	21,555	23,540	26,255
Coffee, Eating House Keepers	5,488	7,425	11,869	15,895
Corn Dealers	11,441	12,379	15,353	17,748
Dealers in Instruments, Toys	1,193	1,839	2,851	5,084
Dealers in Skins, etc.	2,890	4,302	5,339	7,221
Dealers in Works of Art	1,047	1,438	2,165	3,796
Drapers	52,143	58,869	65,719	65,425
Engravers	3,575	3,644	4,050	4,887
Farmers, Graziers	203,308	201,872	202,745	208,750
Farmers' etc. Sons, Relatives	75,042	67,122	83,410	92,294
Fish Curers, Fishmongers	18,107	25,027	30,542	39,681
Furniture etc. Dealers	7,342	10,864	17,444	23,596
Greengrocers	22,230	29,554	39,735	50,979
Grocers	99,434	128,886	145,014	161,528
Hat Dealers	2,950	3,593	3,749	4,376
Horse, Cab etc. Proprieters	8,743	11,006	12,479	10,972
Hosiers, Haberdashers	4,792	5,572	6,672	7,459
Hospital, Institution Service	4,253	6,870	10,590	17,253
Inn, Hotel Keepers	70,199	66,947	76,207	81,670
Ironmongers, Iron Dealers	14,915	19,530	25,540	28,955
Lodging House Keepers	4,482	6,002	6,543	9,137
Merchant Service, Pilots etc.	7,044	7,094	6,506	6,661
Milliners, Dress Makers	2,687	4,130	2,733	5,262
Mineral Water Manufacture	3,571	4,700	8,811	8,598
Navigation Service on Shore	4,525	5,106	4,141	5,147

Class IIA (Continued)

Occupation	1881	1891	1901	1911
Officers of Commercial				
Societies	360	1,463	1,671	3,365
Officers of Local				
Authorities	17,933	19,710	26,337	54,257
Other Dealers in Dress	1,397	1,743	1,999	2,630
Other Dealers in Food	1,230	1,746	3,602	4,388
Other Dealers in Metals	382	1,060	5,132	13,241
Other Dealers in Textiles	15,412	14,675	22,892	34,743
Others in Literature	945	1,526	1,437	7,085
Pawnbrokers	7,215	9,007	9,940	11,927
Photographers	5,231	7,909	10,980	11,765
Provision Dealers	13,517	13,541	16,353	18,309
Railway, Canal				
Contractors	1,173	1,981	573	1,143
Receiving Office Keepers	–	–	–	307
Scripture Readers etc.	2,964	5,115	5,292	4,972
Shirt Makers	1,338	2,089	3,952	4,922
Shop Keepers, etc.,				
Undefined	28,419	27,184	22,928	41,058
Sick Nurses	492	600	1,092	1,257
Stationers and Other				
Paper Dealers	9,938	11,101	12,367	13,806
Timber etc. Dealers	6,627	8,046	8,388	9,812
Tobacconists	5,085	6,041	10,079	11,625
Veterinary Surgeons	2,468	3,191	2,938	2,610
Total Class IIA	885,397	994,009	1,156,161	1,386,702

All attributed to Class II, 1911; and to Class II, 1951.

Class IIB

Occupation	1881	1891	1901	1911
Jewellers, Watch makers	44,770	44,559	48,906	47,974

All attributed to   Class II, 1911; 50 per cent to Class II and 50 per cent to Class III, 1951

	Class IIC			
Occupation	1881	1891	1901	1911
Actors	2,180	3,586	5,994	9,002
Advertising, Bill Posting Agents	708	1,264	2,237	3,402
Art, Music, Theatre Service	1,098	1,968	5,372	13,668
Artificial Flower Makers	665	666	470	607
Bird, Animal Keepers etc.	1,085	1,800	1,037	1,778
Book Publishers, Sellers	9,421	10,957	11,721	13,245
Circular, Envelope Addressers	52	80	93	123
Educational Service	1,755	3,574	3,201	7,635
Engineers' and Surveyors' Assistants	1,224	1,277	1,449	1,025
Milksellers, Dairymen	20,242	27,570	33,004	45,735
Musicians, Singers	13,977	19,262	20,429	22,788
Other Dealers in Sundries	1,835	1,603	1,103	1,426
Other Food Manufacture	611	865	1,922	3,622
Performers, Exhibitors, etc.	4,243	7,725	11,890	27,169
Subordinate Medical Service	2,879	3,457	3,350	4,014
Telegraph, Telephone Service	4,433	6,806	8,858	8,693
Undertakers	1,682	2,393	2,858	3,502
Total Class IIC	68,090	94,853	114,988	167,434

All attributed to Class II, 1911; and to Class III, 1951.

	Class IID			
Occupation	1881	1891	1901	1911
Knackers, Cat's Meat Dealers	1,785	2,049	933	1,266

All attributed to Class II, 1911; and to Class V, 1951

	Class IIE			
Occupation	1881	1891	1901	1911
Newspaper Publishers	574	1,027	1,820	2,768

All attributed to Class II, 1911; and to Class I, 1951

Class IIF

Occupation	1881	1891	1901	1911
Pensioners	21,675	20,988	25,567	70,500
Retired Persons	131,003	192,941	262,175	351,707
Total Class IIF	152,678	213,929	287,742	422,207

All attributed to Class I, 1911; not classified, 1951

Class II — 1911 System of Classification

Sub-Group	1881	1891	1901	1911
IIA	885,397	994,009	1,156,161	1,386,702
IIB	44,770	44,559	48,906	47,974
IIC	68,090	94,853	114,988	167,434
IID	1,785	2,049	933	1,266
IIE	574	1,027	1,820	2,768
IIF	152,678	213,929	287,742	422,207
Total	1,153,294	1,350,426	1,610,550	2,028,351

Class II — 1951 System of Classification

Sub-Group	1881	1891	1901	1911
IB (see above)	11,388	16,992	24,264	34,625
IC (see above)	10,200	12,058	13,695	13,801
ID (see above)	134,881	150,383	196,152	227,064
IIA	885,397	994,009	1,156,161	1,386,702
IIB	22,385	22,279	24,453	23,987
IIID (see below)	19,373	18,194	22,623	22,141
IVC (see below)	5,874	8,656	11,377	20,303
IVD (see below)	—	—	—	1,242
Total	1,089,498	1,222,571	1,448,725	1,729,865

Class IIIA

Occupation	1881	1891	1901	1911
Bag and Box Makers	1,095	1,808	2,974	4,408
Blacksmiths	118,100	136,542	134,414	123,981
Boiler Makers	25,564	35,783	45,414	48,175

Class IIIA (Continued)

Occupation	1881	1891	1901	1911
Bone, Horn etc. Workers	1,899	2,008	1,651	1,147
Bookbinders	9,137	11,014	12,245	12,659
Brassfounders and fitters	23,090	27,822	31,948	23,052
Bricklayers	55,664	63,840	115,141	102,503
Cabinet Makers, etc.	58,836	67,173	83,603	82,712
Carpenters, Joiners	226,214	211,729	259,892	207,253
Cartridge, Firework Makers	743	1,308	3,418	2,854
Chimney Sweeps	6,644	7,648	6,770	7,673
Cooks (not Domestic)	2,846	4,881	6,885	10,312
Coppersmiths	3,706	4,125	4,651	5,041
Cutlers, Scissor Makers	15,846	16,888	14,706	14,102
Cycle and Car Manufacture	1,015	10,126	27,447	69,857
Dealers in Bricks, Earthenware	4,754	4,653	6,101	6,871
Die, Seal, Coin Makers	1,426	1,773	2,206	2,159
Electrical Workers	2,446	11,788	49,116	98,089
Envelope Makers	153	262	352	495
Filemakers	7,468	7,153	6,166	5,286
Fitters	58,227	78,496	143,042	151,903
Footwear Manufacture	178,034	184,702	177,457	164,142
Gamekeepers	12,546	13,654	16,456	16,982
Gasfitters, Locksmiths, etc.	15,946	15,026	17,329	18,085
Gunsmiths	7,302	8,816	9,863	7,054
Hairdressers	13,545	22,554	31,839	41,375
House and Shop Fittings etc.	2,496	3,867	6,845	13,453
Leather Goods Makers etc.	18,188	20,172	25,237	20,664
Lithographers	6,214	8,914	10,342	12,471
Makers of Toys, Sports Equipment	2,674	3,461	3,851	6,432
Masons	70,185	61,213	70,255	50,553
Millwrights	6,881	6,065	5,246	5,488
Motor Drivers, Chauffeurs	–	–	559	38,599
Musical Instrument Makers	8,275	10,983	13,519	15,655
Needle, Pin Makers	2,407	2,240	1,988	2,028
Oil and Colourmen	4,142	6,507	7,859	8,469
Other Dealers in Oils	1,414	1,608	2,409	3,485
Other Vehicle Makers	1,879	3,375	4,182	7,083

Class IIIA (Continued)

Occupation	1881	1891	1901	1911
Painters, Decorators, Glaziers	98,242	121,194	158,222	183,298
Paperhangers, Whitewashers	3,543	3,622	6,366	5,909
Paper Stainers	1,137	1,924	1,885	3,314
Pattern Makers	6,153	7,688	11,827	13,759
Plasterers	22,673	20,254	31,022	24,994
Plumbers	35,951	44,491	63,195	63,958
Printers	54,679	75,962	91,817	111,740
Railway Coach, etc. Makers	30,724	37,243	52,487	61,094
Railway Engine Drivers etc.	22,831	39,816	65,976	69,578
Railway Guards	10,225	12,892	20,827	21,137
Roller, Engravers, Cutters	790	970	1,766	2,437
Saddlers, etc.	20,330	22,172	25,237	20,664
Sawmakers	1,972	1,935	2,240	2,442
Scientific Instrument Makers	3,117	4,056	5,288	8,114
Ships' Platers, Rivetters	9,307	14,460	21,738	31,929
Shipwrights	23,833	25,789	27,002	27,618
Signalmen	24,228	24,574	24,793	25,939
Slaters	7,366	6,668	9,644	8,348
Slaughterers	1,317	2,316	3,562	2,631
Steel Pen Makers	212	273	401	439
Surgical Instrument Makers	1,086	1,372	3,148	6,717
Sword Makers	181	251	398	251
Tailors	98,919	105,592	117,131	120,494
Tobacco Pipe, etc Makers	1,433	1,253	1,314	1,595
Toolmakers	8,940	11,520	15,886	24,490
Type Cutters, Founders	1,072	1,182	1,238	1,312
Umbrella, Stick Makers	3,922	5,100	4,773	5,351
Waiters	3,682	9,037	9,774	22,958
Wheelwrights	28,232	27,345	28,349	23,461
Weighting Instrument Makers	2,182	2,839	4,088	8,228
Well, Mine Sinkers etc.	1,457	1,101	2,914	3,193
Wood Carvers, etc.	10,708	11,389	13,624	11,089
Workers in Textile Machinery etc.	3,823	4,812	8,991	12,725

Class IIIA (continued)

Occupation	1881	1891	1901	1911
Motor Van Drivers	—	—	64	4,456
Post Office				
Telegraphists etc.	2,164	3,322	4,324	4,241
Sea Cooks, etc.	16,399	16,518	15,141	15,444
Seamen	81,602	82,292	75,418	76,940
Total Class III A	1,621,413	1,833,804	2,293,090	2,449,544

Class IIIB

Occupation	1881	1891	1901	1911
Domestic, Indoor				
Servants	51,421	51,636	57,760	52,312
Metal Machinists	14,828	16,773	28,219	35,916
Omnibus Service	5,558	8,401	11,881	11,416
Tobacco Manufacture	5,731	6,143	7,113	7,706
Tramways Service	2,591	6,723	17,996	41,219
Total Class IIIB	80,129	89,676	122,969	148,569

All attributed to Class III, 1911; 50 per cent to Class III and 50 per cent to Class IV, 1951.

Class IIIC

Occupation	1881	1891	1901	1911
Beer Bottlers,				
Cellarmen	5,620	8,443	13,456	14,526
College, Club Service	2,787	5,072	6,667	11,005
Ironfounders	117,986	103,157	97,345	99,784
Others on Roads	1,543	1,555	1,434	1,622
Railway Ticket				
Collectors	1,290	1,812	2,457	3,381
Total Class IIIC	129,226	120,039	121,359	130,318

All attributed to Class III, 1911; and to Class IV, 1951.

Class IIID

Occupation	1881	1891	1901	1911
Farm Bailiffs	19,373	18,194	22,623	22,141

All attributed to Class III, 1911; and to Class II, 1951.

Class III — 1911 system of classification

Sub-groups	1881	1891	1901	1911
IIIA	1,621,413	1,833,804	2,293,090	2,449,544
IIIB	80,129	89,676	122,969	148,569
IIIC	129,226	120,039	121,359	130,318
IIID	19,373	18,194	22,623	22,141
Total	1,850,141	2,061,713	2,560,041	2,750,572

Class III — 1951 systems of classification

Sub-groups	1881	1891	1901	1911
IC (see above)	10,200	12,058	13,695	13,801
IE (see above)	269,208	340,342	461,906	559,520
IIB (see above)	22,385	22,279	24,453	23,987
IIC (see above)	68,090	94,853	114,988	167,434
IIIA	1,621,413	1,833,804	2,293,090	2,449,544
IIIB	40,064	44,838	61,484	74,284
IVD (see below)	—	—	—	1,242
IVE (see below)	494,507	573,311	649,269	736,683
IVF (see below)	40,272	50,686	65,018	76,955
VB (see below)	54,268	69,436	107,296	151,891
VIA (see below)	8,645	8,724	6,740	6,743
VIC (see below)	138,698	149,730	136,550	158,942
VIIA (see below)	1,264	2,112	2,645	3,859
VIIC (see below)	203,113	259,220	320,004	438,862
Total	2,972,127	3,461,393	4,257,138	4,863,747

Class IVA

Occupation	1881	1891	1901	1911
Anchor, Chain Manufacture	3,860	4,319	4,556	5,069
Barmen	27,808	28,090	28,371	28,656
Bedstead Makers	1,802	2,279	3,111	4,612
Bolt, Nut, etc. Manufacture	5,135	6,184	7,032	9,760
Brass Manufacture, Workers	2,625	5,256	10,921	14,677
Brewers	24,034	25,627	27,388	25,589
Carrying Service other than Drivers	4,738	6,418	10,619	11,784
Chemical Manufacture	14,759	19,392	22,930	33,121
Contractors, etc. (undefined)	9,848	10,215	6,622	3,196
Copper Manufacture, Workers	3,028	4,127	5,625	7,227
Cork and other Wood Workers	6,814	8,561	15,826	19,236
Distillers	—	101	698	890
Domestic Coachmen and Grooms	39,523	55,838	74,130	66,713
Domestic Gardeners	34,740	64,521	85,835	116,666
Drainage and Sanitation	1,341	2,167	7,159	9,798
Dye, Paint, Ink, Makers	2,468	3,582	5,457	8,349
Electricity Supply	2,447	11,788	49,116	98,089
Explosive Manufacture	597	1,232	3,008	2,294
Fishermen	28,595	24,338	23,484	25,017
Floor Cloth etc. Manufacture	1,051	1,441	3,246	5,900
Gardeners, not domestic	107,216	104,653	119,169	137,181
Gasworks Service	18,471	30,627	46,940	54,447
Irongoods and other Metal Workers	6,635	10,490	32,569	52,903
Lamp, Candlestick Makers	2,429	2,962	2,145	3,349
Lath, Wooden Fence Makers	2,858	2,373	2,203	1,791
Laundry Workers	3,321	6,743	8,696	12,284
Lead Manufacture, Workers	2,280	2,072	2,595	2,476
Lodgekeepers, Caretakers etc.	3,548	9,065	17,285	23,551
Machinists etc. (undefined)	4,464	8,369	4,864	1,210

Class IVA (Continued)

Occupation	1881	1891	1901	1911
Maltsters	9,429	9,003	9,555	9,335
Match Manufacture	48	107	476	700
Nail Manufacture	9,160	4,905	3,044	2,808
Other, Personal Service	1,454	2,623	9,290	28,976
Other Ship Workers	19,872	27,943	36,126	43,638
Other Workers in Dress	454	567	651	854
Other Workers in Engineering	36,144	95,527	87,193	125,572
Other Workers in Paper	950	1,456	1,709	2,248
Other Workers in Sundry Trades	4,967	5,345	2,210	3,986
Others in Agriculture	2,429	1,772	5,610	8,888
Others in Hotels	3,295	8,089	8,749	20,552
Paper Manufacture	9,318	11,151	14,408	16,534
Rag Gatherers, Dealers	1,856	2,208	2,554	4,336
Salt Makers	2,621	2,625	2,682	2,957
Shepherds	21,903	20,687	24,404	20,478
Stationery Manufacture	1,847	2,914	4,238	6,430
Stone and Slate Workers	46,144	49,285	70,581	59,400
Stove, Grate, etc. Makers	2,660	3,763	5,754	9,555
Tinplate, Tin Goods Manufacture	30,519	36,917	33,337	38,462
Waterworks Service	2,505	3,799	5,672	8,554
White Metalware Manufacture	4,578	4,781	11,073	11,007
Zinc Manufacture, Workers	2,188	3,208	2,069	2,225
Total Class IVA	580,776	761,505	972,985	1,213,330

All Attributed to Class IV, 1911; and to Class IV, 1951.

Class IVB

Occupation	1881	1891	1901	1911
Newspaper Agents, etc.	2,749	4,917	8,710	13,248

All attributed to Class IV, 1911; and to Class V, 1951.

Class IVC

Occupation	1881	1891	1901	1911
Harbour, Dock Officials	5,874	8,656	11,377	20,303

All attributed to Class IV, 1911; and to Class II, 1951.

Class IVD

Occupation	1881	1891	1901	1911
Motor and Garage Proprietors, Workers	—	—	—	3,725

All attributed to   Class IV, 1911; 33.3 per cent to Class II, 33.3 per cent to Class III and 33.3 per cent to Class IV, 1911.

Class IVE

Occupation	1881	1891	1901	1911
Agricultural Machine Attendants	4,190	4,575	6,452	7,262
Architectural etc. Sculptors	2,053	1,780	2,030	1,452
Artisans (undefined)	30,452	49,638	16,635	10,091
Basket Makers	7,960	9,462	9,366	8,610
Bread, Cake, Jam Makers	57,505	66,393	74,565	85,954
Button Makers	2,027	1,872	1,200	1,315
Celluloid Makers, etc.	474	661	1,104	2,364
Chocolate, Cocoa Makers	366	741	2,209	5,061
Coopers	18,331	16,809	15,527	13,860
Creamery Workers	—	162	530	1,222
Curriers, Leather Goods	18,188	20,757	23,079	25,371
Engine Drivers (Unspecified)	65,643	81,268	105,351	110,249
Feather, Quill Dressers	404	413	452	493
Furriers, Skinners	4,368	5,235	5,738	8,410
Glove Makers	1,989	2,508	2,356	2,880
Hat Makers	13,077	15,323	19,122	21,677
Japanners	1,331	1,107	935	289
Lock, Gas Fitting Makers	3,249	4,143	6,609	9,845
Men of the Army	68,009	78,158	99,289	103,898
Men of the Navy	25,881	31,876	50,619	77,938

Class IVE (Continued)

Occupation	1881	1891	1901	1911
Millers	20,366	20,051	22,548	23,533
Pointsmen, etc.	6,019	8,896	13,894	14,479
Police	32,508	39,921	44,904	53,160
Provision Curers	1,556	2,206	3,486	4,862
Sawyers	24,356	22,759	31,489	39,264
Steel Smelting, etc.	22,905	25,304	30,178	39,087
Tanners	9,559	9,501	9,405	10,438
Tube Manufacture	6,821	6,828	7,379	8,660
Warehousemen	27,461	24,297	14,724	9,717
Waterproof Goods Makers	1,095	1,715	3,230	4,101
Wire Drawers, etc.	8,334	9,677	12,955	18,986
Woodmen	8,030	9,275	11,909	12,195
Total Class IVE	494,507	573,311	649,269	736,683

All attributed to Class IV, 1911; and to Class III, 1951.

Class IVF

Occupation	1881	1891	1901	1911
Earthenware Manufacture	26,315	31,881	35,810	38,445
Glass Manufacture	18,762	21,865	25,772	26,803
Postmen, etc.	24,644	35,708	50,180	69,876
Wood Turners, Box Makers	10,823	11,918	18,275	18,786
Total Class IVF	80,544	101,372	130,037	153,910

All attributed to Class IV, 1911; 50 per cent to Class III and 50 per cent to Class IV, 1951.

Class IV — 1911 system of classification

Sub-group	1881	1891	1901	1911
IVA	580,776	761,505	972,985	1,213,330
IVB	2,749	4,917	8,710	13,248
IVC	5,874	8,656	11,377	20,303
IVD	—	—	—	3,725
IVE	494,507	573,311	649,269	736,683
IVF	80,544	101,372	130,037	153,910
Total	1,164,450	1,449,761	1,772,378	2,141,199

Class IV – 1951 system of classification

Sub-group	1881	1891	1901	1911
IIIB (see above)	40,064	44,838	61,484	74,284
IIIC (see above)	129,226	120,039	121,359	130,318
IVA	580,776	761,505	972,985	1,213,330
IVD	–	–	–	1,242
IVF	40,272	50,686	65,018	76,955
VC (see below)	290,613	354,451	453,509	453,596
VD (see below)	37,138	38,724	61,859	56,355
VIB (see below)	75,887	72,571	80,692	104,031
VIC (see below)	138,698	149,730	136,550	158,942
VIIB (see below)	42	72	89	133
VIIC (see below)	203,113	259,220	320,004	438,862
VIII	740,554	670,261	646,138	595,600
Total	2,276,383	2,522,097	2,919,687	3,303,648

Class VA

Occupation	1881	1891	1901	1911
Bricklayers' Labourers	67,711	64,937	96,744	69,555
Builders' Labourers	6,531	11,344	27,176	65,836
Carpenters' Labourers	5,749	5,374	6,596	5,260
Coalheavers	13,376	17,998	25,782	32,317
Costermongers	28,445	39,818	43,722	59,379
Dock Labourers	36,505	54,746	88,360	102,539
Factory Labourers (undefined)	15,438	26,063	22,514	7,368
General Labourers	543,779	581,047	405,014	293,904
Glue, Size, etc. Workers	1,150	2,070	2,214	3,504
Manure Manufacturers	1,080	861	1,617	3,466
Masons' Labourers	23,639	20,132	22,535	15,806
Messengers, Porters, Watchmen	84,417	97,384	106,301	145,458
Plasterers' Labourers	6,199	4,973	6,772	4,789
Porters and Other Railway etc.	37,187	65,029	88,874	106,644
Railway Navvies, etc.	58,512	72,090	117,603	100,344
Scavenging, Dust Disposal	2,644	3,944	8,331	14,364
Total Class VA	932,362	1,067,810	1,070,155	1,030,533

All attributed to Class V, 1911; and to Class V, 1951.

Class VB

Occupation	1881	1891	1901	1911
Brush Makers, etc.	8,790	8,636	8,847	9,504
India Rubber Workers	2,704	3,770	6,295	13,477
Lime, Clay, Quarry Workers	8,407	8,994	14,466	19,755
Pig Iron Manufacturers	5,491	8,017	12,632	21,615
Puddling Furnaces, etc.	9,004	12,076	33,857	53,324
Ships' Painters, etc.	19,872	27,943	31,199	34,216
Total Class VB	54,268	69,436	107,296	151,891

All attributed to Class V, 1911; and to Class III, 1951.

Class VC

Occupation	1881	1891	1901	1911
Bargemen, Watermen	29,108	30,016	29,344	27,583
Cabmen, Grocers, etc.	96,993	108,497	111,350	74,728
Carmen, Carriers, etc.	117,122	158,280	254,380	290,604
Fitters' Labourers etc.	5,430	7,322	13,350	14,163
Galvanised Sheet Manufacturers	601	950	2,951	4,793
Grease, Soap, etc.	4,396	5,047	6,316	9,544
Ironfoundry Labourers, etc.	26,450	31,891	18,647	8,555
Oil Millers, Refiners etc.	4,105	3,754	5,355	10,358
Plaster, Cement Manufacturers	3,498	5,329	9,506	9,848
Sugar Refiners	2,910	3,365	2,310	3,420
Total Class VC	290,613	354,451	453,509	453,596

All attributed to Class V, 1911; and to Class IV, 1951.

Class VD

Occupation	1881	1891	1901	1911
Bill Posters	1,379	2,114	2,481	3,265
Brick, Plain Tile Makers	44,148	38,152	57,660	47,180
Coke etc. Manufacturers	4,843	6,232	7,764	9,783

Class VD (Continued)

Occupation	1881	1891	1901	1911
Drovers	2,551	2,779	2,805	2,868
Paviers, Road Labourers etc.	14,950	21,279	50,157	44,473
Sandwichmen, etc.	6,406	6,893	2,851	5,141
Total Class VD	74,277	77,449	123,718	112,710

All attributed to Class V, 1911; 50 per cent to Class IV and 50 per cent to Class V, 1951.

Class V — 1911 system of classification

Sub-group	1881	1891	1901	1911
VA	932,362	1,067,810	1,070,155	1,030,533
VB	54,268	69,436	107,296	151,891
VC	290,613	354,451	453,509	453,596
VD	74,277	77,449	123,718	112,710
Total	1,351,520	1,569,146	1,754,678	1,748,730

Class V — 1951 system of classification

Sub-group	1881	1891	1901	1911
IID (see above)	1,785	2,049	933	1,266
IVB (see above)	2,749	4,917	8,710	13,248
VA	932,362	1,067,810	1,070,155	1,030,533
VD	37,138	38,724	61,859	56,355
Total	974,034	1,113,500	1,141,657	1,101,402

Class VIA

Occupation	1881	1891	1901	1911
Carpet, Rug, Felt Manufacturers	8,645	8,724	6,740	6,743

All attributed to Class VI, 1911; and to Class III, 1951.

Class VIB

Occupation	1881	1891	1901	1911
Factory Hands, Textiles	4,250	2,395	1,030	303
Other Textile Workers	35,297	33,606	31,010	36,787
Textile Bleachers, etc.	36,340	36,570	48,652	66,941
Total Class VIB	75,887	72,571	80,692	104,031

All attributed to Class VI, 1911; and to Class IV, 1951.

Class VIC

Occupation	1881	1891	1901	1911
Cotton Manufacturers	156,971	176,991	173,139	210,697
Hosiery Manufacturers	18,236	17,365	13,230	14,287
Silk Manufacturers	17,176	14,372	9,448	8,362
Wool and Worsted Manufacturers	85,013	90,732	77,283	84,538
Total Class VIC	277.396	299,460	273,100	317,884

All attributed to Class VI, 1911; 50 per cent to Class III and 50 per cent to Class IV, 1951.

Class VI – 1911 system of classification

Sub-group	1881	1891	1901	1911
VIA	8,645	8,724	6,740	6,743
VIB	75,887	72,571	80,692	104,031
VIC	277,396	299,460	273,100	317,884
Total	361,928	380,755	360,532	428,658

Class VIIA

Occupation	1881	1891	1901	1911
Coal and Shale Service	1,264	2,112	2,645	3,859

All attributed to Class VII, 1911; and to Class III, 1951.

Class VIIB

Occupation	1881	1891	1901	1911
Other Mine Service	42	72	89	133

All attributed to Class VII, 1911; and to Class IV, 1951.

Class VIIC

Occupation	1881	1891	1901	1911
Coal and Shale Miners	355,363	482,525	609,402	843,681
Copper Miners	3,601	1,086	771	278
Iron Miners, Quarriers	25,153	17,823	16,765	22,049
Lead Miners	10,599	5,609	4,328	2,934
Other Mineral Miners	1,982	2,342	2,419	1,770
Tin Miners	9,528	9,055	6,324	7,012
Total Class VIIC	406,226	518,440	640,009	877,724

All attributed to Class VII, 1911; 50 per cent to Class III and 50 per cent to Class IV, 1951.

Class VII — 1911 system of classification

Sub-group	1881	1891	1901	1911
VIIA	1,264	2,112	2,645	3,859
VIIB	42	72	89	133
VIIC	406,226	518,440	640,009	877,724
Total Class VII	407,532	520,624	642,743	881,716

Class VIII — 1911 system of classification

Occupation	1881	1891	1901	1911
Agricultural Labourers	740,554	670,261	646,138	595,600

Class structure — 1911 system of classification

Class	1881	1891	1901	1911
I	920,644	1,108,061	1,338,507	1,484,277
II	1,153,296	1,350,426	1,610,550	2,028,351
III	1,850,141	2,061,713	2,560,041	2,750,572
IV	1,164,450	1,449,761	1,772,378	2,141,199
V	1,351,520	1,569,146	1,754,678	1,748,730
VI	361,928	380,755	360,532	428,658
VII	407,532	520,624	642,743	881,716
VIII	740,554	670,261	646,138	595,600
Total	7,950,063	9,110,747	10,685,567	12,059,103

Class structure — 1911 system, reduced to five classes

Class	1881	1891	1901	1911
I	920,644	1,108,061	1,338,507	1,484,277
II	1,153,294	1,350,426	1,610,550	2,028,351
III + VIA, C + VIIA, C	2,201,861	2,481,499	3,025,980	3,358,978
IV + VIB, C + VIIB, C + VIII	2,322,744	2,601,615	2,955,851	3,438,767
V	1,351,520	1,569,146	1,754,678	1,748,730
Total	7,950,063	9,110,747	10,685,566	12,059,103

Class structure — 1951 system of classification

Class	1881	1891	1901	1911
I	159,756	197,282	246,837	302,753
II	1,089,498	1,222,571	1,448,725	1,729,865
III	2,972,127	3,461,393	4,257,138	4,863,747
IV	2,276,383	2,522,097	2,919,687	3,303,648
V	974,034	1,113,500	1,141,657	1,101,402
Total	7,471,798	8,516,843	10,014,044	11,301,415

The difference in the totals for these three separate approximations to the class structure, 1881–1911, arise on the one hand from the subdivision of items which were rounded off to the nearest whole number or to the lower whole number in cases of 0.5, and on the other hand from the omission of items IF and IIF from the 1951 system of classification.

CHAPTER 7

Education in England and Wales in 1851: the Education Census of Great Britain, 1851

M. GOLDSTROM

When the 1851 population census was projected the Registrar General asked the government if a census of education and of religion could be undertaken as well. He justified his request by pointing out that little additional expense would be involved, since the enumerators being paid for conducting the population census could be used. The government agreed, in spite of hostility in various quarters to the idea of an educational census. There were arguments that it would erode the freedom of the individual, that it would draw an invidious distinction between dissenters and the Church of England, and in the case of the Voluntaryists, that it was yet another unwelcome attempt at state intervention.[1]

The man chosen to supervise both the census of education and of religion was Horace Mann, at the time assistant commissioner for the population census and later to be secretary to the Civil Service Commission.[2] It was Mann's objective to find out the number of schools in England and Wales, their religious and secular affiliations, their income and expenditure and their date of establishment; the number of teachers, their sex, their pay and their level of training; the number of pupils on the schools' books, their sex and age and their attendance on census day; the subjects of instruction and the number of pupils receiving it. In addition, miscellaneous information was sought such as the size of classrooms, the occupations of evening scholars and the manner in which school governors were appointed. The census forms drawn up by Mann and his assistants were to be filled in by the 'heads or keepers' of day schools, Sunday schools, evening schools for adults and 'literary, scientific and mechanics' institutions'.[3] The census was to be spread over three days — evening schools completing their forms on Saturday, 29 March, Sunday schools the following day, and day schools on Monday, 31 March.

Much of the data collected was never published in the *Census Report on Education* (hereinafter referred to as the *Census Report*) and much of what did appear was condensed into short summaries or expressed on a sample basis. If there had been a pilot survey (and none appears to have been undertaken) Mann might have realised that it was beyond the resources of the census office to analyse and publish everything that was collected.

The enumerators were instructed that, when they delivered the householder's form, in order to avoid missing schools they should ask at every house if a school of any kind was conducted on the premises and, if such was the case, to leave the appropriate census form. They were also, because of an ambiguity in the wording of the Census Act, to point out to heads of schools that there was no obligation to complete the form. To check on those who refused or neglected to return the form, each enumerator was asked to list all the schools in his district and the names and addresses of the person with whom the form was left. The lists were sent to the local Registrar, who thus had a means of ascertaining which schools had not completed their form. These schools were approached once more before he forwarded both lists and forms to the census office in London.[4]

When the forms were sorted in London there were more than a thousand lists missing. And when these were eventually secured several thousand schools referred to in them had not filled in the form. Renewed efforts were made, but Mann estimated in the *Census Report* that at least 1,206 day schools, mostly private, and 377 Sunday schools had declined to supply information. After making allowance for non-returns Mann calculated that there were some 46,042 day schools in England and Wales, with 2,144,378 scholars on the books; 23,514 Sunday schools, with 2,407,642 scholars; and 1,545 evening schools, with 39,783 scholars.[5] Day schools were divided into 'public' schools, defined as those 'supported in any degree, from other sources than the payments by scholars, and which are established in any degree for other objects than pecuniary profit to the promoters', and 'private' schools, defined as receiving all their income from pupils or being run for a profit. Public schools were grouped under four headings: those which were supported by the state or local authority, those supported by religious bodies, and 'other public schools'; Sunday schools were listed according to their religious affiliation.[6]

Reliability of the Education Census

Even if we assume that the census was accurately compiled, it has grave deficiencies from the researcher's point of view. With the exceptions of 'literary, scientific and mechanics' institutions', the report does not list individual schools. Instead, schools were grouped within the 624 registration districts into which England and Wales was organized (see above, chap. 2). As some districts contained several hundred schools and few had under thirty it is only occasionally possible to identify a specific school. Nor is there a great deal of information in the *Census Report* about registration districts: we are given the number of day and Sunday schools, their source of financial support, their religious affiliation, the number and sex of pupils 'belonging to the school' and the numbers in attendance on census day. All other information such as the age of scholars, or the number of Sunday school teachers, is available at best on a registration county basis. For the counties of Lancashire and Lincolnshire a little more detail is given, including an analysis of teachers' remuneration. The sources of income of schools and the number and qualifications of teachers is summarised without reference to regional variation. The scantiness of the information published would not matter so much were it possible to go back to the original manuscript census returns, but they have unfortunately been lost. The material was not transferred, as in the case of the religious census, to the Public Record Office. Somerset House has no record of what happened to it, nor even a record of its having been destroyed, though it is all too probable that it no longer exists.[7]

From the point of view of those interested in aggregate

figures, the disappearance of the manuscript sources is not such a serious problem, if he can regard the census forms as having been accurately filled in and accurately analysed. The most reliable figure is undoubtedly the number of public day schools in England and Wales, not least because Mann took care to define a school as a building or range of buildings under one general management.[8] It is possible to compare the *Census Report* figures with subsequent statistics for the second half of the nineteenth century, but this would *not* be possible for figures compiled earlier in the century, when it was not uncommon to list separate classrooms as individual schools, and to leave vague the distinction between Sunday and day schools.[9] Few of the public schools of 1851 were missed by the census enumerators; it is true that some enumerators lacked zeal, that some teachers refused to co-operate, that a few census forms were lost and that workhouse schools were missed altogether (because they were not the responsibility of the enumerators[10]) but most of these omissions were discovered and the figures may be regarded as tolerably accurate.

More doubtful are the figures for private schools: many of the 30,524 schools enumerated (i.e. twice the number of public schools) were little more than child-minding establishments in private houses where at best reading was taught to a handful of pupils. The enumerators must have had great difficulty in distinguishing between a school and such an establishment, especially as they were required to list children of all ages — there was no lower limit. In 708 cases, establishments were styled schools by the enumerators despite the fact that the teacher signed the census form with a mark.[11] In the same category, but at the other end of the scale, were large proprietary schools, boarding schools and commercial schools. Mann attempted to classify them all in three groups and calculate the proportion of each type, but as he admitted himself, it was a rough attempt.[12]

The figure for the number of children 'belonging to the schools' (i.e. on the register), which Mann calculated to be 2,144,378, is highly suspect. It was from this figure that Mann calculated, after allowance for those educated at home or too ill ever to attend school, that the average child spent nearly five years at school (upper and middle class children six years, and children of the labouring classes a little over four). He concluded that 'very few children are *completely* uninstructed'.[13] This on the whole comforting conclusion about the education of the working classes is at variance with the views of informed contemporary observers, not least among them the inspectors of the Committee of Council on Education.[14]

Mann's conclusion can only be sustained if the number of children belonging to the schools was a meaningful figure. Teachers were asked to state the number of scholars 'actually paying for instruction at the time of the Return, or who may be entered on the books of the schools'.[15] If the number of children admitted or leaving the school is relatively small, the figure may have some meaning though it must always be in excess of the number of children genuinely on the school register. It might be some time before the name of a child who had left the school was actually erased from the register. His name might even appear on two registers. In fact the turnover of pupils was very high, especially in the towns. The Committee of Council inspectors always recorded the number of pupils on the day of their inspection and they also tried to obtain figures of the number of children who had been admitted and had left in the previous twelve months.[16] At about this time the Reverend F.C. Cook, one of Her Majesty's Inspectors of Schools, visited schools in the counties of Middlesex, Bedford, Buckingham and Hertford, and his experience is revealing. He managed to obtain figures for 75 schools. On the days he called there were 8,714 children in attendance; the number admitted in the previous twelve months was 9,513 and 8,538 had left.[17] Given this large turnover, the most conscientious teacher could not have kept an accurate register. Mann's figures are certainly inflated: but there is unfortunately no way of estimating the excess.

The average attendance figures, given as 79 per cent of the number of children belonging to public schools and 91 per cent[18] of those at private schools, are impossibly high. If we are correct in assuming that the number of children 'belonging to the school' is an over-estimate, the average attendance figures would be even higher than those calculated by Mann. But even in 1869, when teachers' salaries were based in part on attendance and juvenile employment opportunities had diminished, average attendance in public schools was only 69 per cent of those on the register. Sadler and Edwards[19] thought that in the mid-nineteenth century an average attendance of 50 per cent of the number of children on the register was a realistic assumption.[20] It is interesting to compare the position in Ireland on 25 June, 1868, when the Irish Constabulary was given sealed orders to descend on all schools and count the pupils: of the 967,563 on the registers only 453,615 were present.[21]

There are various ways of accounting for the inflation. The choice of the census date itself could have influenced the figures. The 31st March was a time when attendance would have been high: children would have recovered from winter illnesses and would not yet be engaged in their seasonal summer occupations. More important, it was the custom for teachers to put pressure on their children to attend for an inspector's visit (prior notice was always given) and the same pressure would have been applied for the day of the census. It is likely, too, that some teachers would have succumbed on census day to the temptation of marking pupils present who were absent for a known and unavoidable reason. Teachers had a reputation during this period for exaggerating their attendance, and on the day the inspector called he was invariably told that the attendance was below average.[22] Mann was obliged to defend teachers against allegations of deceit that followed publication of the *Census Report*.[23] Finally, there is the question of clerical errors in the census office, since the clerks were instructed to estimate average attendance figures where these were not supplied on the forms. However, since an elaborate system of double checking was employed by Mann, it is unlikely that the figures were significantly influenced. All in all, perhaps the best course for the researcher would be to take the figure purporting to be the average attendance, and assume it to be the number of children genuinely belonging to the school.

Analysis of the Education Census

The census volume used on its own has serious limitations,

but if it is used in conjunction with other contemporary published and manuscript material it is possible to reconstruct statistical information on education nationally, regionally and locally. A much neglected source is the detailed survey (hereinafter referred to as the *General Inquiry*[24]) undertaken by the National Society in 1846 and 1847 of all schools catering for the children of the poor connected with the Church of England, which in effect meant the overwhelming majority of all day schools. Unlike the census it lists every school individually, gives the number of pupils on the books, the number of teachers, their salaries and emoluments, the income and expenditure of the school and the holder of the title deeds, and quite often the comments on their particular school of teachers or clergymen. The *General Inquiry* has its faults — it does not distinguish adequately between day and Sunday schools, each separate classroom is counted as a school and there are duplicated entries — but it is an immensely valuable document.[25] The *Minutes of the Committee of Council* are a better-known source, again providing information on individual schools of all denominations, but the Committee of Council inspected only those schools in receipt of public money, i.e. a minority of schools. Other annual government reports can provide information on government-inspected schools such as factory, workhouse, prison and military schools.[26] The printed volumes of the census of population and of religion can provide information. The population census gives a breakdown of the ages of children by registration district and lists the occupation of those who are working. The religious census would give a comparison between the strength of the religious denominations in a specific area (see below, chap. 8) and the provisions they made for schooling. If the manuscript enumerators' books of the population census are used in conjunction with surviving school registers an analysis of the social composition of an individual school is possible. The religious societies all issued national annual reports and local reports are not uncommon, especially those issued by the Diocesan Committees of the Church of England. All the major societies had their educational periodicals, which sometimes published statistics.[27] In addition there is printed and manuscript material at local libraries, local public record offices and in the archives of the religious societies. Unfortunately, two major sources of manuscript material have been destroyed — all the records of the British and Foreign School Society and nearly all those of the Committee of Council on Education.

Thus, it is possible to construct studies of the following topics of mid-nineteenth century educational interest.

THE INDIVIDUAL SCHOOL

Where it is known from other sources that a particular school existed in a registration district, it may be possible to identify it in the *Census Report* in spite of the fact that individual schools are not listed by name. If a school happens to be supported by the central or local government, for example a military, naval or workhouse school, it is unlikely that there will be more than one of its kind in the registration district. If that is the case, the table will indicate that there is one such school in the district and will give the number of pupils 'belonging to the school' and their sex. Similarly, an isolated public school — a grammar, endowed, Jewish, Catholic or 'British' school — can usually be identified. So can a Sunday school belonging to a minor denomination. In sparsely populated areas it may be possible to identify even a National school. It is also worth checking footnotes in the *Census Report* because sometimes an individual school is referred to and statistical information supplied. There is no breakdown of private schools by type or religious affiliation and it is impossible to identify such schools in the *Census Report*. However a private school may be listed in the National Society's *General Inquiry* which did not distinguish between public and private: if the school considered itself Church of England it was included. If a school took in boarders, further information will be found in the manuscript returns made by the population census enumerators.[28]

If a school received a Committee of Council grant, attendance figures and the amount of financial assistance received are given in the Council's *Minutes*. Information about schools receiving money from other government departments can sometimes be found by consulting the appropriate annual report. The same applies to factory schools, which were liable to government inspection. It may occasionally be possible to cross-check information supplied to the census enumerators with that noted by the inspectors. This is *not* possible in the case of Poor Law schools because the information contained in the *Census Report* derives from the annual report of the Poor Law Commissioners.[29]

THE REGION

Anyone wishing to study an area involving one or more registration districts will have, in addition to the material referred to above, the aggregate figures on 31 March for each registration district. By using all this material in conjunction with the population and religion censuses (whether in printed or manuscript form) it is possible to reconstruct a statistical picture of the educational facilities of an area and to analyse the age of pupils, the social class of their parents and the occupations of those children at work.[30] From the annual reports of the Registrar General it is even possible to calculate very crudely the literacy rate of a district.[31] On a county basis the *Census Report* lists the ages of scholars and the dates when schools were established. In the case of Lancashire and Lincolnshire, there is a breakdown of the number of scholars attending school and on the books by type of day school, a comparison of the ages of scholars by type of day school and salaries of teachers by type of public day school.

RELIGIOUS AFFILIATION

Even though the number of scholars given in the *Census Report* is clearly inaccurate there is no reason to assume that particular types of schools overstated their numbers more than others. Given this assumption, and the further assumption that the number of schools listed in the *Census Report* is tolerably accurate, it is possible to calculate the relative strengths of the educational societies on a national and local basis, and the relative size of each type of school. But there are a number of complicating factors. The affiliations of some schools were open to doubt. For example, the majority of 'British' schools said they had no link with any denomination, but some said they had. Twelve 'British' schools even stated a link with the Church of England. Accordingly the *Census Report* gives more than one figure for the number of 'British' schools.[32] Some of the private schools were connected with educational societies, yet their affiliations are not recorded in the *Census Report* because they were run on a profit basis. It is likely that the *Census Report* underestimates the number of Nonconformist schools, especially Congregational schools, which were frequently run on a private profit-making basis and therefore were listed as private schools. Furthermore the Congregationalists refused to co-operate with the census officers and this may have led to some of their schools being missed by the enumerators.

TEACHERS' SALARIES

Teachers' salaries are of interest to the historians of the teaching profession and to those who wish to use the material to gauge the quality and social standing of a school, since the best paid teachers were more often found in the more highly regarded schools. It is unfortunate therefore that all that was published in the *Census Report* was the total number of teachers by status and sex and a breakdown of the remuneration of teachers by type of school for only two 'typical' counties.[33] It is tempting to use the average salaries because they confirm what we know from other sources — that Nonconformist schools paid their teachers more than other types of school.[34] In Mann's view this was 'the least satisfactory portion of the Census returns; the omissions being many, and the ambiguities not a few'.[35] The amount teachers said they received in cash was calculated but no account was taken of the value of payments in kind, such as a house, fuel or board and lodging. If this were added, the differential between poorly paid teachers such as Church of England teachers (who frequently had a house) or military teachers (who had uniform and board and lodgings) and highly paid Nonconformist teachers, who usually received no payment in kind, is likely to be less. A further complication is that there is no evidence to show that the two counties were typical or that the sample of teachers was representative. The National Society's *General Inquiry* is a more useful source, since it gives the salary paid in every individual school 'plus allowances for coals etc.' and states if a house is supplied.[36] In the *Minutes of the Committee of Council* the aggregate paid to all teachers in an inspector's district is given. The amount paid by the Committee of Council towards teachers' salaries is listed for each school.

SCHOOL FEES

The range in school fees from a penny a week to a shilling or more is a valuable indicator of the social standing of the school. Public schools were asked to state the sources of their income and the fees they charged, but only half of them supplied the necessary information. In the *Census Report* the total income of public day schools is given, and its sources, including the amount of revenue from fees, but on a national basis only. The table indicates the much lower proportion of income obtained from fees in National schools and confirms the inspectors' reports that National schools catered for the poorer children.[37] Much more detailed information is available in the National Society *General Inquiry* and the *Minutes of the Committee of Council.*

INCOME AND EXPENDITURE

Mann complained in the *Census Report* that returns on the income and expenditure of schools were difficult to obtain. He did not make it any easier for himself by failing to distinguish on the census form between current and capital expenditure. From the incomplete returns he attempted to calculate the total expenditure on public school education.[38]

Unfortunately his figures are not consistent with those given in the National Society *General Inquiry* or with those collected by the Committee of Council. It is perhaps possible to use his figures to make a rough estimate of public school expenditure. For the private sector this is hardly possible, since the only figures we have are those of private schools listed in the National Society *General Inquiry,* and any estimates based on these figures would be of dubious value.

SUNDAY SCHOOLS

The *Census Report* lists the number of Sunday schools by registration district and gives the number of schools and scholars belonging to each denomination. The number in attendance on census Sunday is given by registration district and the number of teachers in each county and large town is listed by denomination (see below, chap. 8).

It is likely that the number of Sunday schools belonging to each denomination is reasonably accurate and that the number of teachers is overstated. Even those who taught occasionally were liable to be counted. The number of scholars on the books, as in the case of day schools, and for the same reasons, is probably exaggerated. The attendance figures for census Sunday, given as 'between 75 and 77 per cent' of those belonging[39] to the schools, are too high to be typical of an average Sunday School. The clergy no doubt managed to secure a particularly high attendance for that day and, moreover, some might have 'improved' the attendances. While the figures themselves are suspect, the proportionate strength of the denominations is probably accurate (for a fuller discussion see below, pp. 244—53).

ADULT EDUCATION

The *Census Report* deals with evening schools for adults, and literary, scientific and mechanics' institutions. Information on evening schools giving the number of schools, scholars, teachers, fees charged, opening hours, subjects taught and occupation of scholars is shown on a county basis. The institutions are listed individually with the number of members, subscriptions charged and nature of the lectures given, but the list is far from complete. Many of the institutions on the enumerators' lists failed to make a return and others, especially those which did not have their own premises, are likely to have been missed by the enumerators. The *Census Report* gives fascinating information but it is likely that it lists only the better-known institutions.[40]

THE GROWTH OF EDUCATIONAL PROVISIONS

An often-quoted table is the one compiled by Mann for a parliamentary return in 1853 comparing the number of schools and scholars for 1818, 1833 and 1851.[41] Despite C. Richson's careful demonstration that the earlier surveys underestimated the number of schools and scholars and his conclusion that the figures were not comparable,[42] Mann reprinted the return in the *Census Report*.[43] He admitted that the earlier returns were deficient, especially that of 1833 which he considered to be 10 per cent deficient, but nevertheless he argued that they were sufficiently complete to show the progress made in educational provision.[44]

Before sharing Mann's optimism it should be borne in mind that the number of pupils in a school can be defined as the number on the books, the number in attendance on a particular day, or the number in average attendance over a period of time. In the 1851 census it was made clear which figures were required, but these distinctions were not made by the investigators in 1818 and 1833. A comparison of the number of schools presents greater difficulties. Some teachers considered a building to be a school, others regarded each separate classroom as a school and in the case of large monitorial schools several 'schools' might have shared a classroom.

Mann attempted another way of measuring the growth of educational provision by listing the number of new schools established during each decade. As he pointed out, this tended to overstate the number of schools established in the later period, since many established earlier — especially private schools — had closed down or re-opened under a new name.[45]

TYPE OF INSTRUCTION

The tables showing the subjects taught in schools are probably reliable, though some of the subjects might have been taught in a token manner.[46] At first sight it is surprising that while 98 per cent of all schools said they taught reading, only 70 per cent taught writing and 62 per cent arithmetic. This is because many private schools catered for very young children and taught only reading. Only 60 per cent of them taught writing as well. The high proportion of children shown to be receiving instruction in 'industrial occupations' is almost entirely accounted for by needlework lessons for girls.

Conclusion

The government decided not to hold an education census in 1861. There would not have been strong opposition to one (as there was in the case of the religious census) but the Royal Commission on Education which had begun its investigations in 1858 decided to undertake its own survey, and there seemed to be no point in duplicating effort and expense.[47] This was a great pity, since the Royal Commission's statistical report dealt only with primary education and was much more limited in scope than the 1851 education census.

NOTES

NB. This chapter was written in 1970 and has been unavoidably delayed in the press. This will explain the absence of reference to relevant sources since that date.

1.   Census of Great Britain, 1851, Education. England and Wales. *Report and Tables.* B.P.P. 1852–3, (1632), vol. XC, xi. (Hereafter referred to as *Census Report*). See also *Return of the Number of Day Schools and Sunday Schools, and the Number of Day Scholars and Sunday Scholars, in England and Wales, with the Population; distinguishing between Public and Private Day Schools, and also distinguishing Male and Female Scholars, according to the Census of 1851; – also similar Return for each of the Cities and Municipal Boroughs in England.* B.P.P. 1852–3 (514), LXXIX.
       There was also a Scottish census: Census of Great Britain, 1851. Religious Worship, and Education. Scotland. *Report and Tables* B.P.P. 1854, (1764), vol. LIX, 301. The discussion that follows is confined to the England and Wales volume. The Voluntaryist position on state intervention is made clear in (Congregational Board of Education) *Crosby-Hall Lectures on Education*, London 1848. Views of those hostile to the census are expressed in the volumes of *The Educator* (ed. W.J. Unwin) published from 1851.
2.   Very little is known about Mann outside his publications, though there is a brief biographical account in Joseph Foster, *Men-At-The-Bar*, (1885), p. 303.
3.   The Education Census forms and the instructions to enumerators are reprinted in the *Census Report*, p. xcvi–cxi.

4. *Census Report*, pp. xciv—c.
5. *Census Report*, p. xiv. For the total number of children in England and Wales in each age group see *Census Report*, p. cxx. For a breakdown of children's ages by Registration District see Census of Great Britain, *Population Tables*, B.P.P. 1852–3, (1691–1–II), vol. LXXXVIII parts i and ii. The population census states the number of 'scholars' to be 1,450,504. This figure is not comparable with that of the education census because many parents when completing their census form stated their children as having no occupation.
6. *Census Report*, p. xcvi.
7. I suspect that the records, which had been 'numbered, and arranged and bound in topographical parochial order' (*Census Report* p. xcv), found their way to the offices of the Committee of Council on Education. If so, they would have been destroyed with most of the other records of this Committee.
8. *Census Report*, p.c.
9. The important surveys of the earlier part of the century are:
    (a) Government investigations:
         A Digest of Parochial Returns made to the Select Committee Appointed to Inquire into the Education of the Poor, (England, Wales, Scotland etc.), B.P.P. 1819 (224), vol. IX parts i—iii.
         Education Enquiry, *Abstract of the Answers and Returns made pursuant to an address of the House of Commons*, 24th May 1833, B.P.P. 1835 (62), vols. XLI, XLII, XLIII.
    (b) Investigations undertaken by the Society for Promoting Christian Knowledge and/or the National Society:
         1826 Survey: *Sixteenth Annual Report of the National Society for Promoting the Education of the Poor in the Principles of the Established Church*, (1827).
         1831 Survey: *21st Report*, (1832).
         1837 Survey: *26th Report*, (1837).
         (National Society) *Result of the Returns to the General Inquiry made by the National Society into the state and progress of Schools for the Education of the Poor in the Principles of the Established Church, during the years 1846—7, Throughout England and Wales*, (1849). (Hereafter referred to as the *General Inquiry*).
    (c) The Statistical Societies:
         The surveys of Birmingham, Bristol, Hull, London, Manchester, Rutlandshire, Staffordshire and West Bromwich, in *Journal of the Statistical Society of London*, vols. I to X, (1839—49). There are many further references to education surveys and to education statistics in the *Journal*. See *Journal of the Statistical Society of London. General Index to the First Fifteen Volumes*, London 1854. See also *Catalogue of the Library of the Statistical Society*, London 1884—6,

2 vols, and Department of Science and Art of the Committee of Council on Education, *Catalogue of the Education Library in the South Kensington Museum*, (10th ed., 1893).

10. *Census Report*, p. xcvi.

11. *Census Report*, p. xxxiii.

12. *Ibid.*

13. *Census Report*, p. xxx.

14. See *Minutes of the Committee of Council on Education*, 1839–58, 8vo ed. The *Minutes* are also to be found in British Parliamentary Papers but with different pagination. Subsequent references to the *Minutes* are to the octavo edition

15. *Census Report*, p. civ.

16. See, for example, *Minutes of the Committee of Council on Education*, 1851–2, 2 vols.

17. Calculated from *Minutes of the Committee of Council on Education* 1851–2, vol. II, pp. 52–69.

18. *Census Report*, pp. xxx–xxxi.

19. Calculated from *Report of the Committee of Council on Education; with Appendix*, 1869–70, p. vii.

20. M.E. Sadler and J.W. Edwards, 'Summary of Statistics, Regulations, etc., of Elementary Education in England and Wales, 1833–1870.' *Special Reports on Educational Subjects, Volume 2*, B.P.P. 1898 (C.–8943), vol. XXIV, 449.

21. *Royal Commission of Inquiry, Primary Education (Ireland), Vol. VI. Educational Census*, B.P.P. 1870, (C.–6.V.), vol. XXVIII part 5, xxxviii. *Thirty-Fifth Report of the Commissioners of National Education in Ireland (For the year 1868) with appendices*, B.P.P. 1868–9, (4193), vol. XXI, 8.

22. The 75 schools F.C. Cook visited in 1851 had 8,714 pupils present when he called, yet he was told that the average attendance was 11,150. Calculated from Cook's report. *Minutes of the Committee of Council on Education*, 1851–52, vol. II, pp. 52–69. Reasons for this kind of exaggeration by teachers are given in Walter Farquhar Hook, *On the Means of Rendering More Efficient the Education of the People*, (1846).

23. Horace Mann, 'On the Statistical Position of Religious Bodies in England and Wales,' *Journal of the Statistical Society*, 18 (1855) p. 143. Horace Mann, 'The Resources of Popular Education in England and Wales: Present and Future', *Journal of the Statistical Society*, 15 (1852), pp. 50–1. See below, chap. 8, for similar accusations relating to the Religious Census of 1851.

24. *General Inquiry, op. cit.*

25. The compilers themselves were only too well aware of its deficiencies. *General Inquiry*, pp. i–iii. For a defence of the accuracy of the *Inquiry* see C.K. Francis Brown, *The Church's Part in Education 1833–1941, with special reference to the work of the National Society* (1942), pp. 40–44.

26. All the annual reports are listed in the alphabetical indexes to

the British Parliamentary Papers, but it is easier to consult P. and G. Ford, *Select List of British Parliamentary Papers*, 1833–1899 (1953).

27. For a list of the more important annual reports and periodicals see my book, *The Social Content of Education 1808–1870: a study of the working class reader in England and Ireland* (1972).

28. I am indebted to Dr W.A. Armstrong for this information.

29. *Census Report*, p. xcvi.

30. For an interesting example of the exploitation of this kind of material see R.J. Smith, 'Education, Society and Literacy: Nottinghamshire in the Mid-Nineteenth Century', *University of Birmingham Historical Journal*, 12 (1969) pp. 42–56.

31. For possible pitfalls when using these figures see my book, *The Social Content of Education 1808–1870*, (1972), ch. 5.

32. *Census Report*, p. liii and pp. cxxiii–cxxiv.

33. *Census Report*, p. cxl.

34. See 'Report of the Board of General Education for 1855', *Congregational Year Book* (1856), pp. 99–100.

35. *Census Report*, p. lii.

36. For an attempt by an H.M.I., the Reverend H. Moseley, to calculate the earnings of teachers see *Minutes of the Committee of Council on Education*, vol. 1, pp. 279–81.

37. *Census Report*, pp. cxxvi–cxxvii.

38. *Census Report*, p. li.

39. *Census Report*, p. clxix.

40. T. Kelly thinks that the census 'is by no means complete'. Thomas Kelly, *A History of Adult Education in Great Britain* (1962), Liverpool, p. 147.

41. *Returns of the Number of Day Schools and Sunday Schools, and of the Number of Day Scholars and Sunday Scholars, in England and Wales, in 1818, 1833 and 1851; etc.*, B.P.P. 1852–3, (487), vol. LXXIX.

42. Rev. C. Richson, 'On the Fallacies involved in certain "Returns of the Number of Day Schools and Day Scholars, in England and Wales, in 1818, 1833 and 1851; etc. Ordered, by the House of Commons, to be printed, 13th May, 1853".' *Transactions of the Manchester Statistical Society* (1853–4), pp. 1–16.

43. Mann refers to Richson's paper in the *Census Report*, p. xvii, but ignores the argument.

44. *Ibid.*

45. *Census Report*, p. xx.

46. *Census Report*, pp. cxxx–cxxxiii.

47. 'Report on the Education in England and Wales in 1858–60, as ascertained by the Education Commission of 1858', *Journal of the Statistical Society* 24 (1861), p. 208.

CHAPTER 8

The Religious Census of 1851

DAVID M. THOMPSON

In 1851 information was sought on religion in a British census for the first and only time. On Sunday 30th March, the day of the national census, a count was made of all those attending worship at churches, chapels or meeting rooms throughout the country.[1] The purpose of the census was to discover

> how far the means of Religious Instruction provided in Great Britain during the last fifty years have kept pace with the population during the same period, and to what extent those means are adequate to meet the spiritual wants of the increased population of 1851.[2]

The results were tabulated by Horace Mann, a twenty-eight year old barrister,[3] and were published in 1854. The figures for England and Wales were prefaced by a long report written by Mann, but the figures for Scotland, which were in any case less complete, had only a brief introduction.[4] The original schedules for England and Wales are available in the Public Record Office, but those for Scotland have apparently disappeared.[5] The Census has become popularly known as the 1851 Religious Census, but strictly it is only a Census of Accommodation and Attendance at Worship: this fact explains much of the subsequent controversy. For all its faults, however, it stands out as a fascinating revelation of the religious state of Britain in the middle of the century.

It is not quite clear where the idea for the census came from. Sir George Lewis, Under-Secretary at the Home Office in 1851, later claimed that he suggested the expediency of extending the census to religion.[6] Certainly it was he who suggested the questions on religious profession in the 1861 census (subsequently dropped) and he had been a member of the Commission which took a census of religious profession in Ireland in 1834.[7] But it seems likely that the form of the enquiry was suggested by the Registrar General, Major George Graham, as he himself claimed.[8] His brother, Sir James Graham, had been responsible for the abortive bill on Factory Education in 1843, and had regretted the lack of information available on provision for education and religious worship.[9] It had become apparent that statistics on these were inadequate in the debates on W.J. Fox's Education Bill in 1850, and this was referred to by Sir George Grey, Home Secretary, when answering a question about the census from Mr H. Goulburn on 14th March 1851.[10] Nevertheless the enquiries were not specifically authorised by the Census Act (13 & 14 Vict. c. 53) and this was one of the later points of grievance.[11]

The taking of and response to the 1851 Religious Census

The procedure for the religious census was simple: each enumerator for the general census was asked to search out every church, chapel or room in his district used regularly as a place of worship, and to give a blank return to a responsible person, usually the minister, in each. Different forms were provided for the Established Church (of England or Scotland) and for other Churches. (Facsimiles of these forms are reproduced in Appendix VII). On all returns questions were asked about the date of the building (if erected after 1800), the number of sittings (distinguishing between free and appropriated sittings), the number of people actually present at each service on 30th March 1851, the number of Sunday scholars present and the average attendances at each time of day for both general congregation and Sunday scholars. Ministers of the Established Church were asked to fill in details of the endowment of the church.[12]

There were some objections to the nature of the questions before the census was taken. In the House of Commons, Goulburn asked whether the questions on income were compulsory, whilst Lord Stanley in the House of Lords objected to the inquisitorial nature of the questions, especially those on endowments and the private accounts of private schools. In both Houses government spokesmen said that failure to answer these questions would not be subject to penalty.[13] Four days later Goulburn returned to the attack and complained that the enquiries were vague and in some respects unwarrantable, citing the questions on average attendance as examples of the former and those on income as examples of the latter. On that occasion Sir George Grey repeated the assurance that penalties would not attach to these questions and also said that the questions on income could be ignored completely.[14] In the House of Lords the Bishop of Oxford, Samuel Wilberforce, presented a petition from the Deanery of Newbury complaining about the questions, arguing that many replies would not be made at all, that others would be necessarily vague, that the general result would be the propagation of error rather than truth, and that the incorrect information thus obtained would be made available to the prejudice of the interests of the Church: his own opinion was to advise the clergy not to answer. Earl Granville, for the government, pointed out that failure to answer would only 'redound greatly to the disadvantage of the ministers of the Established Church'. A short debate followed in which Wilberforce ended by saying that 'it was his opinion that it was, for every reason, better that they should have no information of this kind rather than imperfect information' — an attitude which has characterised many of the attacks on this kind of enquiry since.[15]

In the event the vast majority of returns were completed in England and Wales, and many clergy answered the questions on income. 30,610 lists of places of worship were received and 34,000 returns were sent to London. The Anglican returns were checked against the Clergy List, and a second request was sent to a number of clergy who sent in blanks first time, most of whom responded. The remaining blanks were filled in by returns from the local registrars. Only 390 returns contained no information about sittings or attendance. Mann estimated that 90 per cent of the Anglican clergy had filled in returns themselves.[16] In Scotland, however, the response was not so good.

The publication of the *Report and Tables* for England and Wales in January 1854 revived the controversy. The *Report* showed that Protestant Dissenters provided nearly half the church accommodation in the country, that over 40 per cent of the attendants at worship in the morning and afternoon were Dissenters, that two-thirds of the attendants in the evening were Dissenters, and that the number present at the best attended Dissenting services exceeded the number at the best attended Anglican services (Table 8.1).

TABLE 8.1
Accommodation and attendance at Church: England & Wales, 1851

| | Sittings | Attendances at worship on 30th March 1851 | | | |
		Morning	Afternoon	Evening	Best attended service
Church of England	5,317,915	2,541,244	1,890,764	860,543	2,971,258
Protestant Dissenters	4,661,138	1,839,112	1,225,042	2,105,573	3,110,782
Roman Catholics	186,111	252,783	53,967	76,880	249,389
Other denominations	47,399	14,343	14,362	21,453	24,793
Totals	10,212,563	4,647,482	3,184,135	3,064,449	6,356,222

This table includes estimates for blank returns.
Source: Report, pp. clxxxi–clxxxii.

21,000 copies of the *Report* were sold and it seems to have been much discussed in religious circles.[17] Attention focused on the apparent strength of Dissent. *The Nonconformist* said that 'for the first time, perhaps, in the annals of this country Dissenters are dealt with in a State paper in accordance with their actual professions and deeds'.[18] It went on to argue that the results made it impossible to justify the State Church system. Some Anglicans, however, took these results as proof of their prediction that the census would be inaccurate. They were led by the Bishop of Oxford, who returned to the attack in the House of Lords. He repeated his arguments about the inaccuracy of the census and said that it was wrong for misleading statistics to go out under government authority. He described various Dissenting and Roman Catholic tricks, but suggested that perhaps the lack of education of many Dissenters had led them to exaggerate. He concluded, 'Thank

God, the great majority of people of this country do still belong to the Established Church'. The Bishop of St David's echoed his sentiments.[19] Not all Anglicans were so sceptical. An article in the *Christian Remembrancer* said that 'on the whole the Church of England may accept the general results as not a very untrue picture.'[20] The Rev. A. Hume, though a critic of some of the methods and conclusions of Mann's report, on the whole accepted the census as accurate within its own limits.[21] But these people tended to be exceptional: in most subsequent Anglican discussions of the subject it was the errors of the census that were dwelt upon.[22]

There is no doubt that some Dissenters twisted the figures to use as ammunition in the campaign for disestablishment of the Church of England. The Liberation Society published a long pamphlet entitled *Voluntaryism in England and Wales,* which used the statistics of accommodation to argue that 'the Church of England, as a State Church, has totally failed' and that 'the success of the Voluntary principle in religion has been as unequivocal as has been the failure of its opposite'.[23] The Rev. John Kennedy, in a paper to the Congregational Union's assembly, quoted Mann's estimates of the total number of separate attendants to show the large numbers of Dissenters and their majority position in certain areas.[24] He also drew the conclusion that the Establishment had failed. The Baptist Union Committee noticed that the census figures did not tally with their own and a 'trustworthy person' was permitted to examine the schedules to extract more detailed information. In 1855 they published revised estimates of the number of Baptists, assuming that the original figures had under-represented Baptist strength.[25] For many, this aspect of the returns made more impact than the revelation of the number of people who did not go to church or chapel at all: but non-attendance was not ignored. The Rev. W.R. Stevenson, a minister of the New Connexion of General Baptists, and the Rev. John Kennedy, in the paper referred to, both pointed out the great mission field which had to be opened up, particularly in the towns.[26] But, particularly in the context of parliament, the results of the census became evidence in the battle between Dissenters and the Establishment.

It was primarily because of this that questions on religion were never repeated. In 1860 the government proposed to ask for the religious profession of every individual, on the grounds that this would be a more satisfactory way of obtaining information on religion than that adopted in 1851. Nonconformist MPs objected, and under pressure Sir George Lewis, the Home Secretary, said that he was prepared to exempt this question from penalty. This concession, however, was not sufficient and Edward Baines moved the omission of the question in Committee. The government gave way after a furious debate which was concluded by Lord Palmerston with his famous words, 'We defer to their feelings, but we cannot assent to their reasoning'.[27] A question on religious profession remained in the Irish Census. There is no doubt that Dissenters had conscientious objections to what they regarded as an unwarrantable inquisition into a private matter: but it was also plain that a census of profession would give a much less favourable picture of the position of Dissent than a census of attendance at worship. The matter was raised in the discussion of every census bill up to 1910, but no government ever suggested the question again.[28] Not was there ever any suggestion that the government should repeat a census of attendance at worship. The sad consequence was that the religious census of 1851 was discredited because of the efforts made to use it for purposes not originally intended.

This controversy has also affected the attitude of historians to the religious census of 1851. It is impossible to appreciate the census on its own terms, unless the words of Mann in a letter to *The Times* in 1870 are taken seriously: 'The inquiry undertaken in 1851 related to the provision for religious worship and the extent to which the means provided were made use of. It was not an enumeration of professed adherents to the different sects'.[29] This explains why so much space is spent on accommodation in the report (more than on attendance) and why Mann, in calculating the number of attendants, felt free to use statistical methods which can only be justified on the grounds that regional and denominational errors will balance out. From this point of view Mann's most significant discovery was that lack of accommodation was not a complete explanation of absence from worship:

'Teeming populations often now surround half empty churches, which would probably remain half empty if the sittings were all free'.[30] The census thus provides a good example of the need to understand fully the purposes for which information is gathered before material can be properly used. This should be remembered in the discussion of the ways in which the census can be used to illustrate variations in the level of religious practice later in this chapter.

It is not necessary to give more than a brief outline of the main features of the *Report* here. It began with a history of religious opinions in England from the Druids onwards: detailed descriptions were then given of the main religious bodies and the progress made by the Church of England in church building was noted. A discussion of accommodation followed, beginning with calculations of the number of sittings required for a given population and continuing with comparisons of the situation in town and country, between the various denominations, and at different times of day. The discussion of attendance also began with calculations as to a desirable percentage of attendance and then compared the position in town and country and in the various denominations. The report concluded with an analysis of the causes of non-attendance at worship. A series of general tables and figures for each registration district completed the volume.

Reliability of the Religious Census

Before assessing the *Report* it is perhaps wise to consider the reliability of the information on which it was based. The most important point in its favour is the completeness of the returns. Because enumerators were asked to seek out places of worship 'on the ground', rather than from official lists, many small places were included, especially meeting rooms, that might otherwise have been missed. Of the 34,467 returns received, 2,524 contained no information about sittings and 1,394 contained no information about attendance: however, only 390 contained information about neither. In the two tables of the *Report* which give total sittings and total attendances, the estimates which have been made for the deficient returns are clearly shown.[31] Local historians should remember that even so some places were missed and the location of some chapels is sometimes not precisely identified: these can be checked by referring to directories and denominational records. Some registration districts included workhouse and prison chapels: others did not. But, on the national scale, the completeness is impressive.

The dates of foundation of chapels are less reliable, and the tables based on them not really very helpful. Some Nonconformists gave the date when the building was erected, others the date when it was acquired, others the date when the congregation then occupying it was formed. Each of these pieces of information is individually interesting, but collectively they cause confusion. The Rev. A. Hume made some telling points on this matter in his discussion of the census, pointing out that the tendency of Nonconformist congregations to move made them seem to have expanded more rapidly since 1801 than in fact they had.[32]

The figures given for accommodation are probably the most accurate of any in the census — accurate in the sense that they are precise. In some cases the figure given is apparently the number of pews and a multiplier has been used to give the number of sittings; but these are easily distinguished in the schedules because they are marked in red. The distinction between free and appropriated sittings was widely misunderstood, as Mann admitted: in many country churches sittings were allocated to families and thus counted as 'appropriated', even though they were not rented: in the towns, and in Nonconformist chapels generally, 'appropriated' sittings meant rented ones.[33]

The attendance figures have been most criticised: first, for being inaccurate; and secondly, for being misleading, even if they were accurate in themselves. Some accusations have been made of deliberate exaggeration, though, as Mann observed, it seems unlikely that clergymen, or even humble dissenting ministers, would deliberately falsify their returns.[34] A more cogent objection rests on the fact that no systematic count was made, particularly of the large congregations, and that there was probably a natural tendency to exaggerate the numbers. This is certainly possible.[35] A different kind of objection is that many figures were obviously rounded to the nearest ten or hundred: by adding together these figures and those which purport to be exact, a spurious impression of exactitude is given. This is a real problem and one which is very difficult to solve. The minister of St George's, Leicester, who wrote 'Nearly full, not so full, quite full' in his attendance return may be giving just as accurate a picture as the curate at Melton Mowbray who wrote down 1,050 and added, 'the congregation is given as nearly as I can judge from the size of the church'.[36] One solution is to round all figures to the nearest ten or hundred: but it is not easy to know how to combine rounded congregations of several hundred in the same table as congregations of below fifty. Obviously a lot must depend on what the tables are intended to show.

The view that the attendance figures were misleading, even if accurate, was justified in two ways. First, there were accusations that Dissenters had tried to pack their chapels on Census Sunday; and, secondly, it was argued that local circumstances had reduced attendance – an inopportune shower of rain, the fact that people visited their relatives on mid-Lent Sunday, a local epidemic, and so on. That these circumstances affected the figures in some cases cannot be doubted. But, as Mann pointed out, it is unlikely that they seriously distort the picture. Professor Inglis has remarked that it shows that clergymen were conscientious and tried to explain rather than exaggerate. Dr Pickering has also made the point that the margin of error for these reasons is likely to be equally distributed over the country. On the whole, scholars who have worked with the religious census returns recently have concluded that they do not seriously mislead, if used with care.[37]

Problems of using the Religious Census

There are, however, a number of warnings which ought to be given to those who work from the published tables alone, without referring to the schedules. First, there is a danger of mistakes in addition: some of these are obvious and accidental, like the statement in the *Report* that 'there are in England and Wales 35 different religious communities or sects – 27 native and indigenous, and 9 foreign';[38] others can be discovered by checking the addition in the census tables;[39] yet others can only be discovered by recalculating the tables — for example, the attendance figures for Leicester in the published table overstate any possible combination of the totals on the original returns by 2,000. Secondly, in some cases duplicate returns for the same chapel have been counted as separate returns; and in other cases disused churches have been counted as places of worship.[40] A third snare lies in the use made by Mann of average figures. Although the original returns contain both actual and average attendance figures (in many cases the same), at first sight the published tables look as though they contain only actual figures. In fact, however, what Mann did was to use actual figures where he had them and supplement them with average figures where necessary. Unfortunately no indication is given in the tables of the proportion of actual to average figures. A more sensible method would be to take the average figures as a base and supplement these with actual figures, for no particular interest attaches to the precise number of people present on 30th March 1851 — it is valuable only in so far as it reflects a normal state of affairs. The instructions for filling up the schedules invited those making the return to give average figures if for any reason the number present on 30th March 'should not truly represent the numbers *usually* in attendance', and some churches even admitted that they had put average figures in the 'actual' column because their actual attendance was low.[41] Finally, the denominational identification of some chapels is vague: the published tables for registration districts make no distinction between Particular and General Baptists, for example, and many chapels included as Independents had no connection with the Congregational Union — some were Independent Methodists, others were High Calvinists.[42]

One particularly disappointing feature of the published tables is the failure to distinguish between Sunday scholars and the general congregation. If Sunday scholars were returned for a time of day when there was no service, they were omitted from the tables: but if they were returned for a time of day when there was a service, they were counted in with the general congregation. Whilst it is reasonable to exclude Sunday Schools from tables of attendance at worship on the ground that their purpose was educational, the fact that it has not been done consistently produces confusion. Moreover, as the age structure of the population varies significantly from district to district, no standard allowance for this error can be made. National figures for Sunday Schools may be found in the Educational Census[43] (see also Chapter 7 above), but the only satisfactory way to overcome this difficulty is to consult the schedules.

The other major difficulty remains — that of calculating the number of attendants at worship, as distinct from the number of attendances. This problem was inherent in the method of taking the census. Mann wanted to find out how much of the accommodation for worship was used; but he had to admit that there was no way of calculating how many people attended more than once on Sunday, nor how many people attended less frequently than once a week. He did offer a formula to take account of double attendances, but he told the Statistical Society that there was no way of even forming a probable conjecture as to the irregular attendants. The importance of this problem can easily be seen: if a large number of people attended once a fortnight or once a month, the number who never attended at all is reduced: similarly, if a large number of people attended more than once on 30th March 1851, the total number attending is reduced. Mann therefore devised his famous formula for the number of separate attendants — all the morning congregation plus half the afternoon plus one-third of the evening.[44] In its original context this was a perfectly acceptable statistical method, for Mann explicitly assumed that denominational and regional variations would balance each other out. In view of that assumption, it was extremely misleading — as Mann went on to do — to publish a table which purported to show the number of attendants belonging to each denomination.[45] Naturally this table was widely reproduced as a 'result' of the census, though Mann cannot be wholly blamed for that.

Mann's formula was unfair to Nonconformists; though — as Abraham Hume argued — the morning attendance was the highest total figure, the Dissenters' highest turnout was in the evening, only one-third of which was counted in the estimate of the number of their attendants. Many Dissenting chapels had no morning service at all. Anglicans argued that some people attended the Church of England in the morning and a Dissenting chapel in the afternoon or evening. There is no doubt that this happened: but why should such people be counted as Anglicans rather than Dissenters? Certainly they were different from the 'professed' Dissenters who went nowhere else, but presumably they were also different from convinced Anglicans, who also went nowhere else. This illustrates the dangers of trying to produce a denominational breakdown of the estimated total number of attendants. Hume also argued that 'the morning service may be said to be the service of *necessity,* the afternoon service that of *convenience,* and the evening one that of *devotion'.*[46] This may have been true in those places where there were three services on a Sunday, particularly if they were Anglican. Hume was a town clergyman. But nearly 10,000 places of worship had only one service on Sunday; nearly 9,000 of these were in the countryside, of which half were Anglican. Mann's calculation on this point thus took no account of the number of people who had no opportunity to attend a second service, for 60 per cent of these single services were in the afternoon or evening.[47] Nor was it invariably the case that where there were two services in a church or chapel the morning service was better attended. This was often true for Anglicans, particularly in the towns, but in some country areas afternoon attendances were consistently larger. The Nonconformist pattern was generally quite different in both town and country, with the largest attendance coming in the evening. These differences were some of the most important facts revealed by the religious census and they are inevitably obscured by attempts at national generalisation.

Mann's guess about the total number of irregular attendants was less controversial. He thought that Dissenters were generally more assiduous in church attendance than Anglicans or Roman Catholics, so for his estimate of the total 'religious population' he doubled his figures for Anglicans and Roman Catholics and increased his Nonconformist figures by two-thirds to give the following result:[48]

Church of England	7,546,948
Roman Catholics	610,786

Protestant Dissenters	5,303,609
Total	13,461,343

(The total population of England and Wales in 1851 was 17,927,609.) This estimate does, of course, depend on the accuracy of the first formula because this is how the starting figures for Anglicans, Catholics and Dissenters are calculated.

The analysis and findings of the Religious Census

It is now possible to make some assessment of the *Report* and its tables. The first two sections on the progress of religious opinions and the various denominations in detail are mainly of historical interest: Mann believed that the origins of a sect indicated its particular 'genius' and the section is interesting in showing how much was known about this at the time. From the reactions expressed in several articles it is clear that this was new to some contemporaries. In some cases statistics were included in the descriptions of the various denominations, either from the census or from their own official sources. The most interesting figures in this section are those showing the progress made by the Church of England since 1831 in erecting new churches in Lancashire, Cheshire, the West Riding of Yorkshire, Middlesex and Surrey.[49] The section on the Wesleyan Reformers also comments that their own figures are much higher than the census returns: the crisis in Methodism at that time makes it very difficult to assess the relative position of Wesleyans and Wesleyan Reformers.[50]

ACCOMMODATION

The section on accommodation contains the most tables. It begins with a calculation as to the proportion of the population able to attend worship at any one time (i.e. the amount of accommodation required), which Mann estimated as 58 per cent. More significant than this figure is the subsequent discussion of those places where there is not sufficient accommodation. Tables 2, 3 and 4 of the *Report* show how the amount of accommodation varied according to the size of parish and whether the parish was urban or rural: the position was worst in the large towns.[51] Estimates which follow, of accommodation at previous dates, are unreliable because they depend on the dating of churches and chapels, which was inconsistently done: but the figures given indicate that no substantial improvement in the general position had taken place since 1801 despite the number of churches that had been built, because of the increase in population. Table 8 of the *Report* gave the number of services per Sunday for the urban and rural areas as part of Mann's argument that at no time of day was accommodation sufficient: this very useful table also indicates the varying patterns of worship. The breakdown between the Church of England and Dissent in both town and country on this point is also given (*Report*, table 16). The rest of the section concerns the accommodation provided by the different denominations, amplifying the point that the towns are badly served. Mann's general conclusion was that there was a need to provide more accommodation in the working class areas of towns — the suburbs could fend for themselves — and to make better use of existing buildings by holding special services for the working classes on Sundays and weekdays: 'Week evening services, undoubtedly, are common now;' he added, 'but they are principally of a character adapted mainly to the regular attendants, and they generally terminate about the hour at which the workmen leave their labour'.[52]

ATTENDANCE

The section on attendance is shorter. Beginning with a calculation of what would be a desirable percentage of attendance, it was shown (*Report*, table 21) that accommodation was insufficient, but Mann concluded that this was not the main reason for absence. The percentage of the population attending was higher in the countryside than in the towns (*Report*, table 22), but Mann did not comment on the fact that the same table also showed how low attendance was in the countryside. The estimated number of attendants for each denomination (*Report*, table 23) is also expressed as a percentage of the population, with the argument that the attendance patterns reveal social differences, and the rest of the section is concerned with an analysis of the reasons for the absence of 'the labouring myriads of our country'. It is worth noting that this section is not based on the statistics as such: the reasons given by Mann were general (social distinctions in church, indifference of the Churches to the social condition of the poor, distrust of ministers' motives, and effects of poverty and overcrowding) and not related to detailed differences revealed by the census. The conclusions of Mann's report, in which he defends his impartiality as a reporter, are interesting because they show his own presuppositions — which may indeed be taken as those of the whole enquiry — that religion is essential to a civilised community and more important than education:

> For, whatever the dissuasive influence, from crime and grosser vice, of those refined ideas which in general accompany augmented knowledge, yet undoubtedly it may occur that, under the opposing influence of social misery, increased intelligence may only furnish to the vicious and criminal increased facilities for evil. But the wider and more penetrating influence exerted by religious principle — controlling conscience rather than refining taste — is seldom felt without conferring, in addition to its higher blessings, those fixed views and habits which can scarcely fail to render individuals prosperous and states secure. Applying to the regulation of their daily conduct towards themselves and towards society the same high sanctions which control them in their loftier relations, Christian men become, almost inevitably, temperate, industrious, and provident, as part of their religious duty; and Christian citizens acquire respect for human laws from having learnt to reverence those which are divine.[53]

THE TABLES

Modern students will usually be more interested in the general tables than in the report. The most useful are those giving accommodation and attendance (including estimates) by denominations for England and Wales (*Report,* table A — partly reproduced in Appendix VIII) and those giving similar information (but without estimates) for the registration divisions and counties (*Report,* tables B and C). A summary of the denominational figures for the eleven main regions is given in Appendix IX. There is also a detailed statement of the number of defective returns. Accommodation and attendance by denomination are given for large towns (*Report,* table F), as are the variations in accommodation provided by the denominations in the counties and registration districts

(*Report,* tables G and H). The tables showing districts with the most and the least accommodation and the comparative position of the Church of England and Dissent on accommodation in different parts of the country (*Report,* tables I and K) are particularly interesting. So are those giving the number of services by each religious body at different times of day and the extent to which the various denominations make use of their accommodation (*Report,* tables L and M): Unitarians and Quakers have high morning figures, suggesting that their support came from the middle classes; all Methodists and General Baptists have evening figures which exceed the morning, suggesting a large working class element; whilst Independents and Particular Baptists have figures about equal for morning and evening – a position somewhere in between. Finally, the number of attendants at the best-attended services in registration counties and divisions for Anglicans, Dissenters, Roman Catholics and Others is given in a very useful table (*Report,* table N).

SCOTLAND

The Report and Tables for Scotland are much shorter, because publication was demanded before Mann had had time to make a detailed report. As stated earlier the proportion of defective returns is higher: 481 out of 3395 gave no return for accommodation or attendance, giving Scotland a 14 per cent failure as compared with 1 per cent in England and Wales. There were also more places of worship which were never issued with a return. The reasons for this state of affairs seem to have been that enumerators were less careful in delivering forms in Scotland and clergy were less ready to give answers after it was announced that the enquiry was voluntary. The absence of civil machinery for the registration of births, marriages and deaths in Scotland at that time also made it impossible for the Census Office to remedy the deficiencies by subsequent enquiry as it did in England and Wales.[54]

The number of places of worship in Scotland was very much smaller than in England and Wales, but the proportion of accommodation and attendants to population was higher. Whereas in England and Wales just over one quarter of the

population attended in the morning, in Scotland the figure
was nearly one third. By contrast in Scotland only a very
small percentage attended in the evening, because the
number of evening services was much smaller.[55] The denominational structure of Scotland was, of course, also different
with the three largest bodies all being Presbyterian. The census
showed that the Free Church of Scotland (formed after the
Disruption of 1843) had twice as many attendants in the
evening as the Established Church, and it also emphasised
how rapidly the Free Church had grown in eight years: it
already had only two hundred fewer churches than the
Established Church.[56] A summary of the accommodation
and attendance for the main denominations is given in
Appendix X. Because of the lack of a system of civil registration — not introduced into Scotland until 1855 — there
are detailed tables for only counties and burghs: as in
England, it had been agreed not to publish figures for parishes.

INTERPRETATION

What did the religious census show? Can modern historians
learn anything more from it? Modern research has concentrated on what the census showed about non-attendance at
worship. But recently interest has been moving towards an
investigation of the differences in attendance between
denominations and regions.

Mann had no doubt about what the census had shown:
'The most important fact which this investigation as to
attendance brings before us,' he wrote, 'is, unquestionably,
the alarming number of the non-attendants. Even in the least
unfavourable aspect of the figures just presented, and assuming (as no doubt is right) that the 5,288,294 absent every
Sunday are not always the same individuals, it must be
apparent that a sadly formidable portion of the English people
are habitual neglecters of the public ordinances of religion'.[57]
The fact of non-attendance was not new. Frederick Engels,
the Communist, and Edward Miall, the Congregationalist, had
both discussed the absence of the English working classes
from church in books published in the 1840s and, though
their analyses differed, in many ways they were strikingly

similar. Other Churchmen too were aware of the problem.[58] What the census did was to give a statistical impression of the scale of non-attendance, and this brought home to a statistically-minded age the extent of the problem. Perhaps also clergymen who had comforted themselves with the thought that their own plight was particularly desperate were horrified to discover how typical they were. On the other hand, we should not be misled by the precision of Mann's number of 5,288,294 absentees: the problems of making such a calculation have already been indicated. What we can say, however, is that on the evidence of the census the number of people attending worship can only have significantly exceeded eleven million (in England and Wales) if a good number of them went less often than once a week: and furthermore, that this statement itself is an optimistic one, because we know that a proportion of the eleven million attendances recorded by the census represent double attendances. In other words, statements implying that a majority of nineteenth century Englishmen attended church two or three times on Sunday are simply unacceptable.[59]

Generally the fact of non-attendance is not in dispute, and attention is concentrated on the reasons for it. Mann noted that the lowest levels of attendance were found in large towns; from this he inferred that the decisive differences were those of social class and that 'the labouring myriads' were the chief absentees. The truth of this description, however, does not necessarily imply that people did not attend church *because* they were poor and lived in large towns. Some writers, such as Mann, tended to stress the effects of poverty: for them, large towns were relevant to the explanation because they were the scenes of the most widespread poverty. Others, such as Engels, pointed to the effects of the geographical separation of social groups, to the fact of the sheer size of towns, and to the social problems facing immigrants uprooted from their country origins. These varying lines of explanation have been followed by later commentators: they have been drawn together in a composite explanation which sees industrialisation and urbanisation as twin causes working through the social effects of migration.[60] But there are still several loose ends. Professor Inglis has shown that towns vary

TABLE 8.2
Percentage of the population attending worship in
England and Wales, 1851

	Morning	Afternoon	Evening
Rural areas	28.1	25.5	17.8
Large towns over 10,000	23.9	10.5	15.3

Source: *Report*, Table 22, p.clv.

as to how 'bad' their church attendance level is: traditional
country market towns in the south do better than new
industrial towns in the north.[61] Mann's own figures showed
that levels of attendance in the countryside were not idyllic
(Table 8.2).

Does the difference between the two sets of figures justify
the weight put on the towns as an explanation? In fact the
distinction made here between 'rural areas' and 'large towns'
is far too simple, and the figures in the published report can
be rearranged to produce an even less favourable picture of
the rural situation. But the towns were the real object of
Mann's (and the government's) attention: no one felt that
there was a social problem in the countryside and so there
was little interest in rural religion.

Another point to be considered here is the difference shown
by the census between England, Wales and Scotland. The
Scottish Report noted the higher attendance levels in Scotland
than in England and Wales, but if the percentages for England
and Wales are calculated separately those for Wales are seen
to be much closer to the Scottish ones: indeed the Welsh
evening attendance level is slightly higher than the Scottish
morning one. Why should attendance levels in the 'Celtic
fringe' be higher than in England? An explanation of non-
attendance simply in terms of industrialisation and urbanisation can only take us part of the way here; added point is
given to the question if we remember that attendance levels
in the northern counties of England,[62] counties in many ways
similar in economy and terrain to parts of Wales and Scotland,
are actually lower than the average for England as a whole.
The importance of regional and denominational differences

is therefore clear. In its article on the religious census, the *Christian Remembrancer* said, 'The fact is, that those who do go to church, go with tolerable punctuality, are taken from certain classes and certain ages of life, i.e. from the upper and middle classes, from servants, from a small portion of the old and infirm, and in large numbers from children; other classes and ages do not attend'.[63] As a generalisation this statement has been borne out by subsequent research.[64] But the religious census does not enable us to verify this generalisation with any precision; whereas it does provide us with more material for comparisons between denominations and regions than any other single source.

This was recognised at the time. 'Scarcely anything, indeed, is more curious or more puzzling', Mann told the Statistical Society, 'than the attempt to trace the causes why particular doctrines or religious parties should find one soil favourable and another adverse to their propagation and success'.[65] The evidence comes from the figures both for accommodation and attendance. Mann provided a table showing the relative amounts of accommodation provided by the Church of England and Dissent in counties and selected towns (*Report*, table K). The Rev. A. Hume drew a map to show the relative strength of the Church of England and Dissent based on calculations he made from the religious census for the entire worshipping community.[66] Dr W.S.F. Pickering has prepared similar maps based on the best attended service, and Dr J.D. Gay has prepared maps based on total attendances.[67] These all show that the Church of England was strong in the south, especially south of a line drawn from the Wash to the Bristol Channel (excluding Cornwall), and weak in the north and in Wales. Dissenters were strongest in Wales and Cornwall, and in the East Midlands; and weak in the West Midlands and counties south of London. Roman Catholics were strongest in Lancashire. The most interesting feature was first noted by Hume: 'It does not appear that the injury of one religious body contributes to the success of another ... In other words, the high numbers of one do not indicate low numbers of another; but the contrary'.[68] There is a country-wide variation in religious practice which transcends the division between Church of England and Dissent. Moreover, though it is true that the large towns were concentrated in the north where church-going was weak, it is probable that this variation reflects something deeper than the difference between town and country, and may be similar to the variations in France discovered by Boulard which go back long before industrialisation or even the Revolution.[69]

There are thus three broad types of area where Dissent is stronger than the Church of England: first, where the Church of England is also strong, as in Bedfordshire, Huntingdonshire, the North Riding of Yorkshire and Leicestershire; secondly, where the Church of England is weak, as in Wales, Cornwall, Lincolnshire, Nottinghamshire, Derbyshire and the rest of Yorkshire; and thirdly, where Dissent is weak but the Church of England is weaker, as in Cheshire, Staffordshire, Lancashire, Northumberland and Durham. In the towns, of course, Dissent was often stronger than the Church of England, but the overall religious situation was poor. The analysis can also be taken a stage further so as to differentiate between the success of the 'old' (Baptist and Congregational) and the 'new' (Methodist) Dissent. In general the old Dissent is concentrated in areas of Anglican strength, probably because of its seventeenth century origins, whereas the new Dissent is concentrated in areas of Anglican weakness, probably because these were areas of new economic growth in the late eighteenth and early nineteenth centuries only slowly catered for by the Church of England. A similar analysis can also be made for Methodism itself, showing how the later Methodist denominations — Primitive Methodists and Bible Christians, for example — flourished away from the centres of the Wesleyan revival. This whole field is a fascinating area for study.[70] The religious census offers ideal material because of its unique completeness, and because it was taken at a point in time before the economic changes of the later nineteenth century had begun to produce a different pattern, with a shift of population back to the south and east.

The comparisons between counties so far considered have all been based on the published tables. A study of the original returns enables one to make comparisons between settlements and villages in the same area. Three main conclusions emerged from my own work on Leicestershire.[71] First, the distribution of Nonconformist chapels, and indeed of the Non-conformist denominations, often turns out to have a certain logic about it. It is generally more likely, for example, that Nonconformist chapels will be found in villages where there is no single, large landowner dominating the settlement — in 'open' villages, in other words. Similarly Roman Catholic chapels are usually found near the homes of old Catholic families, or in places which have at some time experienced the presence of a group of Irish labourers. Chapels of the older Dissenting bodies are often found in villages with a number of long-established freehold farmers; Methodist chapels are more likely in villages with an eighteenth century industrial or mining development or in villages with a large number of agricultural labourers (i.e. arable rather than pastoral). None of this is surprising, but the census shows it up. Secondly, the accommodation figures show that by no means all rural parishes had sufficient accommodation for their population. Nonconformist chapels tend to be found in the larger villages where population had grown. This confirms the impression given by Mann's table in the *Report,* based on a sample of 832 parishes.[72] Thirdly, a comparison of the percentage attendance in different villages shows that the Church of England tends to do better than average in places of low population, undivided landownership and agricultural occupations, whilst it tends to do worse than average in places of high population, 'open' villages and industrial villages. The size of population seems to be particularly significant, for in a total of 334 villages attendance was significantly above average in places below 200 in population, and significantly below average in places over 600 in population. More interesting still was the marginal effect which the presence of Dissent had on this pattern. The number of people attending Dissenting places of worship was rarely high enough to offset a significantly low Anglican attendance, though this is partly explained by the fact that clear differences do not emerge from the figures for evening services. Generally there were few Anglican evening services, but those that were held were usually well attended. Only in a handful of cases does it seem that the Church of England actually suffered directly from Dissenting competition; thus Hume's conclusion for counties seems to be valid also for villages — that there is a direct rather than an inverse correlation between the success of different religious groups.[73]

Conclusion

It is in the study of the varying levels of religious practice that the census can most profitably be used. Though it has attracted attention both at the time and since by what it revealed about non-attendance at worship, this information is essentially negative. A comparative study can usefully be linked with what the general census reveals about differences in occupation, age structure and migration patterns. From this combination, religious practice could be linked to a number of demographic variables. Since 1851 there have been a number of unofficial censuses of religious worship conducted with varying degrees of rigour.[74] None has the national coverage of the 1851 census, however, and in no other is there the same opportunity to link religious practice with other demographic information collected at the same time. For this reason the 1851 Religious Census, despite its manifest deficiencies, is likely to remain an important source for nineteenth century social history.

NOTES

1. I.e. Great Britain. No such count was made in Ireland.
2. Circular to the Clergy, 14 March 1851: H.C. 1851, vol. xliii, p. 41.
3. Horace Mann (b. 1823), barrister at law, and Secretary to the Civil Service Commission, 1855—88. His father worked in the Registrar General's office. (*Men of the Time*, 13th ed., (1861), p. 604; J. Foster, *Men at the Bar* (1885), p. 303.)
4. The *Report and Tables* for England and Wales (hereafter referred to as *Report)* are in Parliamentary Paper no. 1690: H.C. 1852—53, vol. lxxxix. An abridged version was also published by Routledge in 1854. The *Report and Tables* for Scotland (hereafter referred to as *Scottish Report)* are in Parliamentary Paper no. 1764: H.C. 1854, vol. lix. It was published early at the request of Scottish MPs who wanted to use it as evidence for the Scottish Education Bill (*Nonconformist*, 10 May 1854, p. 385).
5. A.A. Maclaren, 'Presbyterianism and the working class in a mid-nineteenth century city', *Scottish Historical Review*, vol. 46

(1967), p. 122, n. 4. The series number of the English schedules is in the Home Office Papers: H.O. 129. The University of Wales Press is publishing a two-volume calendar of the returns relating to Wales, of which the first volume has already been published: see I.G. Jones and David Williams, *eds. The Religious Census of 1851: A Calendar of the Returns relating to Wales*, vol. 1. *South Wales* (1976).

6. House of Commons, 11 July 1860: Parliamentary Debates, 3rd Series, vol. clix, col. 1709; cf. W.O. Chadwick, *The Victorian Church*, vol. i, (1966), p. 363. For his career, see *Dictionary of National Biography*.

7. *Parliamentary Debates*, 3rd Series, vol. clix, cols. 1695–1702. The Irish Religious Census of 1834 is in the *First Report of the Commissioners on Public Instruction: Ireland*: H.C. 1835, vol. xxxiii.

8. See Graham's letter to Palmerston at the beginning of the Education Report: H.C. 1852–53, (1692), vol. xc, p. ix: cf. *Report*, pp. vii–viii; H.S. Skeats and C.S. Miall, *History of the Free Churches of England, 1688–1891*, (1891), p. 522.

9. C.S. Parker, *Life and Letters of Sir James Graham* (1907), vol. i, pp. 345–47, especially letter to Peel of 17 September 1843.

10. *Parliamentary Debates*, 3rd Series, vol. cxiv, cols. 1316–17. The debates on Fox's Bill are in *Ibid.*, vol. cix, cols. 38ff, and vol. cx, cols. 438ff. Fox was MP for Oldham: his bill was defeated.

11. The Prefatory Note to the *Report* (p. v) referred to instructions received from the government 'to procure information as to the existing accommodation for religious worship'. Lewis agreed to a motion in the House of Commons for a copy of the instructions but after delay had to confess that 'no copy of the instructions could be produced, for that no such instructions existed'. J.G. Hubbard, *A Census of Religions* (1882), pp. 10–11. See also M. Drake, 'The Census, 1801–1891' in E.A. Wrigley (ed.) *Nineteenth-century Society* (1972), pp. 15–19.

12. Facsimiles of the forms and a note on procedure are to be found at the end of the *Report*. A different form was used for the Society of Friends, but this was not reproduced.

13. 14 March 1851: *Parliamentary Debates*, 3rd Series, vol. cxiv, cols. 1316–17 (House of Commons); cols. 1305–10 (House of Lords).

14. 18 March 1851: *Parliamentary Debates*, 3rd Series, vol. cxv, cols. 113–14.

15. 27 March 1851: *Parliamentary Debates*, 3rd Series, vol. cxv, cols. 629–33.

16. *Report*, p. clxx; H. Mann, 'On the Statistical Position of Religious Bodies in England and Wales', *Journal of the Statistical Society*, vol. 18 (1855), p. 144.

17. Earl Granville gave the number in the House of Lords, 11 July 1854: *Parliamentary Debates*, 3rd Series, vol. cxxxv, col. 32.

W.S.F. Pickering, 'The 1851 Religious Census — a useless experiment?' *British Journal of Sociology*, vol. 18 (1967), p. 405, says that the results did not arouse much comment: Mann implies the contrary in his lecture to the Statistical Society *(Journal of the Statistical Society*, vol. 18 (1855), p. 141). The main Nonconformist denominations referred to the report in their year books and conferences, and the *Nonconformist* commented on the reactions in other national newspapers in its issues of 11 and 25 January 1854.

18.   *Nonconformist*, 4 January 1854, p. 1.

19.   House of Lords, 11 July 1854: *Parliamentary Debates*, 3rd Series, vol. cxxxv, cols. 23—33.

20.   *Christian Remembrancer*, vol. 27 (April 1854), p. 380.

21.   A. Hume, *Remarks on the Census of Religious Worship for England and Wales* (1860), pp. 16, 19, 22—23, 29—30, 35.

22.   E.g. debates in Convocation, 1870, 1880: *Chronicle of the Convocation of Canterbury* (1870), pp. 452—53, 487—91; (1880), pp. 222—25, 225—27. See also G.H. Curteis, *Dissent in its relation to the Church of England* (1873), p. 112, n. 61; C.K.F. Brown, *A History of the English Clergy, 1800—1900* (1953), p. 177.

23.   *Voluntaryism in England and Wales, or, The Census of 1851* (1854), pp. 6, 52, 59.

24.   J. Kennedy, 'On the Census Returns respecting Congregational Worship', *Congregational Year Book* (1855), pp. 33—47.

25.   *Baptist Manual* (1854), p. 70; (1855), pp. 73—75.

26.   W.R. Stevenson, 'Association Letter', *Minutes of the General Baptist Association* (1854), pp. 40—48; J. Kennedy, *Congregational Year Book* (1855), pp. 40—42.

27.   House of Commons, 25 April 1860: *Parliamentary Debates*, 3rd Series, vol. clviii, col. 92; 25 May 1860, *ibid.*, cols. 1762—66; 11 July 1860, vol. clix, cols. 1695—1734.

28.   1870: *Parliamentary Debates*, 3rd Series, vol. ccii, cols. 1356—57, 1711—12; 1880: 3rd Series, vol. cclvi, cols. 1063—86; 1890: 3rd Series, vol. cccxlvii, cols. 402—07; 1900: 4th Series, vol. lxxx, cols. 500—05, 1002—13; 1910: 5th Series, vol. xv, col. 937. For an account of the 1860 agitation see Skeats & Miall, *History of the Free Churches*, pp. 561—63; cf. S. Maccoby, *English Radicalism, 1853—86* (1938), pp. 144—46.

29.   *The Times*, 22 July 1870, p. 4; cf. *The Times*, 11 July 1860, p. 12.

30.   *Report*, p. clxi.

31.   *Report*, pp. clxxii—iii: Supplements I and II to Table A. See also Appendix VIII to this chapter.

32.   Hume, *Remarks on the Census of Religious Worship*, pp. 8—11.

33.   *Report*, pp. cxxxiv—v.

34.   *Journal of the Statistical Society,* vol. 18 (1855), pp. 142—43.

35.   K.S. Inglis, 'Patterns of Religious Worship in 1851', *Journal of Ecclesiastical History*, vol. 11 (1960), p. 76, suggests that in some places people were counted as they entered. Hume, *Remarks*

on the Census of Religious Worship, pp. 30–32, suggested improvements in procedure, and gave examples of suspicious figures.

36. Public Record Office: *H.O. 129:* 418-2-1-1; 417-1-1-2;
37. Mann, *Journal of the Statistical Society*, vol. 18 (1855), pp. 145–46; Inglis, *Journal of Ecclesiastical History*, vol. 11 (1960), p. 77; Pickering, *British Journal of Sociology*, vol. 18 (1967), p. 387; J.D. Gay, *The Geography of Religion in England* (1971), pp. 47–49. Lord Palmerston, answering a question from Mr Pellatt in the House of Commons on 20 July 1854, said 'he reposed entire confidence in the general accuracy of the returns', *The Times*, 21 July 1854, p. 4.
38. *Report*, p. viii. This statement is nevertheless repeated without correction in Skeats & Miall, *History of the Free Churches*, p. 511.
39. E.g. the total estimated number of individuals attending worship adds to 7,261,042 but is given as 7,261,032: Table 23, *Report*, p. clvi.
40. Examples may be found in my article, 'The 1851 Religious Census: Problems and Possibilities', *Victorian Studies*, vol. 11 (1967–68), pp. 89–90.
41. E.g. the Particular Baptist Church at Arnesby, Leicestershire: Public Record Office: *H.O. 129:* 408–1–36–47. I have used average attendances in my own recalculation of the tables: see my unpublished Ph. D. Thesis, Cambridge University: *The Churches and Society in Leicestershire, 1851–1881*, chapter 1. Mann's justification for his method is in *Report*, p. clxxi.
42. *Report*, p. clxxix; *Congregational Year Book*, 1855, p. 111. This is why it is always useful to check the returns against local evidence.
43. Parliamentary Paper No. 1692: H.C. 1852–53, vol. xc. Mann's explanation of his procedure is in *Report*, p. clxxi.
44. Mann stressed that it was only one possible way, *Journal of the Statistical Society*, vol. 18 (1855), pp. 151–52. It was in fact one of four suggestions, each producing approximately the same result:

Morning + half afternoon + one-third evening	= 7,261,042
Mean of the difference between morning attendance (minimum) and total attendances (maximum)	= 7,771,774
Two-thirds of the total attendances	= 7,264,044
Best attended service plus one-third	=8,476,693

Report, p. clii; cf. Hume, *Remarks on the Census of Religious Worship*, p. 15.
45. Table 23, *Report*, p. clvi. This was widely reproduced.
46. Hume, *Remarks on the Census of Religious Worship*, p. 17.
47. Table L, *Report*, p. ccxcviii.
48. Mann, *Journal of the Statistical Society*, vol. 18 (1855), pp. 152–53.

49. Table A, *Report*, p. xxxix.
50. *Report*, p. lxxxviii.
51. *Report*, pp. cxxxvi—ix.
52. *Report*, pp. cxlix—cl.
53. *Report*, pp. clxvii—viii.
54. *Scottish Report*, pp. vii, 2, 4. Civil registration was not introduced into Scotland until 1855.
55. *Scottish Report*, Table 3, p. ix.
56. *Scottish Report*, p. x.
57. *Report*, p. clviii.
58. F. Engels, *The Condition of the Working Class in England* (1844); E. Miall, *The British Churches in relation to the British People* (1849). Cf. the discussions at the Congregational Union Assembly of 1848 *(Congregational Year Book*, 1848) and the actions of the Christian Socialist group — Maurice, Ludlow, Kingsley etc.
59. E.g. R.C.K. Ensor, *England, 1870–1914* (1936), p. 139.
60. E.g. E.R. Wickham, *Church and People in an Industrial City*, (1957).
61. Inglis, *Journal of Ecclesiastical History*, vol. 11, (1960), pp. 80–81.
62. Durham, Northumberland, Cumberland and Westmorland.
63. *Christian Remembrancer*, vol. 27, (1854), pp. 405–6.
64. E.g. R. Mudie-Smith, *The Religious Life of London* (1904), especially pp. 193–201; B.S. Rowntree & G.R. Lavers, *English Life and Leisure* (1951), pp.341–45; Hugh McLeod, *Class and Religion in the Late Victorian City* (1974), especially pp. 23–35.
65. *Journal of the Statistical Society*, vol. 18 (1855), p. 155.
66. Hume, *Remarks on the Census of Religious Worship*, frontispiece.
67. Pickering, *Journal of British Sociology*, vol. 18 (1967): these are based on *Report*, Table N, p. ccc; Gay, *Geography of Religion in England*: these are more comprehensive than Pickering's.
68. Hume, *Remarks on the Census of Religious Worship*, p. 33.
69. F. Boulard, *An Introduction to Religious Sociology* (Eng. trans. 1960), ch. 3. A first attempt at doing something similar for England has now been made by J.D. Gay, *Geography of Religion in England*, but Dr Gay devotes most of his space to the examination of denominational differences rather than variations in religious practice in general.
70. See Gay, *Geography of Religion in England;* R. Currie, 'A Micro-Theory of Methodist Growth', *Proceedings of the Wesley Historical Society*, vol. 36, (1967), pp. 65–73, and his book, *Methodism Divided*, (1968), ch. 3; B. Greaves, *An Analysis of the Spread of Methodism in Yorkshire during the 18th Century and early 19th Century*, unpublished M.A. thesis, Leeds University, 1960–61.
71. *The Churches and Society in Leicestershire, 1851–1881*, (unpublished Cambridge Ph. D. thesis, 1969). I.G. Jones has done some similar work on the Swansea Registration District: 'Denominationalism in Swansea and District: a Study of the Ecclesiastical Census of 1851', *Morgannwg, Journal of the Glamorgan History*

Society, vol. 12, (1968), pp. 67—96.

72.   *Report*, p. cxxvii.

73.   I hope to develop this line of enquiry in future research.

74.   E.g. the newspaper censuses of 1881, collected by Andrew Mearns, *The Statistics of Attendance at Public Worship* (1882); and R. Mudie-Smith, *The Religious Life of London* (1904).

APPENDIX VII
Facsimiles of the Religious Census forms, 1851

Different forms were provided for the established and non-established Churches, and for England and Wales, and Scotland

(a) **Established Church: England and Wales.**

FORM A.

CENSUS OF GREAT BRITAIN, 1851.
(13 & 14 Victoriæ, Cap. 53.)

A RETURN of the several Particulars to be inquired into respecting the under-mentioned Church or Chapel in England, belonging to the United Church of England and Ireland.

A similar Return (*mutatis mutandis*) will be obtained with respect to Churches belonging to the Established Church in Scotland, and the Episcopal Church there, and also from Roman Catholic Priests, and from the Ministers of every other Religious Denomination throughout Great Britain, with respect to their Places of Worship.]

I.	NAME AND DESCRIPTION OF CHURCH OR CHAPEL.			
II.	WHERE SITUATED.	Parish, Ecclesiastical Division or District, Township, or Place.	Superintendent Registrar's District.	County and Diocese.
III.	WHEN CONSECRATED OR LICENSED.	UNDER WHAT CIRCUMSTANCES CONSECRATED OR LICENSED.		

IN THE CASE OF A CHURCH OR CHAPEL CONSECRATED OR LICENSED SINCE THE 1st JANUARY 1800 ; STATE

IV.	HOW OR BY WHOM ERECTED.	COST, HOW DEFRAYED.
		By Parliamentary Grant - - - Parochial Rate - - - - Private Benefaction or Subscrip-} tion, or from other Sources -} Total Cost - - £

V.		VI.
HOW ENDOWED.		SPACE AVAILABLE FOR PUBLIC WORSHIP.
Land - - - £ Tithe - - - Glebe - - - Other Permanent En-} dowment - -}	Pew Rents - - - £ Fees - - - Dues - - - Easter Offerings - Other Sources -	Free Sittings - - - Other Sittings - - - Total Sittings -

	ESTIMATED NUMBER OF PERSONS ATTENDING DIVINE SERVICE ON SUNDAY, MARCH 30, 1851.				AVERAGE NUMBER OF ATTENDANTS during Months next preceding March 30, 1851. (See Instruction VII.)			
VII.		Morning.	Afternoon.	Evening.		Morning.	Afternoon.	Evening.
	General Congre-} gation - -} Sunday Scholars -				General Congre-} gation - -} Sunday Scholars -			
	Total -				Total -			

VIII.	REMARKS.

I certify the foregoing to be a true and correct Return to the best of my belief.
Witness my hand this_____ day of_____ 1851.
IX. (*Signature*)_____
   (*Official Character*) _____ *of the above-named.*
   (*Address by Post*) _____

(b) Non-established churches: England and Wales.

FORM B.

CENSUS OF GREAT BRITAIN, 1851.

(13 & 14 Victoriæ, Cap. 53.)

A RETURN of the several Particulars to be inquired into respecting the under-mentioned Place of Public Religious Worship.

[N.B.—A similar Return will be obtained from the Clergy of the Church of England, and also from the Ministers of every other Religious Denomination throughout Great Britain.]

I.	II.			III.	IV.	V.	VI.	VII.			VIII.				IX.
Name or Title of Place of Worship.	Where situate; specifying the			Religious Denomination.	When erected.	Whether a separate and entire Building.	Whether used exclusively as a Place of Worship (except for a Sunday School).	Space available for Public Worship.			Estimated Number of Persons attending Divine Service on Sunday March 30, 1851.				REMARKS.
	Parish or Place.	District, County.						Number of Sittings already provided.				Morning.	Afternoon.	Evening.	
								Free Sittings.	Other Sittings.						
	(1)	(2)	(3)					(4)	(5)		General Congregation				
											Sunday Scholars				
											TOTAL -				
								Free Space or *Standing Room* for			Average Number of Attendants during Months. (See Instruction VIII.)				
											General Congregation				
											Sunday Scholars				
											TOTAL -				

I certify the foregoing to be a true and correct Return to the best of my belief. Witness my hand this _____ day of _____ 1851.

X. (*Signature*) _____ of the above-named Place of Worship.

(*Official Character*) _____

(*Address by Post*) _____

The Particulars to be inserted in Divisions I. to VI. inclusive, and in IX., may be written either along or across the Columns, as may be more convenient.

(c) Established Church: Scotland.

CENSUS OF GREAT BRITAIN, 1851.
(13 & 14 Victoriæ, Cap. 53.)

A RETURN of the several Particulars to be inquired into respecting the under-mentioned Church or Chapel in SCOTLAND, belonging to the Established Church of Scotland.

[A similar Return (*mutatis mutandis*) will be obtained with respect to Churches belonging to the Established Church in England, and also from Roman Catholic Priests, and from the Ministers of every other Religious Denomination throughout Great Britain, with respect to their Places of Worship.]

I.	NAME AND DESCRIPTION OF CHURCH OR CHAPEL.		
II.	WHERE SITUATED.	Parish, *Quoad Sacra* Parish, or Burgh.	County.
III.	WHEN OPENED FOR WORSHIP.	UNDER WHAT CIRCUMSTANCES OPENED FOR WORSHIP.	

IV.	IN THE CASE OF A CHURCH OR CHAPEL OPENED FOR WORSHIP SINCE THE 1st JANUARY 1800; STATE	
	HOW OR BY WHOM ERECTED.	COST, HOW DEFRAYED.
		By Parliamentary Grant - - - Church Extension Fund - - Contribution of Heritors - Private Benefaction or Subscription, or from other Sources - } Total Cost - - £

V.	VI.
STIPEND OF MINISTER.	SPACE AVAILABLE FOR PUBLIC WORSHIP
£ Grain Stipend - - Salary - - - £ Money Stipend - - Land Mortified, &c. - Glebe - - - Other Permanent En- } Manse - - - dowment - }	Free Sittings - - - Other Sittings - - - Total Sittings -

VII.	ESTIMATED NUMBER OF PERSONS ATTENDING DIVINE SERVICE ON SUNDAY, MARCH 30, 1851.				AVERAGE NUMBER OF ATTENDANTS during Months next preceding March 30, 1851. (See Instruction VII.)			
		Morning.	Afternoon.	Evening.		Morning.	Afternoon.	Evening.
	General Congregation - } Sunday Scholars -				General Congregation - } Sunday Scholars -			
	Total -				Total -			

VIII.	REMARKS.	

I certify the foregoing to be a true and correct Return to the best of my belief.

Witness my hand this _____ day of _____ 1851.

IX. (*Signature*) _____

(*Official Character*) _____ *of the above-named.*

(*Address by Post*) _____

(d) Non-established churches: Scotland.

CENSUS OF GREAT BRITAIN, 1851.

(13 & 14 Victoriæ, Cap. 53.)

SCOTLAND.

A RETURN of the several Particulars to be inquired into respecting the under-mentioned Place of Public Religious Worship.

[N.B.—A similar Return will be obtained from the Clergy of the Church of England, and also from the Minister of every other Religious Denomination throughout Great Britain.]

I.	II.		III.	IV.	V.	VI.	VII.			VIII.				IX.
Name or Title of Place of Worship.	Where situate; specifying the		Religious Denomination.	When erected.	Whether a separate and entire Building.	Whether used exclusively as a Place of Worship (except for a Sunday School).	Space available for Public Worship. Number of Sittings already provided.			Estimated Number of Persons attending Divine Service on Sunday, March 30, 1851.				REMARKS.
	Parish, *Quoad Sacra* Parish, or Burgh.	County.					Free Sittings. (4)	Other Sittings. (5)		Morning.	Afternoon.	Evening.		
	(1)	(2)							General Congregation ⎰⎱ Sunday Scholars ⎰⎱				TOTAL -	
							Free Space or *Standing Room* for			Average Number of Attendants during _____ Months. (See Instruction VIII.) General Congregation ⎰⎱ Sunday Scholars ⎰⎱				
													TOTAL -	

I certify the foregoing to be a true and correct Return to the best of my belief. Witness my hand this _____ day of _____ 1851.

X. (*Signature*) _____

(*Official Character*) _____ of the above-named Place of Worship.

(*Address by Post*) _____

The Particulars to be inserted in Divisions I. to VI. inclusive, and in IX., may be written either along or across the Columns, as may be more convenient.

APPENDIX VIII
Total Number of Places of Worship, Sittings and Attendances by Denomination: England and Wales

1. Places of Worship and Sittings

Religious Denomination	Places of Worship	Defective Returns	Sittings
Church of England	14,077	1,026	5,317,915
Presbyterians:			
Church of Scotland	18	1	13,789
United Presbyterian Church	66	2	31,351
Presbyterian Church in England	76	2	41,552
Reformed Irish Presbyterians	1	—	120
Independents or Congregationalists	3,244	186	1,067,760
Baptists:			
General	93	9	20,539
Particular	1,947	100	582,953
Seventh Day	2	—	390
Scotch	15	3	2,547
New Connexion, General	182	5	52,604
Undefined	550	64	93,310
Society of Friends	371	9	91,599
Unitarians	229	17	68,554
Moravians	32	2	9,305
Methodists:			
Wesleyan	6,579	386	1,447,580
New Connexion	297	16	96,964
Primitive Methodists	2,871	309	414,030
Bible Christians	482	42	66,834
Wesleyan Methodist Association	419	34	98,813
Independent Methodists	20	2	2,263
Wesleyan Reformers	339	51	67,814
Calvinistic Methodists:			
Welsh	828	53	211,951
Lady Huntingdon's Connexion	109	5	38,727
Sandemanians	6	2	956
New Church (Swedenborgians)	50	1	12,107
Brethren	132	20	18,529
Isolated Congregations	539	71	104,481
Foreign Churches	16	1	4,457
Roman Catholics	570	48	186,111
Catholic Apostolic Church	32	1	7,437
Latter Day Saints (Mormons)	222	53	30,783
Jews	53	3	8,438
Total	34,467	2,524	10,212,563

Defective Returns are those giving no information about sittings. The number of Places of Worship given in the first column includes defective returns. The number of Sittings given in the last column includes an estimate for the defective returns based on the average for the denomination concerned.

This Table is based on Supplement I to Table A in the *Report*, p. clxxxi.

2. Attendance

Religious Denomination	Defective Returns	Attendance in the Morning	Afternoon	Evening
Church of England	939	2,541,244	1,890,764	860,543
Presbyterians:				
Church of Scotland	–	6,949	960	3,849
United Presbyterian Church	2	17,725	5,085	8,818
Presbyterians Church in England	1	22,908	3,390	10,826
Reformed Irish Presbyterians	1	–	–	–
Independents	59	524,612	232,285	457,162
Baptists:				
General	3	5,404	8,130	8,562
Particular	38	292,656	175,572	272,524
Seventh Day	–	27	40	16
Scotch	–	649	986	312
New Connexion, General	2	23,951	15,718	24,652
Undefined	24	38,119	23,822	39,050
Society of Friends	9	14,364	6,619	1,495
Unitarians	7	28,483	8,881	12,697
Moravians	2	4,993	2,466	3,415
Methodists:				
Wesleyan	133	492,714	383,964	667,850
New Connexion	3	36,801	22,620	39,624
Primitive Methodists	61	100,125	176,435	234,635
Bible Christians	8	14,902	24,345	34,612
Wesleyan Methodist Association	5	32,308	21,140	40,655
Independent Methodists	1	601	1,311	1,208
Wesleyan Reformers	5	30,470	16,080	44,953
Calvinistic Methodists:				
Welsh	–	79,728	59,140	125,244
Lady Huntingdon's Connexion	7	21,103	4,380	19,159
Sandemanians	–	439	256	61
New Church (Swedenborgian)	2	4,846	2,404	3,102
Brethren	2	5,699	4,509	7,384
Isolated Congregations	33	36,969	24,208	43,498
Foreign Churches	2	2,257	316	410
Roman Catholics	27	252,783	53,967	76,880
Catholic Apostolic Church	2	3,176	1,659	2,707
Latter Day Saints (Mormons)	9	7,517	11,481	16,628
Jews	7	2,910	1,202	1,918
Total	1,394	4,647,482	3,184,135	3,064,449

For total number of Places of Worship, see previous table. Defective Returns are those giving no information about attendance. The number of Attendances given includes an estimate for the defective returns based on the average for the denomination concerned, except for the Reformed Irish Presbyterians who only had one congregation and that with no information about attendance.

Total population: 17,927,609   Total Attendances: 10,896,066.

This Table is based on Supplement II to Table A in the *Report*, p. clxxxii.

APPENDIX IX

Total number of Places of Worship, Sittings and Attendances by Denomination in the registration divisions of England and Wales

1. Places of Worship and Sittings

Religious Denomination	LONDON Places of Worship	Sittings	SOUTH EAST Places of Worship	Sittings	SOUTH MIDLANDS Places of Worship	Sittings
Church of England	458	409,834	1,616	541,940	1,414	438,167
Presbyterians	23	18,211	–	–	–	–
Independents	161	100,436	362	88,547	299	80,950
Baptists	130	54,234	298	60,342	426	104,395
Society of Friends	9	3,157	34	6,344	48	10,548
Unitarians	9	3,300	14	4,509	7	1,445
Wesleyan Methodists	98	44,162	432	72,767	493	91,485
Primitive Methodists	21	3,380	156	16,565	188	22,386
Other Methodists	35	6,856	98	10,534	21	3,701
Calvinistic Methodists	11	6,298	18	5,807	13	1,689
Others	57	10,936	90	11,715	79	14,143
Foreign Churches	13	3,657	2	280	–	–
Roman Catholics	35	18,230	47	7,566	30	3,830
Catholic Apostolic	6	2,700	6	980	4	285
Mormons	20	2,640	17	1,565	21	1,807
Jews	11	3,692	8	627	3	50
Total	1,097	691,723	3,198	830,088	3,046	774,881
Defective Returns	35		325		73	

LONDON = the 36 Metropolitan registration districts. SOUTH EAST = Surrey (extra-Metropolitan), Kent (extra-Metropolitan), Sussex, Hampshire and Berkshire. SOUTH MIDLANDS = Middlesex (extra-Metropolitan), Hertfordshire, Buckinghamshire, Oxfordshire, Northamptonshire, Huntingdonshire, Bedfordshire and Cambridgeshire.

This Table is based on Table B in the *Report*, pp. clxxxiv–vi.

No estimate is included for defective returns.

Religious Denomination	EASTERN		SOUTH WEST		WEST MIDLANDS	
	Places of Worship	Sittings	Places of Worship	Sittings	Places of Worship	Sittings
Church of England	1,629	429,637	2,006	628,450	1,783	658,270
Presbyterians	–	–	–	–	6	2,500
Independents	264	85,940	437	113,431	319	95,322
Baptists	236	57,045	340	74,012	260	68,260
Society of Friends	41	10,855	41	9,055	38	8,575
Unitarians	10	3,020	28	7,232	33	9,633
Wesleyan Methodists	346	56,954	1,029	206,068	614	131,441
Primitive Methodists	338	35,426	200	22,744	446	53,107
Other Methodists	56	9,067	531	76,280	142	38,718
Calvinistic Methodists	4	1,908	9	2,464	38	10,880
Others	49	7,108	146	24,136	78	14,514
Foreign Churches	–	–	–	–	–	–
Roman Catholics	19	3,412	33	5,235	101	24,951
Catholic Apostolic	2	158	5	900	5	970
Mormons	18	1,351	16	1,398	26	4,160
Jews	3	186	5	376	5	745
Total	3,015	702,067	4,826	1,171,781	3,894	1,122,046
Defective Returns	237		427		133	

EASTERN = Essex, Suffolk and Norfolk. SOUTH WEST = Wiltshire, Dorset, Devon, Cornwall and Somerset. WEST MIDLANDS = Gloucestershire, Herefordshire, Shropshire, Staffordshire, Worcestershire and Warwickshire.

This Table is based on Table B in the *Report*, pp. clxxxvii–ix.

No estimate is included for defective returns.

Religious Denomination	NORTH MIDLANDS Places of Worship	Sittings	NORTH WEST Places of Worship	Sittings	YORKSHIRE Places of Worship	Sittings
Church of England	1,499	395,003	791	507,434	1,119	430,366
Presbyterians	–	–	28	18,445	4	1,789
Independents	157	47,742	238	101,490	233	95,419
Baptists	257	65,125	131	40,160	126	44,355
Society of Friends	22	4,197	37	10,445	55	16,300
Unitarians	20	4,809	49	15,616	23	6,472
Wesleyan Methodists	963	169,706	496	146,797	1,168	263,075
Primitive Methodists	470	59,268	238	39,451	482	67,485
Other Methodists	126	25,266	199	57,111	195	45,614
Calvinistic Methodists	4	860	32	12,520	–	–
Others	38	4,789	82	16,876	75	12,341
Foreign Churches	–	–	1	86	–	–
Roman Catholics	39	8,030	131	61,548	60	14,380
Catholic Apostolic	1	400	1	100	1	320
Mormons	30	2,592	24	2,279	11	1,780
Jews	1	50	7	1,138	4	735
Total	3,627	787,837	2,485	1,031,496	3,556	1,000,431
Defective Returns	241		190		335	

NORTH MIDLANDS = Leicestershire, Rutland, Lincolnshire, Nottinghamshire and Derbyshire. NORTH WEST = Lancashire and Cheshire. YORKSHIRE = West, East and North Ridings.

This Table is based on Table B in the *Report*, p. cxc–cxcii.

No estimate is included for defective returns.

Religious Denomination	NORTHERN Places of Worship	Sittings	WALES Places of Worship	Sittings
Church of England	582	204,198	1,180	279,113
Presbyterians	100	42,498	–	–
Independents	74	24,354	700	168,876
Baptists	52	10,536	533	127,199
Society of Friends	38	10,301	8	774
Unitarians	8	2,134	27	5,600
Wesleyan Methodists	441	84,919	499	94,069
Primitive Methodists	214	36,244	118	12,160
Other Methodists	112	23,740	42	5,229
Calvinistic Methodists	–	–	808	191,026
Others	31	4,784	35	5,801
Foreign Churches	–	–	–	–
Roman Catholics	54	12,089	21	5,393
Catholic Apostolic	–	–	1	160
Mormons	7	449	32	2,930
Jews	4	250	2	112
Total	1,717	456,946	4,006	898,442
Defective Returns	123		387	

NORTHERN = Durham, Northumberland, Cumberland and West-morland. WALES = Wales and Monmouthshire.

This Table is based on Table B in the *Report*, pp. cxciii–iv.

No estimate is included for defective returns.

2. Attendance

Religious Denomination	LONDON Number of attendants			SOUTH EAST Number of attendants		
	Morning	Afternoon	Evening	Morning	Afternoon	Evening
Church of England	261,426	76,666	157,135	314,713	243,130	81,682
Presbyterians	10,527	100	7,244	–	–	–
Independents	69,631	6,684	61,863	48,917	18,265	42,283
Baptists	32,801	5,466	32,440	32,729	17,883	25,512
Society of Friends	1,049	417	49	1,028	599	98
Unitarians	1,545	–	693	1,767	419	1,231
Wesleyan Methodists	24,507	2,454	23,135	29,522	20,641	39,849
Primitive Methodists	1,306	551	1,735	5,758	8,833	12,691
Other Methodists	4,573	95	4,086	3,771	4,726	6,366
Calvinistic Methodists	5,363	220	3,227	3,383	272	3,811
Others	5,448	703	3,327	4,828	2,755	4,166
Foreign Churches	1,980	240	360	–	21	–
Roman Catholics	35,994	4,660	14,394	6,867	2,392	1,115
Catholic Apostolic	1,700	980	1,130	388	160	459
Mormons	846	1,080	1,685	404	506	880
Jews	1,472	539	813	255	81	223
Total	460,168	100,855	313,316	454,330	320,683	220,366
Percentage Population	19.5	4.3	13.3	27.8	19.7	13.5
Population	2,362,236			1,628,386		
Defective Returns	53			174		

This Table is based on Table B in the *Report*, pp. clxxxiv–v.

No estimate is included for defective returns.

Religious Denomination	SOUTH MIDLANDS Number of attendants			EASTERN Number of attendants		
	Morning	Afternoon	Evening	Morning	Afternoon	Evening
Church of England	231,599	221,037	57,286	178,585	241,769	29,511
Presbyterians	–	–	–	–	–	–
Independents	39,913	25,967	34,368	44,781	46,648	27,422
Baptists	53,697	52,063	51,146	31,535	35,668	18,867
Society of Friends	1,356	522	573	1,115	549	24
Unitarians	694	337	414	1,355	127	845
Wesleyan Methodists	35,000	50,106	59,364	18,515	24,570	22,781
Primitive Methodists	7,064	14,063	16,124	11,404	26,004	21,334
Other Methodists	1,997	1,480	2,490	3,463	3,799	4,537
Calvinistic Methodists	1,285	708	1,019	436	255	230
Others	6,073	5,264	7,581	2,019	3,174	3,379
Foreign Churches	–	–	–	–	–	–
Roman Catholics	3,195	798	890	3,209	1,192	567
Catholic Apostolic	150	20	135	70	78	43
Mormons	410	750	942	165	600	635
Jews	10	–	–	50	–	46
Total	382,443	373,115	232,332	296,792	384,433	130,221
Percentage Population	31.0	30.2	18.8	26.6	34.5	11.7
Population		1,234,332			1,113,982	
Defective Returns		58			93	

This Table is based on Table B in the *Report*, pp. clxxxvi–vii.

No estimate is included for defective returns.

Religious Denomination	SOUTH WEST Number of attendants			WEST MIDLANDS Number of attendants		
	Morning	Afternoon	Evening	Morning	Afternoon	Evening
Church of England	306,181	276,155	102,701	313,637	198,649	108,740
Presbyterians	–	–	–	1,213	–	975
Independents	53,005	23,926	57,622	47,377	13,599	44,368
Baptists	36,130	20,566	36,883	34,890	15,093	32,099
Society of Friends	1,061	402	104	1,634	600	200
Unitarians	2,755	893	1,725	5,125	884	1,873
Wesleyan Methodists	72,514	42,032	115,548	51,988	31,282	62,080
Primitive Methodists	5,681	10,657	17,237	15,602	25,607	32,638
Other Methodists	19,749	22,739	42,405	17,065	8,867	22,031
Calvinistic Methodists	1,052	346	1,654	5,180	1,337	5,200
Others	11,238	5,016	12,379	5,383	1,442	6,900
Foreign Churches	–	–	–	–	–	–
Roman Catholics	4,808	2,514	987	24,755	8,325	11,149
Catholic Apostolic	297	146	222	212	123	323
Mormons	434	760	1,253	1,431	1,188	2,645
Jews	137	70	118	321	79	228
Total	515,042	406,222	390,838	525,813	307,075	331,449
Percentage Population	28.5	22.5	21.6	24.7	14.4	15.5
Population		1,803,291			2,132,930	
Defective Returns		217			196	

This Table is based on Table B in the *Report*, pp. clxxxviii–ix.

No estimate is included for defective returns.

Religious Denomination	NORTH MIDLANDS Number of attendants			NORTH WEST Number of attendants		
	Morning	Afternoon	Evening	Morning	Afternoon	Evening
Church of England	154,357	137,250	49,205	244,523	161,327	88,190
Presbyterians	–	–	–	9,777	3,365	5,024
Independents	20,565	10,333	16,030	50,785	22,003	33,031
Baptists	24,223	16,881	30,553	16,817	13,243	11,236
Society of Friends	550	266	70	1,909	797	–
Unitarians	1,672	239	943	7,331	4,268	1,406
Wesleyan Methodists	41,745	49,398	80,163	67,566	36,140	60,763
Primitive Methodists	9,491	26,022	40,673	11,294	17,508	17,575
Other Methodists	10,055	6,063	16,216	20,943	14,893	19,996
Calvinistic Methodists	368	218	297	5,903	2,136	6,401
Others	2,008	770	2,250	5,779	4,577	4,589
Foreign Churches	–	–	–	–	–	–
Roman Catholics	8,020	2,131	3,542	110,694	21,319	27,860
Catholic Apostolic	Defective return			70	–	60
Mormons	325	1,096	1,961	950	1,710	1,969
Jews	27	15	14	313	118	157
Total	273,406	250,682	241,917	554,714	303,404	278,257
Percentage Population	22.4	20.6	19.9	22.2	12.2	11.2
Population	1,214,538			2,490,827		
Defective Returns	194			134		

This Table is based on Table B in the *Report*, pp. cxc–cxci.

No estimate is included for defective returns.

Religious Denomination	YORKSHIRE Number of attendants			NORTHERN Number of attendants		
	Morning	Afternoon	Evening	Morning	Afternoon	Evening
Church of England	170,248	124,430	55,186	95,510	35,137	33,943
Presbyterians	895	116	544	24,332	5,655	9,297
Independents	43,011	26,865	26,141	9,849	1,305	9,192
Baptists	20,561	19,292	10,951	4,388	1,184	4,603
Society of Friends	2,960	1,519	256	1,252	744	85
Unitarians	2,527	715	1,710	711	25	587
Wesleyan Methodists	90,805	84,079	103,526	20,289	15,966	33,410
Primitive Methodists	17,925	28,015	40,387	9,202	11,799	22,068
Other Methodists	22,617	15,605	24,711	8,157	4,617	12,831
Calvinistic Methodists	–	–	–	–	–	–
Others	3,901	5,974	4,761	1,065	827	1,695
Foreign Churches	–	–	–	–	–	–
Roman Catholics	19,863	3,404	6,871	17,555	3,366	4,531
Catholic Apostolic	140	100	250	–	–	–
Mormons	460	778	1,053	162	160	192
Jews	147	103	21	82	17	30
Total	396,060	310,995	276,368	192,554	80,802	132,464
Percentage Population	22.1	17.4	15.4	19.9	8.3	13.7
Population	1,789,047			969,126		
Defective Returns	133			74		

This Table is based on Table B in the *Report,* pp. cxcii–iii.

No estimate is included for defective returns.

	WALES		
Religious	*Number of attendants*		
Denomination	*Morning*	*Afternoon*	*Evening*
Church of England	100,953	49,091	39,662
Presbyterians	–	–	–
Independents	87,237	32,465	96,527
Baptists	65,290	22,068	83,324
Society of Friends	102	43	–
Unitarians	2,130	703	979
Wesleyan Methodists	30,302	19,534	53,730
Primitive Methodists	3,274	3,625	7,184
Other Methodists	1,204	1,483	3,195
Calvinistic Methodists	76,724	57,747	121,334
Others	2,349	1,541	3,221
Foreign Churches	–	–	–
Roman Catholics	5,742	1,305	1,326
Catholic Apostolic	50	–	–
Mormons	1,625	2,388	2,739
Jews	34	21	23
Total	377,016	192,014	413,244
Percentage Population	31.8	16.2	34.8
Population		1,188,914	
Defective Returns		91	

This Table is based on Table B in the *Report*, p. cxciv.

No estimate is included for defective returns.

APPENDIX X

Total number of Places of Worship, Sittings
and Attendances by Denomination : Scotland

1. Places of Worship and Sittings

Religious Denomination	Places of Worship	Defective Returns	Sittings
Presbyterians:			
Church of Scotland	1,183	366	767,088
Reformed Presbyterian Church	39	7	16,969
Original Secession Church	36	8	16,424
Relief Church	2	—	1,020
United Presbyterian Church	465	55	288,100
Free Church of Scotland	889	132	495,335
Episcopal Church	134	34	40,022
Independents	192	44	76,342
Baptists	119	39	26,086
Society of Friends	7	3	2,152
Unitarians	5	1	2,437
Moravians	1	—	200
Methodists:			
Wesleyan	70	14	19,951
Primitive Methodists	10	—	1,890
Independent Methodists	1	—	600
Wesleyan Reformers	1	1	—
Sandemanians	6	1	1,068
New Church (Swedenborgian)	5	—	710
Evangelical Union	28	8	10,319
Isolated Congregations	61	15	11,402
Roman Catholics	117	26	52,766
Catholic Apostolic	3	1	675
Latter Day Saints (Mormons)	20	11	3,182
Jews	1	—	67
Total	3,395	766	1,834,805

Defective Returns are those giving no information about
sittings. The number of Places of Worship given in the first
column includes defective returns. The number of Sittings
given in the last column includes an estimate for defective
returns based on the average of the denomination concerned.

This Table is based on Supplements I and II to Table A in the
Scottish Report, pp. 4—5.

2. Attendance

Religious Denomination	Defective Returns	Attendance in the Morning	Afternoon	Evening
Presbyterian:				
Church of Scotland	413	351,454	184,192	30,763
Reformed Presbyterian Church	8	8,739	7,460	2,180
Original Secession Church	7	6,562	5,724	1,629
Relief Church	—	220	250	275
United Presbyterian Church	46	159,191	146,411	30,810
Free Church of Scotland	112	292,308	198,583	64,811
Episcopal Church	29	26,966	11,578	5,360
Independents	31	26,392	24,866	17,273
Baptists	26	9,208	7,735	4,015
Society of Friends	1	196	142	—
Unitarians	1	863	130	855
Moravians	—	16	—	55
Methodists:				
Wesleyan	13	8,409	2,669	8,610
Primitive Methodists	—	327	404	715
Independent Methodists	—	190	150	180
Wesleyan Reformers	—	11	—	11
Sandemanians	—	429	554	100
New Church (Swedenborgian)	—	211	67	120
Evangelical Union	1	3,895	4,504	2,171
Isolated Congregations	5	2,882	2,061	3,053
Roman Catholics	28	43,878	21,032	14,813
Catholic Apostolic	—	272	126	190
Latter Day Saints (Mormons)	1	1,304	1,225	878
Jews	—	28	—	7
Total	722*	943,951	619,863	188,874

For total number of Places of Worship, see previous table. Defective Returns are those giving no information about attendance. The number of Attendances given includes an estimate for the defective returns based on the average for the denomination concerned.

Total population: 2,888,742   Total Attendances: 1,752,688

This Table is based on Supplements I and II to Table A in the *Scottish Report*, pp. 4—5.

*On p. 2 of the *Scottish Report* the number of returns which failed to state the number of attendants (other than the 481 where neither attendance nor accommodation was given) is given as 242. In fact, the sum of the denominational figures which follow is 241 and that figure has been used here.

APPENDIX XI

The Guide to Official Sources

APPENDIX XI

The Guide to Official Sources

Selected Data from nineteenth century Census Reports for England and Wales

The following extracts are taken from the pamphlet produced under the direction of the Interdepartmental Committee on Social and Economic Research in 1951, *Guides to Official Sources No. 2. Census Reports of Great Britain, 1801–1931*. Written by the late L.M. Feery of the General Register Office (now the Office of Population Censuses and Surveys), this remarkable pioneer enterprise has long been a key reference for those seeking to follow a reliable track through the Census jungle. We have all benefited from it in writing the various chapters of the present book (in which it is referred to, simply, as the *Guide*) and are greatly indebted to the Controller of Her Majesty's Stationery Office for permission to reproduce the following sections.

The *Guide*, which outlines briefly the history of Census enquiry, has a useful list of tables of Census Reports published (see below, Section D), of tabulations of Occupations (Section E), Birthplaces (Section F) and Areas (Section C) together with selected examples of Census Schedules and forms annexed to the Schedule. It has unfortunately been out of print for many years, but a recent revision has been published jointly by the Office of Population Censuses and Surveys and the General Register Office, Edinburgh: *Guide to Census Reports Great Britain 1801–1966*, HMSO (1977).

A. List of Census Dates 1801–1931
And References to Relevant Acts of Parliament

Census			Act of Parliament
Year	Day	Scope	Reference and Date
1801	Monday, 10th March	Great Britain	41 Geo. III. c. 15, 31 December, 1800.
1811	Monday, 27th May	Great Britain	51 Geo. III. c. 6, 22 March, 1811.
1821	Monday, 28th May	Great Britain	1 Geo. IV. c. 94, 24 July, 1820.
1831	Monday, 30th May	Great Britain	11 Geo. IV. & 1 Gul. IV. c. 30, 23 June, 1830.
1841	Sunday, 6th June	Great Britain	3 & 4 Vict. c. 99, 10 August, 1840. 4 & 5 Vict. c. 7, 6 April, 1841.
1851	Sunday, 30th March	Great Britain	13 & 14 Vict. c. 53, 5 August, 1850.
1861	Sunday, 7th April	England and Wales	23 & 24 Vict. c. 61, 6 August, 1860.
		Scotland	23 & 24 Vict. c. 98, 20 August, 1860.
1871	Sunday, 2nd April	England and Wales	33 & 34 Vict. c. 107, 10 August, 1870.
		Scotland	33 & 34, Vict. c. 108, 10 August, 1870.
1881	Sunday, 3rd April	England and Wales	43 & 44 Vict, c. 37, 7 September, 1880.
		Scotland	43 & 44 Vict. c. 38, 7 September, 1880.
1891	Sunday, 5th April	England and Wales	53 & 54 Vict. c. 61, 18 August, 1890.
		Scotland	53 & 54 Vict. c. 38, 14 August, 1890.
1901	Sunday, 31st March	Great Britain	63 Vict. c. 4, 27th March, 1900.
1911	Sunday, 2nd April	Great Britain	10 Edw. 7 & 1 Geo. 5. c. 27, 3 August, 1910.
1921	Sunday, 19th June*	Great Britain	10 & 11 Geo. 5, c. 41,
1931	Sunday, 26th April*		16 August, 1920.

* Dates determined by the Census Orders in Council, see below.

In accordance with this new procedure, the Census Order, 1920, made on 21st December, 1920, directed the taking of the 1921 Census, and the Census Order, 1931, made on 12th February, 1931, (S.R. and O. 1931 No. 73) directed the taking of the 1931 Census.

References to these Acts are given above with a list of dates on which the Censuses were taken.

B. Questions and Schedules

A summary statement of the information obtained at each occasion of the Census from 1801 to 1931 will be found on pages 4 and 5.* It will be seen that in the main the scope of the enquiry at each Census has been the same throughout Great Britain and that, apart from enquiries into languages spoken by those enumerated in Scotland and Wales, the only significant variations between schedules used north and south of the Border have been in questions on education and housing.

The schedules and forms annexed to the Population Act of 1800 are reproduced in the Appendix (see pages 104—109), together with specimens of the householder's schedules used throughout Great Britain in 1851 and in Scotland in 1861. The forms used by enumerators in 1811, 1821 and 1831 followed the pattern of those issued for use in England and Wales in 1801. Specimens of householder's schedules, which were first used at the Census of 1841, will be found in the following Census Reports:

GREAT BRITAIN

1841 *Enumeration Abstract*. Preface, page V.
1851 *Population Tables I:* Vol. I, p. cxxxvii.

<table>
<tr><td>ENGLAND AND WALES</td><td>SCOTLAND</td></tr>
<tr><td>1861 General Report, p. 75</td><td>Not Published.</td></tr>
<tr><td>1871 General Report, p. 167</td><td>Report, Vol. I, p. lxii.</td></tr>
<tr><td>1881 General Report, p. 117</td><td>Report, Vol. I. p. xxx.</td></tr>
<tr><td>1891 General Report, p. 139</td><td>Report, Vol. I. p. xxx.</td></tr>
<tr><td>1901 General Report, p. 321</td><td>Report, Vol. I. p. xxxviii.</td></tr>
<tr><td>1911 General Report, p. 258</td><td>Report, Vol. III, p. cxii.</td></tr>
<tr><td>1921 General Report, p. 203</td><td>Report, Vol. II, p. lii.</td></tr>
<tr><td>1931 General Report, p. 193</td><td>Report, Vol. II, p. liv.</td></tr>
</table>

* Reproduced on pp. 290—1, below.

Questions asked at each occasion of the Census, 1801–1931

X = England, Wales and Scotland   E = England   S = Scotland   W = Wales and Monmouthshire

#	Question	1801	1811	1821	1831	1841	1851	1861	1871	1881	1891	1901	1911	1921	1931
1	Name and Surname	–	–	–	–	X	X	X	X	X	X	X	X	X	X
2	Sex	X	X	X	X	X	X	X	X	X	X	X	X	X	X
	Age—														
3	To nearest quinquennial age-group	–	–	X	–	X	–	–	–	–	–	–	–	–	–
4	In years	–	–	–	–	X	X	X	X	X	X	X	X	–	–
5	In years and months[1]	–	–	–	–	–	–	–	–	–	–	–	–	X	X
6	Relationship to head of household	–	–	–	–	–	X	X	X	X	X	X	X	X	X
7	Condition as to Marriage	–	–	–	–	–	X	X	X	X	X	X	X	X	X
8	Birthplace	–	–	–	–	X[2]	X	X	X	X	X	X	X	X	X[1]
9	Nationality	–	–	–	–	X[2]	X	X	X	X	X	X	X	X	X
	Occupations—														
10	Personal Occupation	X	–	–	X	X	X	X	X	X	X	X	X	X	X
11	Family Occupation	–	X	X	–	–	–	–	–	–	–	–	–	–	–
12	Whether Employer	–	–	–	–	–	–	–	–	–	X	X	X	X	X
13	Employed	–	–	–	–	–	–	–	–	–	X	X	X	X	X
14	Working on own account	–	–	–	–	–	–	–	–	–	X	X	X	X	X
15	At home	–	–	–	–	–	–	–	–	–	–	X	X	–	–
16	Unemployed	–	–	–	–	–	–	–	–	–	–	–	–	X	X
	Industry—														
17	Employer's Name	–	–	–	–	–	–	–	–	–	–	–	–	X	X
18	Business	–	–	–	–	–	–	–	–	–	–	–	X	X	X
19	Business Address	–	–	–	–	–	–	–	–	–	–	–	–	–	X
	Language spoken—														
20	Gaelic	–	–	–	–	–	–	–	–	S	S	S	S	S	S
21	Welsh	–	–	–	–	–	–	–	–	–	W	W	W	W	W
	Housing—														
22	Houses inhabited —Number of	X	X	X	X	X	X	X	X	X	X	X	X	X	X
23	Houses inhabited — By how many families occupied	X	X	X	X	–	–	–	–	–	X	X	X	X	X
24	Houses being built	–	–	–	–	X	X	X	X	X	X	X	X	X	–

Item												
25 Houses uninhabited	X	X	X	X	X	X	X	X	X	X	X	X
26 Number of rooms in household	—	—	—	—	—	—	—	EW³	EW³	EW	EW	EW
27 Number of rooms with one or more windows	—	—	—	—	—	s	s	s	s	s	s	s
28 Usual Residence	—	—	—	—	s	—	—	—	—	—	—	X
29 Place of Work	—	—	—	—	—	—	—	—	—	—	X	—
Education—												
30 Separate Voluntary Enquiry	—	—	—	—	—	—	—	X	—	—	—	—
31 Attending school part or whole-time	—	—	—	—	X	X	s	X	X	X	X	X
32 Receiving regular instruction at home	—	—	—	—	X	s	s	s	X	X	—	—
Religion—												
33 Separate Voluntary enquiry	—	—	—	—	X	—	—	—	—	—	—	—
Fertility—												
34 Children born alive, still living or died, of present marriage	—	—	—	—	—	—	—	—	—	X	—	—
35 Duration of present marriage	—	—	—	—	—	—	—	—	—	X	—	—
Dependency—												
36 Number of children under 16 years	—	—	—	—	—	—	—	—	—	—	X	X
Orphanhood—												
37 Father, Mother or both parents dead	—	—	—	—	—	—	—	—	—	—	X	X
Infirmity—												
38 Deaf, Dumb, Blind, Lunatic, etc.	—	—	—	—	X	X	X	X	X	X	X	—
39 Eligibility to medical benefit under National Health Insurance Acts	—	—	—	—	—	—	—	—	—	X	s	s
40 Number of baptisms, burials and marriages	X	EW	EW	EW	EW	—	—	—	—	—	—	—

(1) Length of residence also asked in Scotland. (2) Only required in cases of Scottish or Irish birth. (3) Only required if under 5 rooms.

C. Principal Areas of England and Wales for which Populations have been given in Census Reports, 1801 – 1931.

	1801	1811	1821	1831	1841	1851	1861	1871	1881	1891	1901	1911	1921	1931	
1. Ancient Counties	X	X	X	X	X	X	X	X	X	X	X	–	–	–	1
2. Hundreds, Wapentakes, etc.	X	X	X	X	X	X	X	X	X	–	–	–	–	–	2
3. Ancient Parishes	X	X	X	X	X	X	X	X	X	–	–	–	–	–	3
4. Tythings, Chapelries, Townships, Hamlets, Precincts, Extra-Parochial Places, etc.	X	X	X	X	X	X	X	–	–	–	–	–	–	–	4
5. Boroughs	X	X	X	X	X	–	X	–	–	–	–	–	–	–	5
6. Parliamentary Boroughs	–	–	–	–	X	X	X	X	X	X	X	X	X	X	6
7. Parliamentary Counties	–	–	–	–	–	X	X	X	X	X	X	X	X	X	7
8. Parliamentary County Divisions	–	–	–	–	–	X	X	X	X	X	X	X	X	X	8
9. Parliamentary Borough Divisions	–	–	–	–	–	–	–	–	–	X	X	X	X	X	9
10. Provinces	–	–	–	–	–	–	–	–	X	X	X	X	X	X	10
11. Dioceses	–	–	–	X	–	X	X	X	X	X	X	X	X	X	11
12. Ecclesiastical Districts, Parishes	–	–	–	–	–	X	X	X	X	X	X	X	X	X	12
13. Registration Districts	–	–	–	–	X	X	X	X	X	X	X	X	X	–	13
14. Registration Sub-Districts	–	–	–	–	–	X	X	X	X	X	X	X	X	–	14
15. Registration Counties	–	–	–	–	–	X	X	X	X	X	X	X	X	–	15
16. Registration Divisions	–	–	–	–	–	X	X	X	X	X	X	X	X	–	16
17. Poor Law Unions	–	–	–	–	–	X	X	X	X	X	X	X	–	–	17
18. Municipal Boroughs	–	–	–	–	–	X	X	X	X	X	X	X	X	X	18

	19	20	21	22	23	24	25	26	27	28	29	30	31	32	33
	–	–	–	X	X	X	X	X	X	X	X	X	X	–	X
	–	–	–	X	X	X	X	X	X	X	X	X	X	X	–
	–	–	–	X	X	X	X	X	X	X	X	X	X	–	–
	–	–	–	X	X	X	X	X	X	X	X	X	X	–	–
	–	–	–	X	X	X	X	X	X	X	X	–	–	–	–
	–	X	–	X	X	X	X	–	–	X	–	–	–	–	–
	–	X	–	X	X	X	–	–	–	–	X	–	–	–	–
	X	X	–	–	–	–	–	–	–	–	–	–	–	–	–
	–	–	–	–	–	–	–	–	–	–	–	–	–	–	–
	–	–	–	–	–	–	–	–	–	–	–	–	–	–	–
	–	–	–	–	–	–	–	–	–	–	–	–	–	–	–
	–	–	–	–	–	–	–	–	–	–	–	–	–	–	–
	–	–	–	–	–	–	–	–	–	–	–	–	–	–	–

19. Towns of 2,000 inhabitants not being Corporate or Parliamentary
20. Sub-Divisions of Lieutenancy
21. Local Board Districts—Towns with Improvement Commissions
22. Petty Sessional Divisions
23. Boroughs having separate Courts of Quarter Sessions and Commissions of Peace
24. Civil Parishes
25. Urban Districts
26. Rural Districts
27. Administrative Counties
28. County Boroughs
29. Wards of Municipal Boroughs
30. Metropolitan Boroughs
31. County Court Circuits and Districts
32. Geographical Divisions
33. Geographical Regions

D. Census Reports 1801 — 1911

The *Abstracts of Answers and Returns* ordered by Parliament to be printed after the first census consisted entirely of tables compiled from information given on the forms completed by the enumerators. The *Abstracts* of the second and third censuses were prefaced by preliminary observations in which changes in scope and in method were described, the results appraised and summary tables presented. As the scope of the census widened the task of preparing tables became more lengthy. The practice of publishing first results in advance of the more detailed Reports began in 1811 when populations enumerated at the census of that year were shown in parallel columns with those of the first enumeration. The *Comparative Account of the Population of Great Britain, 1801, 1811, 1821, 1831* contained (facing p. 12) the interesting coloured map of the Metropolis. A useful precedent, which has not always been followed, was set by the publication of an Index to the Names of Places at the end of the second volume of the *Enumeration Abstract* of 1831. The series of reports on the censuses taken in Scotland since 1861 have consistently followed the method adopted in 1851 when commentary and tables on particular aspects of enquiry were comprised in the same volume. With important exceptions, critical commentary on the results of each census taken in England and Wales from 1861 has been given in the *General Report*. Notable exceptions include the reports on the census of 1911, each of which gave an historical account of the information obtained at previous censuses on the subject to which it related. The format of the reports remained unchanged throughout the period under review except in the case of three volumes which were no doubt printed in octavo in order to distinguish them from the main series. they were *Religious Worship in England and Wales, Education in England and Wales* and *Religious Worship and Education in Scotland* in which the results of *voluntary* enquiries made in 1851 were published. A list of census reports, in which year of publication is noted, will be found below.

List of Census Reports for Great Britain, 1801 — 1911

Reports	Year of Publication	Order Paper ( ) or Command [ ] No.
1801. GREAT BRITAIN		
Abstracts of the Answers and Returns:		
Enumeration. Part I England: Part II		
Scotland	1801, 1802	(140, 9, 112)
Parish Registers	1801	—
1811. GREAT BRITAIN		
Comparative Statement of Population etc.,		
Gt. Britain, 1801, 1811.	1812	(12)

Reports	Year of Publication	Order Paper ( ) or Command [ ] No.
Abstracts of the Answers and Returns: Preliminary Observations ⎫ Enumeration Abstract ⎬ Parish-Register Abstract ⎭	1812	(316, 317)
1821. GREAT BRITAIN		
Comparative Statement of Population etc., Gt. Britain, 1801, 1811, 1821.	1822	(8)
Abstracts of the Answers and Returns: Preliminary Observations ⎫ Enumeration Abstract ⎬ Parish-Register Abstract ⎭	1822	(502)
1831. GREAT BRITAIN		
Comparative Account of the Population of Great Britain, 1801, 1811, 1821, 1831.	1831	(348)
Abstracts of the Answers and Returns: Enumeration. Vols. I & II with Index to the Names of Places at the end of Vol. II.	1833	(149, Appendix to 612)
Parish Registers	1833	–
1841. GREAT BRITAIN		
Statements on Population[1]	1841	(52)
Abstracts of the Answers and Returns: Enumeration. Part I England and Wales: Part II Scotland with Index to Names of Places at end of each Part.	1843	(496)
Index to Names of Places, England and Wales	1843	(511)
Index to Names of Places, Scotland	1843	(498, 506)
Age. Part I England and Wales: Part II Scotland	1843	(497)
Occupations. Part I England and Wales: Part II Scotland.	1844	(587–588)
Parish Registers	1845	–
Introductory Remarks to the Census Abstracts (Reprinted as a separate volume)	1844	–

(1) The full title is '*Accounts of the Total Population 1841, of each country of Gt. Britain; distinguishing males and females and showing the rate per cent. increase or decrease in each county compared with population 1831; also the number of houses inhabited, uninhabited and building according to the Census, 1841; similar returns for Channel Islands, Isle of Man; also, comparative statements of the population and number of houses, 1801, 1811, 1821, 1831, for each county in Gt. Britain; also population of each city and Royal and Parliamentary Burgh in Scotland*'.

Reports	Year of Publication	Command No.
1851. GREAT BRITAIN		
Forms and instructions for the use of persons employed in taking an account of the population of Gt. Britain	1851	[1339]
Tables of Population and Houses	1851	[1339]
Population Tables I. Vols. I & II. Numbers of Inhabitants.	1852	[1631, 1632]
Population Tables II. Vols. I & II. Ages, Civil Conditions, Occupations and Birthplaces.	1854	[1691, I–II]
Index to Names of Places in the Population Tables	1852	[1633]
Religious Worship. England and Wales	1853	[1690]
Education. England and Wales.	1854	[1692]
Religious Worship and Education. Scotland.	1854	[1764]
1861. ENGLAND AND WALES		
Tables of Population and Houses	1861	[2846]
Reports: Population Tables. Number and Distribution of the People (Vol.I).	1862	[3056]
Population Tables. Ages, Civil Condition, Occupations and Birthplaces (Vol. II).	1863	[3221]
General Report (Vol. III).	1863	[3221]
1861. SCOTLAND		
Tables of Population, etc.	1861	[2870]
Population Tables and Report: Vol. I Population of various types of areas, Houses.	1862	[3013]
Vol. II. Ages, Civil Condition, Occupations, Birthplaces.	1864	[3275]
1871. ENGLAND AND WALES		
Preliminary Report and Tables of Population and Houses	1871	c. 381
Population Tables: Vol. I. Ancient Counties	1872	c. 676
Vol. II. Registration or Union Counties, with Index to Names of Places in Population Tables.	1872	c. 676–1
Population Abstracts: Vol. III. Ages, Civil Condition, Occupations and Birthplaces.	1873	c. 872
General Report	1873	c. 872–1

Reports	Year of Publication	Command No.
1871. SCOTLAND		
Tables of Population, etc.	1871	c. 380
Population of Scotland with Report:		
Vol. I. Population of various types of areas, Houses	1872	c. 592
Vol. II. Ages, Education, Civil Conditions, Birthplaces, Occupations.	1874	c. 841
1881. ENGLAND AND WALES		
Preliminary Report	1881	c. 2955
Tables:		
Area, Houses and Population in Ancient Counties (Vol. I).	1883	c. 3562
Area, Houses and Population in Registration Counties (Vol. II).	1883	c. 3563
Ages, Marital Condition, Occupations and Birthplaces (Vol. III).	1883	c. 3722
Islands in the British Seas.	1883	c. 3643
General Report (Vol. IV).	1883	c. 3797
1881. SCOTLAND		
Tables of Population etc.	1881	c. 2957
Population of Scotland with Report:		
Vol. I. Population of various types of areas, public institutions.	1882	c. 3320
Vol. II. Ages, Education, Civil Condition, Birthplaces, Occupations, General Index.	1883	c. 3657
1891. ENGLAND AND WALES		
Preliminary Report	1891	c. 6422
Area, Housing and Population:		
Administrative and Ancient Counties (Vol. I).	1893	c. 6948
Registration Areas and Sanitary Districts (Vol. II).	1893	c. 6948–1
Ages, Marital Condition, Occupations, Birthplaces and Infirmities Vol. III).	1893	c. 7058
General Report (Vol. IV).	1893	c. 7222
Islands in the British Seas	1893	c. 7133
Index to Population Tables	1893	c. 7216
1891. SCOTLAND		
Tables of Population, etc.	1891	c.6390
Population of Scotland with Report:		
Vol. I. Report with Appendices, Population of various types of areas, Houses.	1892	c. 6755

Reports	Year of Publication	Command No.
Supplement to Vol. I.	1893	c.6936
Vol. II. Ages, Education, Civil Condition, Birthplaces, Occupations, Working Status, Indices.	1893	c. 6937, c. 7134

1901. ENGLAND AND WALES

Preliminary Report.	1901	Cd. 616
Series of County Parts	1902–3	See Appendix
Index to Population Tables in the		
County volumes	1903	Cd. 1826
Islands in the British Seas	1903	Cd. 1473
Summary Tables.	1903	Cd. 1523
General Report, with Appendices	1904	Cd. 2174

1901. SCOTLAND

Preliminary Report	1901	Cd. 644
Parliamentary Burghs, Counties,		
Population, etc. 1901 *and* 1891	1902	Cd. 898
Population of Scotland with Report:		
Vol. I. Population of various types of areas, Houses.	1902	Cd. 1257
Vol. II. Ages, Marital Condition, Education and Birthplaces.	1903	Cd. 1481
Vol. III. Report, Occupations.	1903	Cd. 1798

1911. ENGLAND AND WALES

Preliminary Report[2]	1911	Cd. 5705
Area, Families and Population:		
Administrative Areas (Vol. I)	1912	Cd. 6258
Registration Areas (Vol. II).	1912	Cd. 6259
Parliamentary Areas (Vol. III).	1912	Cd. 6343
Ecclesiastical Areas (Vol. IV).	1912	Cd. 6360
Index to Population Tables Vols. I–IV (Vol. V).	1913	Cd. 6576
Buildings of various kinds (Vol. VI).	1913	Cd. 6577
Ages and Condition as to Marriage (Vol. VII).	1913	Cd. 6610
Tenements (Vol. VIII).	1913	Cd. 6910
Birthplaces (Vol. IX).	1913	Cd. 7017
Occupations and Industries, Parts I & II.	1913–14	Cd. 7018, 7019
Appendix. Classification of Occupations and Rules adopted for such a Classification (Vol. X).	1915	Cd. 7660

(2) This publication also included preliminary reports for Scotland, Ireland, Isle of Man and Channel Islands.

Reports	Year of Publication	Command No.
Infirmities (Vol. XI).	1913	Cd. 7020
Languages spoken in Wales and Monmouthshire (Vol. XII).	1913	Cd. 6911
Fertility of Marriage, Parts I & II (Vol. XIII).	1917 & 1923	Cd. 8678
Islands in the British Seas	1913	Cd. 6922
Summary Tables.	1915	Cd. 7929
General Report with Appendices	1917	Cd. 8491

1911. SCOTLAND

Preliminary Report.	1911	Cd. 5700
Reports and Tables:		
Vol. I. City and County Parts	1912	Cd. 6907 to Cd. 6907–XXXVI
Vol. II. Population, Ages and Conjugal Condition, Occupations, Birthplaces, Housing, Gaelic-speaking	1913	Cd. 6896
Vol. III. Occupations by birthplace, Nationalities, Infirmities, Fertility.	1913	Cd. 9163

E. Tabulations of Occupations

OCCUPATIONS: 1851 GREAT BRITAIN

VOLUME AND TABLE No. Classification Area *Population and Characteristics*	The Divisional Tables listed below (D) are similar for each Division and are unnumbered in the published volumes. Tables with Arabic numerals are included in the Report section of Vol. I and tables with Roman numerals in the Summary Tables section of the same volume. The Tables show Males and Females separately unless otherwise indicated.

POPULATION TABLES II (AGES, CIVIL CONDITION, OCCUPATIONS, ETC.), VOLS. I AND II.

Classes, Sub-Classes and Groups

Great Britain, with Islands in the British Seas
54 and Supp.

*Age-groups: all ages, under 20, 20+; 0—99 in quinquennia,
100+*

Registration Counties of England and Wales, Scotland

(D)   *Age-groups: 0—99 in quinquennia, 100+*

England and Wales, Scotland, Islands in the British Seas

XXV—XXVII

*Age-groups: all ages, under 20, 20+; 0—84 in quinquennia,
85+*

Great Britain, etc., England and Wales, Scotland, Islands in the
British Seas, Registration Divisions and Counties of England and
Wales. Scottish Counties, Isle of Man, Jersey, Guernsey with
adjacent islands

XXVIII—XXIX

Males and females aged 20+

Counties of Scotland, Islands in the British Seas, Isle of Man,
Jersey, Guernsey etc.

(D)   *Age-groups: 0—24 in quinquennia, 25—74 in decennia, 75+*

Registration Districts of England and Wales

(D)   *Males and females aged 20+*

Principal towns of Great Britain

(D)   *Age-groups: under 20, 20+*

England and Wales and Registration Divisions, Scotland (9
principal towns), Islands in the British Seas (3 principal towns)

XXX—XXXII

and (D)   *Employers by number of employees (trade and manufacture)*

England and Wales, Scotland, Islands in the British Seas

XLIII—LXII

*Blind persons, inmates of workhouses, prisons, lunatic
asylums and hospitals—occupations or former occupations
by age-groups: 0—99 by quinquennia, 100+*

Groups (alphabetical order)

Great Britain, with Islands in the British Seas

53   *Age-groups: under 20, 20+*

Classes and Sub-Classes

Great Britain, with Islands in the British Seas

18   *Proportions in each Class and Sub-Class per 100,000 aged
20 and 20+*

Great Britain, England and Wales, Scotland, Islands in the British
Seas

XXIV   *Age-groups: under 20, 20+*

Registration Divisions of England and Wales, Scotland, Islands
in the British Seas

(D)   *Age-groups: under 20, 20+*

Farmers

Great Britain etc., England and Wales, Scotland, Islands in the
British Seas, Registration Divisions and Counties, Scottish
Counties, Isle of Man, Jersey, Guernsey etc.

XXXIII—XXXVI

and (D)   *Farmers by number of male labourers employed and
acreage of farm*   ·

OCCUPATIONS: 1861 ENGLAND AND WALES

VOLUME AND TABLE No. Classification Area *Population and* *Characteristics*	The Divisional Tables listed below (Arabic numerals under Vol. II) are similar for each Division, but the table numbers vary according to the number of counties in each Division. For reasons of space the table numbers are quoted for *Division V only.* The Tables show Males and Females separately unless otherwise indicated.

POPULATION TABLES, VOL. II (AGES, CIVIL CONDITION, OCCUPATION, ETC.)

Classes, Orders and Sub-Orders
England and Wales

XVIII   *Age-groups: under 20, 20+, all ages*
XXIX   *European aliens in age-groups: under 20, 20+, all ages*
XL   *The Blind, Deaf-and-Dumb, paupers in workhouses,*
prisoners, lunatics in asylums, patients in hospitals—occupa-
tions or former occupations: persons at all ages

Orders, Sub-Orders and Groups
England and Wales

XIX, XX   *Age-groups: all ages, under 20, 20+; 0—100+ in quinquennia*
XXX, XXXI
European aliens by country of birth (18 countries) in age-
groups: under 20, 20+
XLI—XLVII
The Blind, Blind from birth, Deaf-and-Dumb, etc. (as in
Table XL above)—occupations or former occupations by
age-groups: under 20, 20+

Islands in the British Seas
XXII, XXIII
Age-groups: under 20, 20+ (Islands collectively and sepa-
rately)
LV   *The Blind, Deaf-and-Dumb, etc. (as Table XL above)—occu-*
pations or former occupations by age-groups: under 20, 20+
(Islands shown collectively)

Groups (alphabetical order)
England and Wales

XVII   *Persons, males, females at all ages*

Islands in the British Seas (collectively)
XXI   *Age-groups: under 20, 20+*

Classes, Orders and Sub-Orders
Registration Divisions

10   *Age-groups: under 20, 20+, all ages*

Orders, Sub-Orders and Groups
Registration Counties
11—16   *Age-groups: 0—24 in quinquennia, 25—94 in decennia, 95+*
Registration Districts
17, 18   *Males and females aged 20+*
Principal Towns
19, 20   *Age-groups: under 20, 20+*

Selected Sub-Orders and Groups
Registration Divisions
26, 27   *European aliens in age-groups: under 20, 20+*

VOL. III (GENERAL REPORT): APPENDIX

Classes
England and Wales, Registration Divisions, Counties and Districts
82, 83   *Persons aged 20+, numbers and proportions in each Class*

Principal Occupations
England and Wales
84   *Persons at all ages: occupations in order of numerical importance*
85   *Males, 15—19, 20—39 years: occupations in order of numerical importance*

Registration Districts (with locally important occupations)
86   *Males and females aged 20+*

Farmers and Farm Labourers
10 counties, together and individually
87—98   *Farmers by number of male labourers employed and acreage of farm, and comparison with 1851*

All Occupations
England and Wales
102, 103   *Juveniles and children: 0—, 5—, 10—, 15—19, numbers and proportions (1) at school (2) at home (3) in occupations: 1851, 1861*

OCCUPATIONS: 1871 ENGLAND AND WALES

VOLUME AND TABLE No. Classification Area *Population and* *Characteristics*	The Divisional Tables listed below (Arabic numerals in Vol. III) are similar for each Division, but the table numbers vary according to the number of counties in each Division. For reasons of space the table numbers are quoted for *Division V only*. The Tables show Males and Females separately unless otherwise indicated.

VOL. III (AGES, CIVIL CONDITION, OCCUPATIONS, ETC.)

Classes, Orders and Sub-Orders

England and Wales
XVII	*Age-groups: under 20, 20+, all ages*
XXV	*European aliens in age-groups: under 20, 20+*
XXXVII	*The Blind, Blind from birth, Deaf-and-Dumb—occupations or former occupations*

Orders, Sub-Orders and Groups

England and Wales
XVIII, XIX
Age-groups: all ages, under 20, 20+; 0—24 in quinquennia, 25—74 in decennia, 75+

XXVI, XXVII
European aliens by country of birth (17 countries) in age-groups: under 20, 20+

XXXVIII—XL
The Blind, Blind from birth, Deaf-and-Dumb—occupations or former occupations by age-groups: under 20, 20+

Registration Counties, Islands in the British Seas (collectively and and separately)
11—16   *Age-groups: 0—24 in quinquennia, 25—74 in decennia, 75+*

Principal Towns
18—19   *Males and females aged 20+*

Classes, Orders and Sub-Orders

Registration Divisions, Islands in the British Seas (collectively)
10   *Age-groups: under 20, 20+*

Classes and Orders

Registration Divisions, Counties and Districts
17   *Males and females aged 20+*

Selected Sub-Orders and Groups

Registration Divisions
24, 25   *European aliens in age-groups: under 20, 20+*

VOL. IV (GENERAL REPORT): APPENDIX A

Groups (alphabetical order)

England and Wales, Islands in the British Seas (collectively)
99, 178 *Persons, males, females at all ages*

Classes, Orders and Sub-Orders

England and Wales
100   *Age-groups: all ages, under 20, 20+*

Orders, Sub-Orders and Groups

England and Wales
101, 102 *Analysis as in Tables XVIII, XIX above, with further occupational detail in footnotes*

Islands in the British Seas
179, 180   *Age-groups: under 20, 20+*

Principal Occupations

England and Wales
103   *Persons at all ages: occupations in order of numerical*
           importance
104   *Males aged 20—44: occupations in order of numerical*
           importance
107   *Serial table for 1861, 1871: males and females at all ages*

Registration Districts (with occupations of local importance)
108   *Males and females aged 20+*

17 counties, together and individually
109—127   *Farmers by number of male labourers employed and acreage*
           of farm, and comparison with 1851

All Occupations

England and Wales
105, 106   *Juveniles and children: 0—, 5—, 10—, 15—19, numbers and*
           proportions (1) at school (2) at home (3) in occupations:
           1851, 1861, 1871

OCCUPATIONS: 1881 ENGLAND AND WALES

VOLUME AND TABLE No.
Classification
  Area
       Population and
       Characteristics

VOL. III (AGES, CONDITION AS TO MARRIAGE, OCCUPATIONS,
ETC.) (containing Summary Tables (S) and uniform Divisional
Tables (D))

Classes, Orders and Sub-Orders

England and Wales
4(S)   *Persons, males, females at all ages*

Orders, Sub-Orders and Groups

England and Wales
5(S)   *Age-groups: under 5, 5—, 15—, 20—, 25—, 45—, 65+: males*
           and females
13(S)   *European aliens by country of birth (20 countries): males*
           and females

XVII—XIX(S)
           Blind, Blind from birth, Deaf-and-Dumb: males and females

Registration Divisions and Counties, Urban Areas with populations
exceeding 50,000
10(D)   *Males and females at all ages*

Groups (alphabetical order)

England and Wales
6(S)   *Persons, males, females at all ages*

VOL. IV (GENERAL REPORT)

Classes

England and Wales, Registration Counties
32   *Proportion of persons in each class per 1,000 enumerated*

OCCUPATIONS: 1891 ENGLAND AND WALES

VOLUME AND TABLE No. Classification Area *Population and* *Characteristics*	Where not further specified below—Tables show Males and Females separately, with a lower age limit of 10 years; Industrial status distinguishes employers, working on own account, others or no statement.

VOL. III (AGES, CONDITIONS AS TO MARRIAGE, OCCUPATIONS, ETC.) (containing Summary Tables (S) and uniform Divisional Tables (D))

Classes, Orders and Sub-Orders

England and Wales
4(S)   *Persons, males and females aged 10+*

Orders, Sub-Orders and Groups

England and Wales
5(S)   *(1) Industrial status (2) age-groups: 10—, 15—, 20—, 25—,*
           35—, 45—, 55—, 65+
14(S)   *European aliens by country of birth (20 countries)*
18—20(S) *Blind, Blind from childhood, Deaf-and-Dumb*

Registration Divisions and Counties, Urban Areas with populations exceeding 50,000
7(D)   *Males and females aged 10+*

Groups (alphabetical order)

England and Wales
6(S)   *Persons, males, females aged 10+*

VOL. IV (GENERAL REPORT)

Classes

England and Wales, Registration Counties
31   *Proportion of persons in each class per 1,000 enumerated*

OCCUPATIONS: 1901 ENGLAND AND WALES

VOLUME AND TABLE No. Classification Area *Population and* *Characteristics*	Where not further specified below—Tables show Males and Females separately, with a lower age limit of 10 years: Marital condition distinguishes unmarried, married or widowed; Industrial status distinguishes employers, working for employers, working on own account, others or no statement.

SUMMARY TABLES

Orders, Sub-Orders and Groups

England and Wales

XXXV   *(1) Industrial status (2) working at home (3) marital condition of females (all conditions; married or widowed) (4) age-groups: 10−, 14−, 15−, 20−, 25−, 35−, 45−, 55−, 65−, 75+*

XXXVII   *Children aged 10 and under 14, by individual years of age*

XXXVIII   *Pensioners or Retired, former occupations by (1) inmates of workhouses (2) inmates of lunatic asylums (3) marital condition of females*

XLII   *Pauper inmates of workhouses by (1) marital condition of females (2) age-groups: under 25, 25−74 in decennia, 75+, −occupations or former occupations*

XLIII   *Prisoners in local and convict prisons by (1) marital condition (2) age-groups: under 20, 20−, 25−, 35−, 45+, −occupations or former occupations*

LI   *Blind, Blind from childhood, Deaf-and-Dumb. Marital condition of females*

XLVIII   *European aliens by country of birth*

Groups (alphabetical order)
XXXVI   *Persons, males, females*

Orders and Selected Groups

Urban District and Rural District aggregates in England and Wales
XXXIX A, B

(1) Marital condition (2) age-groups as in Table XXXV

Administrative Counties and County Boroughs
XL A, B   *Males and females, with marital condition of females (all occupations)*

XLI   *Children aged 10 and under 14, with total and total occupied in two age-groups: 10−12, 13*

GENERAL REPORT with Appendices

Orders, Sub-Orders and Groups

England and Wales

34   *Serial table for 1881, 1891, 1901: ages under 15, 15+, and total*

Orders, Sub-Orders, and Selected Groups

United Kingdom, England and Wales, Scotland, Ireland
35   *Serial table for 1881, 1891, 1901: persons, males, females— numbers and proportions per million occupied*

Orders and Selected Sub-Orders

England and Wales, Administrative Counties, County Boroughs
29,30   *Proportion per 10,000 occupied*

All Occupations
31   *Marital condition, proportions of unmarried and of married or widowed females engaged in occupation by age-groups: 10+; 10–, 15–, 20–, 25–, 35–, 45–, 55–, 65–, 75+*
32   *Children under 15, proportions engaged in occupations by age-groups: under 14; 10–, 13–, 14*

COUNTY PARTS

Orders, Sub-Orders and Groups

London Administrative County, Yorkshire (East, North and West Riding Administrative Counties with associated County Boroughs), Lancashire (Administrative County with associated County Boroughs)
32   *(1) industrial status (2) working at home (3) marital condition of females (4) age-groups as in Summary Tables, XXXV*

Other Administrative Counties (with associated County Boroughs)
32   *Males and females with marital condition of females. (Additional detail of age, industrial status, etc. as for London, etc. above, given under some counties for certain occupations of local importance.)*
33   *Children 10 and under 14, by individual years*
34   *Pensioners or Retired by (1) inmates of workhouses and lunatic asylums (2) marital condition (3) age-groups: under 35, 35–, 45–, 55–, 65–, 75+, –former occupations*

Orders, Sub-Orders, and Selected Groups

County Boroughs, Metropolitan Boroughs, County aggregates of Urban and Rural Districts
35   *(1) Marital condition of females (2) age-groups: 10–, 15–, 25–, 45–, 65+*

Orders and Selected Sub-Orders

County Boroughs, Municipal Boroughs and Urban Districts with population exceeding 5,000
35A   *(1) Males and females aged 10+ (2) numbers and proportions of children under 14 engaged in occupations (3) numbers and proportions of married or widowed females engaged in occupations (4) proportion of domestic servants to numbers of separate occupiers or families*

OCCUPATIONS: 1911 ENGLAND AND WALES

VOLUME AND TABLE No. Classification Area *Population and* *Characteristics*	Where not further specified below—Tables show Males and Females separately, with a lower age limit of 10 years; Marital condition distinguishes unmarried, married, widowed; Industrial status distinguishes employers, working for employers, working on own account, others or no statement.

OCCUPATIONS AND INDUSTRIES (T), SUMMARY TABLES (S), INFIRMITIES (IN.)

Orders, Sub-Orders and Groups

England and Wales

T1, S48   *Persons, males, females, with marital condition of females*

T3, S50   *(1) Industrial status (2) working at home (3) working at home by industrial status (4) age-groups: 10–, 15–, 20–, 25–, 35–, 45–, 55–, 65–, 75+*

T7, S51   *Married males by (1) industrial status (2) working at home by industrial status (3) age-groups: 10–, 20–, 21–, 25–, 35–, 45–, 55–, 65–, 75+*

T8, S52   *Marital condition of females by (1) industrial status (2) working at home by industrial status (3) age-groups as in Table T3*

T14(A), S54

   Juveniles 10 and under 21 years by individual years of age

T17, S53   *Pensioners and Retired, former occupations by (1) inmates of workhouses (2) inmates of lunatic asylums (3) marital condition of females (4) age-groups under 35, 35–74 in decennia, 75+*

T18, S55   *Pauper inmates of workhouses, occupations or former occupations by (1) marital condition of females (2) age-groups under 25, 25–74 in decennia, 75+*

T19, S56   *Prisoners in local and convict prisons by (1) marital condition (2) age-groups: under 20, 20–, 25–, 35–, 45+*

T20, S58   *Proportion per 1,000 males aged 20+ in age-groups, and proportion married in each age-group: 20–, 25–, 35–, 45–, 55–, 65+*

T26, S64   *Serial table for 1881, 1891, 1901, 1911: numbers under 15, 15+*

S89, IN.5   *Blind, Deaf-and-Dumb, by marital condition*

S79   *All aliens by place of birth*

   London Administrative County, Lancashire Administrative County with associated County Boroughs, Yorkshire (East, West and North Riding Administrative Counties with associated County Boroughs)

T4–6   *Detail as for T3 above*

T9–11   *Detail as for T8 above*

T14(B)–(D)

   Detail as for T14(A) above

Administrative Counties with associated County Boroughs
T12   *Males and females aged 10+, with marital condition of
          females (Additional detail of age, etc. as in T3 above,
          given under some counties for certain occupations of local
          importance)*

Orders and Sub-Orders

England and Wales
T27, S65 *Serial table for 1881, 1891, 1901, 1911, persons, males,
           females: numbers and proportions per million total popu-
           lation aged 10+*

England and Wales, national Urban and Rural District aggregates,
Administrative Counties, County Boroughs, Metropolitan
Boroughs, Urban Districts with a population exceeding 50,000,
Rural District aggregates in Administrative Counties
T13   *(1) marital condition of females (2) age-groups: single years
          10−, 20−, 25−, 35−, 45−, 55−, 65+
          (includes separate selected occupational groups of local
          importance)*

National Urban and Rural District aggregates
S57(A)(B) *Detail as for T13*

Orders and Selected Groups

England and Wales, national Urban and Rural District aggregates,
Administrative Counties, County Boroughs, Metropolitan
Boroughs, Urban Districts with a population exceeding 5,000,
County aggregates of other Urban Districts and of Rural Districts
T15(A)   *Males aged 10+
           Females aged 10+, with (1) numbers and proportions in
           marital condition categories engaged in occupation (2)
           proportion of female domestic servants to separate occupiers
           or families*

England and Wales, Administrative Counties, County Boroughs,
Metropolitan Boroughs, Urban Districts with a population exceed-
ing 50,000
T16   *Children aged 10−12, and 13 years*
T22, S60, S61
          *Proportions of males and females in occupation Groups per
           10,000 in all Groups, and for females proportions by
           marital status*

All Occupations
T21, S59 *Proportion per 1,000 at ages: 10−, 15−, 20−, 25−, 35−,
           45−, 55−, 65−, 75+: 10+ engaged in occupations, in
           marital condition categories*
T23, S62 *Proportion of males and females occupied per 1,000 at
           ages: 10−, 13−19 by single years*

England and Wales, Administrative Counties, County Boroughs,
Metropolitan Boroughs, Urban Districts with a population exceed-
ing 5,000, County aggregates of other Urban Districts and of
Rural Districts
T24   *Children aged 10 and under 14, by (1) total number (2)
          number occupied (3) proportion occupied per 1,000 total
          (additional age detail where proportions are high)*

GENERAL REPORT with Appendices

  Orders and Selected Groups

  United Kingdom, England and Wales, Scotland, Ireland
9(APPX.C) *Serial table for 1881, 1891, 1901, 1911, persons, males, females: numbers and proportions per million total population*

  Orders, Sub-Orders

  British Empire
6(APPX.D) *Males, females (or persons) in various colonies, etc.*

BIRTHPLACES

  Orders, Sub-Orders and Groups

  England and Wales, London Administrative County, Lancashire Administrative County, with associated County Boroughs, Administrative Counties of East, North and West Ridings of Yorkshire with associated County Boroughs
5   *All aliens by place of birth*

F. Tabulations of Birthplaces

Birthplace and Nationality, 1841–1931. A question on birthplace was first introduced with the householder's schedule in 1841 when it was required to be stated whether each person was born (a) in the county of enumeration or, if elsewhere, whether (b) in England, Wales, Scotland, Ireland, British Colonies or foreign parts. At the Census of 1851 householders were asked to state the county and town or parish against the names of those born in the county of enumeration, while a statement of country of birth was asked in respect of those born in another part of Great Britain, in Ireland, the British Colonies, the East Indies or in foreign parts, and British subjects born in foreign parts had to be specified as such. From 1861 British subjects by birth born in foreign parts had to be distinguished from those who were naturalised and from 1901 country of nationality, as distinct from birth, had to be given. The schedules used from 1911 to 1931 provided separate columns for birthplace and nationality; in addition, the particulars obtained enabled foreign residents to be distinguished from visitors.

The subject of birthplace and the study of migration movements was given extensive treatment in the Census reports, especially in those published on the Censuses of Scotland. Details of the analyses published in Census tables are given below.

BIRTHPLACES

Census of Great Britain: 1841 and 1851
Census of England and Wales: 1861—1891

PLACE OF BIRTH
   Where Enumerated
      Characteristics
      Year, Volume and
           Table No.
	Unless otherwise stated:
	1. British subjects are shown separately in tables where foreign countries are grouped;
	2. Tables showing those born in foreign countries relate to foreigners;
	3. Males and females are distinguished except in tables marked †; age-groups under 20 and 20+ are given except in tables marked*.

ENGLAND AND WALES, (SAME COUNTY AND IN OTHER COUNTIES), SCOTLAND, IRELAND, BRITISH COLONIES, FOREIGN PARTS (UNSPECIFIED)

    England, Wales, Counties
      Numbers and proportion per cent. of both sexes
      1841. Enumeration Abstract, p. 14

    Hundreds, Principal Towns
      1841. Enumeration Abstract, County Tables.

SCOTLAND, (SAME COUNTY AND IN OTHER COUNTIES), ENGLAND, WALES, IRELAND, BRITISH COLONIES, FOREIGN PARTS (UNSPECIFIED)

    Scotland, Counties
      Numbers and proportion per cent. of both sexes
      1841. Enumeration Abstract, p. 16

ISLANDS IN THE BRITISH SEAS (SAME OR OTHER ISLANDS), ENGLAND, SCOTLAND, IRELAND, WALES, BRITISH COLONIES, FOREIGN PARTS (UNSPECIFIED)

    Islands in British Seas (given separately)
      Numbers and proportion per cent. of both sexes
      1841. Enumeration Abstract, p. 16

ENGLAND, WALES, SCOTLAND, ISLANDS IN THE BRITISH SEAS, IRELAND, BRITISH COLONIES, FOREIGN PARTS, AT SEA

    England and Wales, Scotland, Islands in British Seas
      †1851. *Population Tables II.* Summary Table XXXVIII.

    England and Wales
      1861. *Population Tables II.* Summary Table XXV.
      1871. *Population Abstracts III,* Summary Table XXI.

British distinguished from foreign subjects born at sea, with figures for previous Census
    *1881. *Volume III*, Summary Table 7.

With figures for previous Census
    *1891. *Volume III*, Summary Table 7.

COUNTIES OF SCOTLAND, ENGLAND, WALES, ISLANDS IN BRITISH SEAS, IRELAND, BRITISH COLONIES, FOREIGN PARTS, AT SEA

Scotland, Northern and Southern Counties Grouped, Counties
    †1851. *Population Tables II*, Summary Table XL and pp. 1038–1040.

Scotland: Principal Towns
    †1851. *Population Tables II*, p. 1041.

LONDON, COUNTIES OF ENGLAND AND WALES, SCOTLAND, ISLANDS IN THE BRITISH SEAS, IRELAND, BRITISH COLONIES, FOREIGN PARTS, AT SEA

England and Wales, Registration Divisions and Registration Counties
    †1851. *Population Tables II*. Summary Table XXXIX.

Registration Divisions, Counties and Districts, Principal Towns
    †1851. *Population Tables II*, County Tables.

England and Wales
    1861. *Population Tables II*, Summary Table XXIV
    1871. *Population Abstracts III*, Summary Table XX.

Ancient Counties of England and Wales
    1861. *Population Tables II*, County Table 21.
    1871. *Population Abstracts III*, County Table 20.

Registration Districts of England and Wales
    1861. *Population Tables II*, County Table 22.

Principal Towns of England and Wales
    1861. *Population Tables II*, County Table 23.
    1871. *Population Abstracts III*, County Table 23.

Divisions, Counties and Urban Districts of Population 50,000+ in England and Wales
    *1881. *Volume III*, County Table 11.
    *1891. *Volume III*, County Table 8.

ISLANDS IN THE BRITISH SEAS (CLASSIFIED), ENGLAND, WALES, SCOTLAND, IRELAND, BRITISH COLONIES, FOREIGN PARTS, AT SEA.

Islands in the British Seas (Classified)
    †1851. *Population Tables II*, Summary Table XLI and p. 1071.
    1861. *Population Tables II*, Summary Table XXVI.
    1871. *Population Abstracts III*, Summary Table XXII.

ENGLAND AND WALES (IN SAME COUNTY, ELSEWHERE)

    County, Township, Parish and Place
        *†1841. *Enumeration Abstract,* County Tables.

REGISTRATION DIVISIONS OF ENGLAND AND WALES

    England and Wales
        *1881. *Volume III,* Summary Table 8.

COUNTIES OF ENGLAND AND WALES

    England and Wales
        *1891. *Volume III,* Summary Table 8.

    Counties of England and Wales
        *1881. *Volume III,* County Table 12.
        *1891. *Volume III,* County Table 9.

SCOTLAND, IRELAND, FOREIGN PARTS

    England and Wales, Registration Divisions, Counties
        *1881. *Volume III,* Summary Table 10.
        *1891. *Volume III,* Summary Table 10.

BRITISH COLONIES: CLASSIFIED

    London Registration Division
      British Subjects
        †1851.*Population Tables II,* p. 36.

FOREIGN COUNTRIES: CLASSIFIED

    England and Wales
        *1881. *Volume III,* Summary Table 9.
        *1891. *Volume III,* Summary Table 9.

    Registration Divisions of England and Wales
        *1861.*Population Tables II,* Summary Table XXVII.
        *1871.*Population Abstracts III,* Summary Table XXIII.

    Registration Divisions and Counties of England and Wales
      Foreigners
        *1861.*Population Tables II,* County Table 24.
        *1871.*Population Abstracts III,* County Table 22.

    Registration Divisions, Counties, and Urban Sanitary Districts
    of Population 50,000+
        *1881.*Population Tables II,* County Table 13.
        *1891. *Volume III,* County Table 10.

    London Registration Division
      British subjects distinguished
        †1851.*Population Tables II,* p. 36.

London Registration Districts
*1871.*Population Tables II*, London County Table 15.
*1881.*Population Abstracts III*, London County Table
13a.

EUROPEAN STATES: CLASSIFIED

England and Wales

21 age-groups
1861. *Population Tables II*, Summary Table XXVIII.

11 age-groups
1871. *Population Abstracts III*, Summary Table XXIV.

6 age-groups
1881. *Volume III*, Summary Table 12.

12 age-groups
1891. *Volume III*, Summary Table 12.

8 age-groups by marital condition
1891. *Volume III*, Summary Table 13.

Registration Divisions of England and Wales
European foreigners

by 21 age-groups
1861. *Population Tables II*, County Table 25.

by 11 age-groups
1871. *Population Abstracts III*, County Table 23.

Registration Divisions and Counties of England and Wales
*†1881. *Volume III*, Summary Table 11.
*†1891. *Volume III*, Summary Table 11.

London Registration Division

Those residing with their families (children distinguished).
Others.
*1861.*Population Tables II*, London County Table 18.

BIRTHPLACES: Census of England and Wales 1901–1931

PLACE OF BIRTH Where Enumerated *Characteristics* Year, Volume and Table No.	Unless otherwise stated British subjects by birth and British subjects by naturalization are distinguished from aliens. In some tables separate figures for N. Ireland and Eire are given in 1921 and 1931.

ENGLAND AND WALES, AND TOTAL OUTSIDE ENGLAND AND WALES; SCOTLAND, IRELAND, ISLANDS IN BRITISH SEAS, BRITISH COLONIES, FOREIGN COUNTRIES, AT SEA

England and Wales
    Population at each Census from 1851
        1901. *General Report*, Appendix A, No. 36.
        1911. *Volume IX*, No. 8.
        1921. *General Tables*, No. 52.
        1931. *General Tables*, No. 36.

    Proportion per 100,000 of population at each Census from 1851
        1901. *General Report*, Appendix A, No. 37.
        1911. *Volume IX*, No. 9.
        1921. *General Tables*, No. 53.
        1931. *General Tables,* No. 37.

ENGLAND, WALES, SCOTLAND, IRELAND, ISLANDS IN THE BRITISH SEAS, BRITISH COLONIES, FOREIGN COUNTRIES, AT SEA

Ancient Counties of England and Wales
    Proportion per 100,000 of population enumerated in Ancient Counties
        1901. *General Report*, Appendix A, No. 39.

England and Wales, Administrative Counties
        1921. *General Tables*, No. 45

Administrative Counties and Urban Areas with Populations exceeding 50,000
    Males and females
        1921. *General Tables*, No. 47.
        1921. *County Parts*, No. 21.
England and Wales, Regions, Administrative Counties, Metropolitan Boroughs, County Boroughs and Urban Areas with Populations exceeding 50,000
    Males and females
        1931. *General Tables*, No. 32.

COUNTIES OF ENGLAND AND WALES, SCOTLAND, IRELAND, ISLANDS IN THE BRITISH SEAS, BRITISH COLONIES, FOREIGN PARTS, AT SEA

England and Wales
    Males and females
        1901. *General Report*, Summary Table XLIV.

Ancient Counties and London
    Males and females
        1901. *General Report*, Summary Table XLV.

Administrative Counties, County Boroughs, Metropolitan Boroughs and Urban Districts with Populations exceeding 50,000
    Males and females
        1911. *Volume IX*, No. 10.

Certain Counties and Large Towns
    Males and females by 8 age-groups
        1911. *Volume IX*, No. 12

ENGLAND AND WALES

England and Wales, Scotland, Ireland, Islands in the British Seas
Population at each Census from 1851.
1901. *General Report*, Appendix A, No. 38.
1911. *Volume IX*, No. 7.
1921. *General Tables*, No. 51.
1931. *General Tables*, No. 38.

ANCIENT COUNTIES OF ENGLAND AND WALES

Ancient Counties, County Boroughs and/or Urban Areas with
Populations exceeding 50,000
Males and females
1901. *Volumes I to VI*, County Tables 36.

ENGLAND AND WALES; ADMINISTRATIVE COUNTIES AND
LARGE TOWNS OF (a) ENGLAND, (b) WALES; COUNTIES OF
(a) SCOTLAND AND (b) IRELAND; ISLE OF MAN; CHANNEL
ISLANDS; BRITISH COLONIES AND FOREIGN COUNTRIES
(BOTH SPECIFIED); AT SEA

England and Wales
Males and Females
1911. *Volume IX*, No. 1.

ENGLAND AND WALES; COUNTIES AND LARGE TOWNS OF
ENGLAND AND WALES; SCOTLAND, IRELAND, ISLANDS IN
THE BRITISH SEAS; BRITISH COLONIES (CLASSIFIED);
FOREIGN COUNTRIES; AT SEA

Administrative Counties, County Boroughs, Metropolitan
Boroughs and Urban Districts with Populations exceeding 50,000
Males and females
1911. *Volume IX* No. 2.

HUNTINGDON, MERIONETH, SOMERSET, WESTMORLAND
(SEPARATELY)

Other Counties, Large Towns
Males and females by 8 age-groups
1911. *Volume IX*, No. 15.

OUTSIDE ADMINISTRATIVE COUNTY OF LONDON

County of London, Metropolitan Boroughs
Males and females by 8 age-groups
1911. *Volume IX*, No. 13

LONDON (ADMINISTRATIVE COUNTY)

Administrative Counties, County Boroughs and Urban Districts
with Populations exceeding 50,000

Males and females by 8 age-groups
1911. *Volume IX*, No. 14.

COUNTIES OF SCOTLAND AND IRELAND, CLASSIFIED ISLANDS IN THE BRITISH SEAS, CLASSIFIED BRITISH DOMINIONS AND COLONIES

England and Wales
  Residents and visitors, males and females
  1911. *Volume IX*, No. 6.

BRITISH EMPIRE AND FOREIGN PARTS: ALL CLASSIFIED

England and Wales, Regions, Administrative Counties, County Boroughs, Metropolitan Boroughs and Urban Areas with Populations exceeding 50,000
  Males and females
  1931. *General Tables*, No. 30.

SCOTLAND, NORTHERN IRELAND, IRISH FREE STATE, ISLANDS IN THE BRITISH SEAS, BRITISH DOMINIONS, FOREIGN COUNTRIES AND AT SEA

England and Wales
  Males and females of British nationality by 17 age-groups
  1931. *General Tables*, No. 35.

BRITISH DOMINIONS (CLASSIFIED)

England and Wales
  Residents and visitors, males and females
  1921. *General Tables*, No. 50.

FOREIGN COUNTRIES (CLASSIFIED)

England and Wales
  Males and females by 17 age-groups and marital condition
  1931. *General Tables*, No. 33.

England and Wales, Ancient Counties
  Males and females, 1891, 1901.
  1901. *General Report*, Summary Table XLVI.

England and Wales (and Regions in 1931)
  Males and females by 10 age-groups and marital condition
  1901. *General Report*, Summary Table XLVII.

  Residents and visitors. Males and females: British by (a) birth (b) naturalization; aliens;
  1921. *General Tables*, No. 46.

  Males and females by 18 age-groups and marital condition
  1921. *General Tables*, No. 48.

  Males and females by 17 age-groups and marital condition
  1931. *General Tables*, No. 34.

Index